Highly Recommended

For **ICSE & ISC** Exams

OSWAAL BOOKS®
LEARNING MADE SIMPLE

WITH AT

GRAMMATICALLY YOURS

ON IN

The Best
English Grammar Book
for ICSE & ISC Exams

Classes 9 to 12

oswaal.ai
LEARNING MADE SMARTER

Smart guidance that helps you learn, practise and improve.

Sudhir Sir

Published by

OSWAAL BOOKS &
LEARNING PVT. LTD.

First Published 2025

ISBN: 9789373016856

Head Office
Oswaal House
1/11, Sahitya Kunj, M.G. Road,
Agra-282002 (UP), India
+91-562-2857671
contact@oswaalbooks.com

From the Author's Desk

Having been an educator and a writer for over three decades, I can completely understand the fear, anxiety and uncertainty students experience when it comes to English grammar. Regrettably, with reading habits on the decline, many students resort to rote learning of grammar rules without really knowing how to apply them correctly.

That is the reason I have written this book. No doubt, there are scores of grammar books available in the market, but what makes this book unique is that it is tailor-made for ICSE and ISC Classes 9 to 12 students, keeping in mind the specific kind of questions that are asked in the exams. The aim was to create a one-stop destination for ICSE and ISC-level grammar, where every rule is explained in a clear, simple, and structured way, supported with examples. Instead of running from one guide to another or memorising shortcuts without proper understanding, students will now have a reliable resource that guides them from basics to mastery.

This book is, however, not just a collection of rules. I would call it your ticket to self-confidence, so that when you enter the exam hall, the certainty that you can attempt the grammar section without hesitation or doubt is priceless. The intention is to ensure you score full marks in grammar.

The English Language exam for students of CISCE Classes 9 to 12 is one of the most critical papers. Being the first exam, it sets the tone for the rest. In addition, its marks count towards the final score. Within this paper, the grammar section alone accounts for 20 marks in the ICSE and 15 marks in ISC – crucial for the overall score. To attempt it without knowing the rules and practising enough questions is akin to a surgeon entering the operating theatre without preparation.

This book covers the rules for transformation, tenses and verbs, and synthesis. Prepositions are explained in detail with clear examples on how to use them. For Classes 11 and 12, an extensive list of phrasal verbs has been included, making it ideal preparation material. Students can also test themselves with 20 ICSE format tests and 20 ISC format tests, all supported by detailed answer keys with explanations.

Along with my other titles, *Write English Right - Compositions, Letters, Notices & Emails Made Easy* and *60 English Essays for ISC,* this grammar book will give you the support you need for a top score in the English language exam. Paired appropriately, they form a well-rounded toolkit for your exam preparation.

In 2019, my daughter, Tejaswini Uma Sudhir and I launched our YouTube venture 'Study with Sudhir' (SWS), to support Telangana State Board students. This initiative was to help students struggling with their Intermediate (Class 11 and 12) exams, where the highest failure rates were in English, Maths, and Economics. To achieve this, we recorded the entire Intermediate English syllabus on YouTube, blending simple English with Telugu. Eventually, the Telangana Board of Intermediate Education broadcast the videos on *Doordarshan*, benefiting nearly 10 lakh students during the COVID-19 pandemic.

Since then, we have branched into CISCE, CBSE, and Maharashtra State Board. Many All-India rank holders, as well as state, district, city and school toppers, have emerged through SWS, which gives me immense satisfaction and pride. The testimonials and messages I receive from grateful students and parents are worth all the effort and leave me truly humbled.

This book is a product of the last six years of working closely with thousands of students. In the process, I have identified the common difficulties and doubts that students face, and have addressed them in this book.

I believe this book will be a game-changer for both students and teachers of ICSE. School librarians will also find it to be an extremely useful resource. I am confident that this book will serve as an invaluable companion as you strive for excellence in English grammar.

I am thankful to Prashant Jain and Swaati Jain of Oswaal Books, Shrijana Subba, Lead Editorial Manager, Assistant Editorial Manager Jyotsna Chauhan, Copy Editor Naga Aparna Komarraju, and all the designers and proofreaders who worked diligently in helping make this book the quality product it has turned out to be.

The wonderful title was suggested by my friend and former colleague, Mona Ramavat.

With increasing emphasis on competency-focused questions, it is important to note that grammar questions will no longer be plain vanilla. Examiners now expect precision, application, and conceptual clarity. My book is designed specifically to meet those expectations. I would greatly appreciate your feedback on how well it helps you achieve this.

Best wishes

Sudhir Sahasranaman

Frequently Asked Questions

1. **How do I improve my grammar?**

   The long-term solution is to read, read and read. The short-term solution is to master all the relevant rules of grammar and practise with reliable practice tests to ensure you learn to use the rules correctly. This book will help you achieve this effectively. Even readers with a good instinct for what sounds right can rely on grammar rules to verify their answers.

2. **How can I determine the correct preposition to use in a sentence?**

   Prepositions are tricky because their usage often depends on convention rather than logic. For example, we say "interested in", not "interested at". The safest approach is to:

   (a) Learn collocations (common word + preposition pairings)
   (b) Read widely to observe correct usage
   (c) Revise the lists of prepositional phrases provided in this book.

In the exam hall, always read out the entire sentence to check if it sounds right.

Author's Tip: Prepositions are best mastered by habit. Whenever you encounter a new phrase, note the preposition that follows it. This memory will help you in exams.

3. **Phrasal verbs are even more difficult. How do I remember so many phrasal verbs?**

   A phrasal verb is a verb followed by a preposition or adverb that changes its meaning. For example, "give up" (quit) or "look after" (take care).

   Make it a habit to read at least one or two pages of this book every day and try to use phrasal verbs in your interactions with friends, classmates, and family members. Doing so will help make them a part of your vocabulary and everyday communication.

Author's Tip: Treat phrasal verbs like vocabulary words. Collect them in a notebook, including their meanings and your own example sentences.

4. **How do I know whether to use the past perfect tense or the simple past tense?**

   ☞ Use the simple past to describe a completed action.
   e.g., He left the house at 7.

   ☞ Use the past perfect when one past action occurred before another.
   e.g., He had left the house before I arrived.

A Simple Trick: If you are narrating two past events, ask yourself, *"Which happened first?"* The earlier action takes the past perfect.

Author's Tip: Use the timeline trick. Always place the earlier event in the past perfect and the later one in the simple past.

5. **What are the most common errors made in transformation of sentences?**

   - Changing the structure but altering the meaning.
   - Forgetting tense consistency when shifting from direct to indirect speech.
   - Changing from active to passive voice without ensuring the subject and object are correctly swapped.

Author's Tip: After transforming, read both sentences side by side. Check that the transformed sentence preserves the exact meaning of the original. If the sense changes even slightly, revise.

6. **How do I avoid mistakes in subject-verb agreement, especially with collective nouns and indefinite pronouns?**

   There is no shortcut. The key is to remember the rules. All rules are explained in detail with examples in the book. One fundamental rule is to identify the 'true subject' of the sentence, as that will determine the correct verb form.

Author's Tip: First, locate the subject, cover up the rest of the sentence, and then choose the verb. This strategy resolves most confusion.

7. **Are there any 'must-know' phrasal verbs that always come up in exams?**

   Yes. Certain phrasal verbs, such as *give up, look after, call off, put up with,* and *break down*, frequently appear in exams. Rather than relying on rote memorisation, learn them using short example sentences. This approach will help you remember their usage in context and reduce the chance of mistakes.

8. **What is the best way to practise grammar to score full marks: memorising the rules or solving past year papers?**

   Both approaches are necessary, but balance is key. Learning the rules gives you the foundation, while past year papers train you to apply those rules under exam conditions. In this book, 20 Test papers for ICSE and 20 Test papers for ISC have been provided, giving you ample practice.

   A suggested approach is to revise the rules, then immediately solve exercises that test those exact concepts. Over time, you will develop both accuracy and speed.

Author's Tip: Study one rule → attempt five practice questions → review answers. This cycle works better than cramming.

9. **Is it advisable to solve the grammar questions during the 15 minutes of reading time before the writing begins?**

   The reading time is best used to plan your composition and other long-answer writing tasks. Once you have decided on those, you can use the remaining reading time to look over the grammar questions.

What does the ICSE Syllabus say?

Several short-answer questions will test the candidates' knowledge of functional grammar, structure and usage. All the items in this question will be compulsory. They will assess the correct use of prepositions, conjunctions, verbs and the structure of sentences.

What does the ISC Syllabus say?

All the items in this question are compulsory, and their number and type/pattern may vary from year to year. They will include transformation of sentences, phrasal verbs, and verbs/tenses. These questions will test the candidates' knowledge of the key aspects of functional English grammar and structure.

Contents

Chapter 1: Verbs and Tenses

What is a Verb?

A verb is a *doing* word. It shows an action or a state of being.

> ***For example:***
> I read a book.
> I run fast.
> I walk to school.
> I sleep early.

Is / am / are - He is happy. I am happy. They are happy.

In short, verbs are words that show *what someone is doing* or *what condition they are in.*

Note: "Is", "am", and "are" are also verbs. These are known as auxiliary verbs, linking verbs or helping verbs. Other auxiliaries include "was" and "were" (used in past forms). They come from the verb "to be". By themselves, they are used to show a state of being rather than an action.

What are Tenses?

Tenses tell us about the time of an action. They express *when* something happens and the degree of its completeness.

So, when we describe an action, we consider:

- Is it happening now?
- Has it already happened?
- Will it happen in the future?

In English, time is generally described in three broad categories:

- **Past** – for actions that have already happened
- **Present** – for actions happening now
- **Future** – for actions that will happen later

Let us take the verb `study' as an example.

- **Present Tense:** I *am studying* Chemistry. (happening now)
- **Past Tense:** I *studied* Chemistry. (already happened)
- **Future Tense:** I *will study* Chemistry (yet to happen)

So, while the verb stays the same in meaning, the *tense* tells when it happened.

Each of these tenses can further be divided into four categories:

(a) Simple (Indefinite):	Used for general facts, habits, or events without focusing on duration or completion
(b) Continuous:	For actions in progress
(c) Perfect:	For completed actions
(d) Perfect Continuous:	For ongoing actions that started earlier and may still be happening

Let us explore these twelve combinations in detail.

THE PRESENT TENSES

1. **Simple Present *(Indefinite)*:**
   - Structure: Subject + base verb (V_1)
   - Used for habits, routines or general facts, universal truths
   - Does not use *-ing* forms

Examples:
I read novels.
I sing every day.
He does not exercise daily.
He works as a carpenter.

2. **Present Continuous**:
   - Structure: Subject + is/are/am + verb (-ing form)
   - Used to describe actions happening at the moment of speaking
   - Also used to describe ongoing developments or temporary events

Examples:
I am studying now.
They are dancing.
We are playing football in the park.
She is writing a letter.
The price of onions *is* rising. (a developing event)

3. **Present Perfect**:
   - Structure: Subject + has/have + past participle (third form of verb V_3)
   - Used to describe an action completed in the past, but which still has relevance to the present

Examples:
I have completed my project.
The students have learned a lot about fractions.
The worker has finished the carpentry work in the house.

4. **Present Perfect Continuous**:
   - Structure: Subject + have/has been + verb + *ing* + time (since/for)
   - Describes an action that started in the past and is still continuing

Examples:
They have been studying for four hours.
I have been teaching at this school for 10 years.
It has been drizzling since morning.

Note: In this form, if "have" or "has" is used with an *-ing* form of the verb, then "been" is essential. It connects the helping verb to the continuous action.

Here, ***'since'*** is used for definite time while ***'for'*** is used for indefinite time.

The Past Tenses

5. **Simple Past *(Indefinite)***:
   - Structure: Subject + verb (past form -V_2)
   - Describes complete actions in the past

Examples:
I studied yesterday.
She played the piano.

Difference: Present Perfect and Simple Past

Present Perfect	Simple Past
Used when time is unspecified or unimportant.	Used when the action is clearly finished and time is mentioned or implied.
Focuses on the result or relevance to the present.	Focuses on the specific time the action happened.
Structure: have/has + past participle	Structure: verb + -ed or irregular form

Example: I have studied for the exam. *(Implies the studying has a connection to now; perhaps you are prepared for the exam)*	Example: I studied for the exam a month ago. *(Emphasises when the studying happened, with no connection to the present)*

6. Past Continuous:
- Structure: Subject + was/were + verb (-ing form)
- Describes an ongoing action in the past

Examples:
I was studying yesterday.
They were playing cricket.

7. Past Perfect:
- Structure: Subject + had + past participle (third form of verb V_3)
- Describes an action completed *before* another past action

Examples:
I had studied before I left home.
She had already left the house when I called her.
They had finished their homework before the teacher arrived.

8. Past Perfect Continuous:
- **Structure:** Subject + had been + verb (-ing form) + time (since/for)
- Describes an ongoing action that was happening in the past before another action occurred

Examples:
I had been studying when the power went off.
He had been driving near Rajkot when the bridge collapsed.

The Future Tenses

Here, **In normal situation:** 'shall' is used with the 1st Person (I & We) and 'will' is used with the 2nd (You) & 3rd Person (He, She, It, They). **In compulsion,** 'shall' & 'will' will be interchanged

9. Simple Future *(Indefinite)*:
- **Structure:** Subject + will/shall + base verb
- Describes decisions or actions that will happen in the future

Examples:
I will call you tomorrow.
They will arrive later.
We shall leave for London next week.
I shall go to school. *(Normal situation)*
I will go to school. *(In compulsion)*

10. Future Continuous:
- **Structure:** Subject + will/shall + be + verb (-ing)
- Describes an action that will be in progress at a specific time or over a duration in the future; emphasises the continuity of action in the future

Examples:
I will be studying tomorrow
They will be travelling to Delhi next week.

11. Future Perfect:
- **Structure:** Subject + will/shall + have + past participle (V_3)
- Describes an action completed before a specific time in the future; emphasises the completion of the action in the future

Examples:
I will have studied by evening tomorrow.
She will have left the office by the time we arrive.
By next year, they will have built the new library.

Important Points to Remember:
- Focus is on completion before a future point in time.
- Often used with time markers like *by*, *before*, or phrases like *by the time*.

12. Future Perfect Continuous:
- Structure: Subject + will/shall + have been + verb (-ing).
- Describes actions that will have been ongoing for a certain duration before a specific point in the future; emphasises the duration or continuity of the action up to that future moment.

Examples:
I will have been studying for 10 hours by the time you come.
By 6 p.m., she will have been waiting at the station for two hours.
They will have been working on the project for a month by next week.

Important Points to Remember:
- Focus is on how long an action will have continued before a particular future time.
- Often used with time markers like *by*, *for*, *since*, or phrases like *by the time*.
- Here, ***'since'*** is used for definite time while ***'for'*** is used for indefinite time.

Difference: Future Continuous, Future Perfect, and Future Perfect Continuous

Future Continuous	Future Perfect	Future Perfect Continuous
Describes an action in progress at a specific time in the future.	Describes an action that will be completed before a certain future time.	Describes how long an action will have been happening up to a point in the future.
Emphasises continuity of the action.	Emphasises completion of the action.	Emphasises the *duration* of the action.
Structure: will/shall + be + verb(-ing).	Structure: will/shall + have + past participle.	Structure: will/shall + have been + verb(-ing).
e.g., I will be waiting for you by 6 p.m.	*e.g., I will have waited for two hours by 6 p.m.*	*e.g., I will have been waiting for two hours by 6 p.m.*

Chapter 2: The World of Prepositions

What are Prepositions?

Suppose you want to tell your friend where something is, when it happened, or how one event relates to another. You do this using a preposition.

A preposition is a word that shows the relationship between a noun or pronoun and another word in the sentence.

It tells us:

- *where* something is (place),
- *when* something happens (time), and
- *how* things are connected (cause, direction, manner).

There are various types of prepositions. For example:

1. Prepositions of Place: e.g., *in, on, under, above, behind*

Example: The phone is on the table.

2. Prepositions of Time: e.g., *at, in, on, before, after*

Example: The movie starts at 10 a.m.

3. Prepositions of Direction or Movement: e.g., *to, into, towards, out of*

Example: The teacher walked into the classroom.

4. Prepositions of Manner or Instrument: e.g., *with, by*

Example: The principal signed with a fountain pen.

5. Prepositions of Cause or Reason: e.g., *because of, due to*

Example: He was late because of the heavy traffic.

6. Prepositions of Comparison: e.g., *as, like*

Example: He is slow like a tortoise.

- **What is a Prepositional Phrase?**

Most prepositions are followed by a noun or pronoun to complete the meaning. Together, they form a prepositional phrase.

For example, I jog in the neighbourhood park.

Here, "in" is the preposition, "the neighbourhood park" is the object of the preposition, and "in the neighbourhood park" is the **prepositional phrase.**

Prepositions are important because they hold the sentence together like glue and give it meaning.

Imagine the sentence: Manav walked the road. Does it make sense? No! The correct sentence would be: Manav walked on the road.

The preposition "on" connects the action to a place, making the sentence complete.

- **Prepositions of Place**

Prepositions of place show *where* someone or something is located. They answer the question "Where?"

1. **In:** Used to convey inside something, as in an enclosed space.
   We use it when referring to something located **within** a box, room, building, state, or country.
   (a) Malathi is in the library.
   (b) My lunchbox is in my bag.
   (c) My best friend lives in Delhi.
2. **On:** Used to show something is resting on the surface of something else.
   It is used when there is physical contact with the surface.
   (a) The book is on my table.
   (b) Do not sit on the teacher's chair.
   (c) I love your portrait on that wall.
3. **At:** To show a specific point or place. It is used when referring to a fixed location or address.
   (a) The Prime Minister lives at 7, Lok Kalyan Marg.
   (b) The postman is at the door.
   (c) We met at a friend's place.
4. **Under:** To convey something is lower than or directly beneath something.
   (a) You will find my shoes under the bed.
   (b) The pup is hiding under my table.
   (c) The cat is under the sofa.
5. **Over:** Shows something is directly above, but not touching.
   (a) A lovely painting hangs over the fireplace.
   (b) The artefact is hanging over the TV set.
   (c) The fan is over the bed.
6. **Above:** Higher than something but not necessarily directly over it.
   (a) The clouds are above the mountains.
   (b) His marks are above average.
   (c) The clock is hanging above the blackboard. (*The clock is at a higher position than the blackboard but not directly over it.*)
7. **Below:** Lower than something, but not directly under it.
   (a) The temperature in Srinagar is below zero.
   (b) The rank of a captain is below that of a colonel in the Army.
   (c) His marks are below expectations.
8. **Next to / Beside:** Means by the side of something or someone
   (a) He sat beside his sister.
   (b) The lamp is next to the bed.
9. **In front of:** To show something is ahead of or facing something.
   (a) The car is parked in front of the house.
   (b) The accused stood in front of the judge.
10. **Behind:** At the back of something.
    (a) He hid behind the curtain.
    (b) The broom is behind the door.
11. **Inside:** Similar to "in" but emphasises being deep within something.
    (a) There is someone inside the hut.
    (b) The keys are inside the box.
    (c) The letter is inside the envelope.
12. **Outside:** Refers to the outer side
    (a) Stand outside the classroom.
    (b) I saw some students standing outside the school.

- **Prepositions of Time**

Prepositions of time show *when* something happens. They answer the question "When?"

1. **At:** Used to refer to a specific point of time.
   Used with clock timings:
   (a) The guests left at midnight
   (b) The meeting starts at 9 a.m.
   Used when referring to a specific time of the day, a specific point in time or festive occasions:
   (a) You will find me working at lunchtime.
   (b) Both players arrived at the same time.
   (c) The architect is free at the moment.
   (d) We had a party at Diwali.

Important distinction:
Are you leaving Ranchi at *the weekend*? (British usage)
Are you leaving Ranchi on *the weekend*? (American usage)

2. **In:** Used for months, years, seasons and extended periods of time
   (a) Were you born in 2012?
   (b) We always travel to the hills in summer.
   (c) I will visit Jamshedpur in October.
   (d) I worked with Kabir Khan in 1994.
   It is also used for parts of the day, the length of time needed or future time references.
   (a) Urmila will study in the evening.
   (b) The doctor managed to cure the pain in a week.
   (c) You can go to Chennai and return in a day.
   (d) The meeting will get over in a few minutes.

Exception: Night takes "at" (not "in")
Although we use "in" for parts of the day (like *in the morning*, *in the evening*), we say "at night" when referring to night in general.

× Incorrect: I sleep in the night.

✓ Correct: I sleep at night.

Use "in the night" only for specific events that occur during the night, usually unusual or noticeable.

✓ Correct: I heard a noise in the night.

✓ She had a terrible dream in the night.

3. **On:** Used for names of days, specific or special days and exact calendar dates.
   (a) The priest performs a special puja on Sundays.
   (b) I will visit the museum on Friday evening.
   (c) We celebrate Republic Day on January 26.
4. **For:** Used to show duration of time, to talk about how long something has continued.
   (a) He waited for two hours.
   (b) The minister has been resting for the past thirty minutes.
   (c) They lived in Delhi for a long time.

Tip to remember: "for" always answers the question "How long?"
Think '*for how long*?' = time span

5. **Since:** Used to show the starting point of action. "Since" refers to a specific time or date and is used *only with perfect tenses*.
   (a) Kavita has been living here since 2015.
   (b) Vinu had been ailing since January.

Tip to remember: Think '*since when*?' = exact time

6. **By:** Used to show that something happens on or before a particular time; something must happen *no later than* a specific time.
   (a) The carpenter needs to finish the work by tomorrow.
   (b) I hope to return your money by Sunday.

Tip to remember: Think '*deadline*' = by

7. **Before:** Indicates something happening earlier than a set time.
   (a) The students left the venue before 5 p.m.
   (b) It is surprising that Aanya slept before sunset.
8. **After:** Refers to any moment later than a specific time
   (a) Shall we go shopping after lunch?
   (b) His brother returned after 11 p.m.
   (c) Arun reached the theatre after the movie started.
9. **From... to:** Used to show starting and ending points in time; show duration
   (a) The museum is open from 10 a.m. to 5 p.m.
   (b) We have computer classes from August to December.
10. **During:** Refers to something that happens within a particular time period
   (a) We stayed indoors during the COVID-19 pandemic.
   (b) He was silent during the meeting.
   (c) Phones are not allowed during the examinations.
11. **About / Around:** Used to show an approximate time.
   (a) We arrived at the venue around 5 p.m.
   (b) The bus usually arrives at about 11 a.m.

Note: We say "*at* about 11 a.m." (not just "about 11 a.m.") when we do not know the exact time.

12. **Within:** Refers to anything happening inside a time limit or before the time is up.
   (a) I will complete the assignment within two days.
   (b) He returned within an hour.

Tip to remember: Think 'by when?' = within

13. **Till / Until:** Used to show something continues up to a point in time
   (a) I will wait till Saturday.
   (b) The pharmacy is open till midnight.
   (c) You cannot leave until the exam is over.

Note: Both 'till' and 'until' mean the same. 'Till' is more common in everyday speech; 'until' is used in formal writing.

- **Prepositions of Depth**

  The Hindi word *neeche* can be expressed in English using the words *below*, *beneath*, *under*, or *underneath*.
  These words suggest:
  → in a lower place or position and
  → sometimes covered by something else
  However, they are not always used in the same way. Let us see the difference.

1. **Under**: Most commonly used preposition of depth.
   Used when something is almost immediately below the other or covered by something else.
   (a) You will find my shoes under the bed.
   (b) The pup is hiding under my table.
   (c) The cat is under the sofa.
2. **Below:** Used when something is lower than something else but not necessarily touching. It is the opposite of "above."
   (a) Read the instructions below before you start answering.
   (b) His name is below mine on the merit list.
   (c) The sun disappeared below the horizon.
3. **Beneath:** Means under or lower than something, often when the lower surface touches the upper object. "Beneath" is a more formal synonym for "under."
   (a) He wore a T-shirt beneath the jacket. ("under" or "underneath" are also acceptable here)
   (b) I have kept money beneath the books. ("under" or "underneath" can also be used)
   (c) The ground beneath my feet began to shake.

4. **Underneath:** A slightly formal alternative to "under", often used for emphasis; used when we want to focus on something hidden or covered.
   (a) The books are in the box underneath the bed.
   (b) He got out of the car and looked underneath.

- **Other Context for "under":**

"Under" is not used just for position. It has many other meanings too!

1. *It is used to convey a state of mind.*
   (a) With exams approaching, I am under a lot of work pressure.
   (b) The Indian team will be under pressure to win the match.
2. *Used to convey age or quantity*
   (a) There were under 50 people at the concert last night. (means fewer than 50 people)
   (b) This movie is not for children under 18. (means younger than 18)
3. *Used to show something is being controlled or managed by someone.*
   (a) The firm will be under a new management from November.
4. *Used to describe an ongoing state.*
   (a) My house is under construction.
5. *As a prefix to indicate something is less than normal or not enough*
   (a) The doctor said that my child is underweight. (opposite of overweight)
   (b) We must never underestimate our potential.
   (c) You are underage to drive.
   (d) The rice is slightly undercooked today.
6. *In idioms*
   (a) Under the weather – feeling unwell
   (b) Under one's breath - speaking very softly with a whisper

- **Other Contexts for "below":**

1. *Used to indicate a level lower than a reference point, such as height, temperature or standard.*
   (a) Temperatures in July were below average.
   (b) Her score was below the required percentage.
   (c) This city is 300 metres below sea level.
2. *In idioms*
   (a) Below the belt – an unfair or hurtful comment (origin: boxing, where hitting below the belt is not allowed)

- **Other Contexts for "beneath":**

1. *To talk about people's emotions or hidden feelings*
   (a) He seemed calm, but beneath that, he was nervous about the text.
2. *To express something is at a lower level of ability, role or expectation, to mean not good enough or not worthy*
   (a) Chores like sweeping or washing dishes are not beneath anyone.

- **Usage of "Between" and "Among"**

1. **Between:** Used when referring to two elements – two people, objects, places or points in time.
   (a) The property was divided between Akbar and Aamir.
   (b) Vedika sat between her parents. *(We can assume there are two.)*
   (c) Varanasi lies between Lucknow and Patna.
   (d) The manager will be in the office between 9 a.m. and 5 p.m.
   (e) The Vande Bharat Express runs between Chennai and Bengaluru.

   Exception: "Between" can also be used for more than two elements when they are seen as separate or distinct from each other.
   (a) Anil had to choose between Mechanical Engineering, Biochemistry, Data Analytics and Cyber Security for his college project.
   (b) Navin is trying to decide between IIT Madras, IIT Kanpur and IIT Delhi.

(c) Talks between the political parties have broken down.

2. **Among:** Used when there are more than two elements that are not considered individually, but rather as part of a group.
   (a) The property was divided among the five children.
   (b) Ravish cannot decide among his shirts.
   (c) The minister sat among the students during the event.
   (d) Deepa has several artists among her friends.

   "Among" implies being part of a group, rather than positioned separately.
   (a) There was unanimity among the residents.
   (b) Panic spread among the residents during COVID-19.
   (c) Share these sweets among yourselves.

Did You Know?

The title of Jeffrey Archer's bestseller, *Honour Among Thieves,* is an old expression that means even people who engage in wrongdoing may follow their own rules or loyalty *within their group.*

The word "among" here shows that the thieves are seen as a group with shared understanding — even if their actions are dishonest.

This is a good reminder that "among" is used when someone is part of a group, even an unusual one!

Quick Ways to Remember

(a) Between – In the middle of two distinct things.
E.g. My phone fell between the books. (just two books)

(b) Among - Surrounded by more than two things, seen as a group
E.g. My phone fell among the books. (a pile of books, more than two)

Important Points to Remember:

(1) Among is not used with "and"
- ✗ Incorrect: Among Ravi and Neha
- ✓ Correct: Between Ravi and Neha

(2) Certain words are commonly followed by "between":
   a. distinguish between
   b. divide between
   c. difference between
   d. differentiate between
   e. choose between
   f. link between
   g. connection between
   h. relationship between

   (a) I did not want to choose between the musicians.
   (b) There is no connection between all the murders taking place in the city
   (c) Is there any difference between the sisters?
   (d) Are you able to distinguish between Vinnu and Sona?

(3) Distribute is usually followed by "among".

Let us distribute the clothes among those in need.

(4.1) Divide can be followed by either "between" (for two) or "among" (for more than two).
   (a) The property was divided between the two brothers.
   (b) The chocolates were divided among the children.

(4.2) *Between* and *Among* for Location and Direction.
   (a) *Between* may also indicate position or direction:
   Vellore lies between Chennai, Bengaluru and Tirupati.
   (b) *Among* may indicate inclusion:
   Among those present at the concert was Prime Minister Narendra Modi.

(c) *Among* can also mean one of many:
The IPL is among the most prestigious sporting events in the world.

(d) Among + Others:
The phrase "among others" means "as well as" or "one of the several"
Her teachers, among others, were worried about her delicate health.
Among other things, I still have to finish my homework.

5. What is Amongst?
Amongst means the same as among. It is more formal or literary and used less commonly in modern English.

- **Prepositions in Real-Life Contexts**
Prepositions can change meaning based on context. Let us explore how prepositions behave in different settings. Below are some common themes and the prepositions that often go with them.

1. Legal Context

a. WITH
- The man was charged with murder.
- The younger daughter was entrusted with the property.

b. UNDER
- The police told the suspect that they were under arrest.
- The accused was booked under Section 103 of the BNS.

c. TO
- He did not confess to the crime.
- The notice was issued to the accused.
- The defendant did not plead guilty to the charges.
- The convict was sentenced to four years in prison.

d. ON
- The thief was arrested on charges of burglary.
- The witness testified on oath.
- The prisoner was released on bail.
- The verdict was passed on Wednesday.

e. INTO
- The parties entered into a contract.
- The culprit was taken into custody.

f. FOR
- The driver was fined for violating the traffic rule.
- The accountant was arrested for fraud.

g. OF
- He was convicted of theft.
- The burden of proof lies on the prosecution.

h. FROM
- The offender was banned from entering the premises.
- The verdict restrained them from selling the property.

i. OVER
- The dispute was over the land near the pond.
- The High Court has jurisdiction over the matter.

j. BETWEEN
- The agreement between the parties was declared null and void.
- The contract was signed between the buyer and the seller.

k. BY
- The defendant was represented by an eminent lawyer.
- A case of fraud was filed by six victims.
- The culprit was found guilty by the Supreme Court.

l. AGAINST
- The charges against the minister were dropped.
- A complaint was lodged against the polluting factory.

m. IN
- The police found no evidence in the suspect's possession.
- The case was heard in the Supreme Court today.

n. ABOUT
- The officer raised questions about the authenticity of the documents.
- There was a debate about the interpretation of the new law.

o. BEFORE (used to convey in the presence of a legal authority or under consideration by a legal body)
- The accused was brought before the judge for the hearing.
- The case is now pending before the Supreme Court.

2. Transport

1. ON FOOT (Walking)
- The children go to school on foot every day.

Explanation:
"On" implies direct contact. When walking, we are "on" our feet, using them as the direct means of locomotion. Other similar phrases include *on your knees, on your back* – all referring to parts of the body in direct contact with a surface.

2. PUBLIC TRANSPORT or LARGE VEHICLES
- Mallika travelled by *bus*.
- Mallika sat on *the bus*.
- Mallika went to Ranchi by *train*.
- Mallika was on *the train* when she heard the news.
- Mallika travelled by *plane*.
- Mallika was on *the plane* that got delayed.
- The cargo was sent by *ship*.
- The tourists stayed on *the ship* for a week.
- Mallika commutes by *metro*.
- Mallika was on *the metro* to Mehrauli.

Explanation:
Use "on" when someone is physically on/in the vehicle. It is often used for public or large vehicles, especially those where people can stand or walk inside.
Use "by" when no article or adjective is used. In this case, you are simply naming the mode of travel.

3. PRIVATE or SMALL, ENCLOSED VEHICLES
- Mallika arrived by *car*.
- Mallika had to sit in *the car* for six hours.
- Mallika reached Mumbai by *taxi*.
- Mallika arrived in a *taxi*.

Explanation:
Use "in" for smaller, enclosed vehicles or private vehicles, where you sit *inside* the space.
Use "by" to describe the mode of travel generally.

4. TWO-WHEELERS (Bike, Scooter, Motorcycle)
- Mallika goes to work by bike.
- Mallika went to the market on *a bike*.

Explanation:
Use "on" when referring to a vehicle you mount on, like a bicycle or motorcycle. You are seated on top; you do not step *into* a bike the way you would a car.
Use "by" when referring to the mode of travel.

3. Body Parts

1. Use of "on" - Direct contact, support or position
   (a) Lie on *your back* for better quality of sleep.
   (b) Many people sleep on *their stomachs* even though it is not advisable.
   (c) I stood on *my feet* for over three hours at the meeting.
   (d) He is always on *his feet* at the workplace. (constantly moving or staying active)
   (e) The future of the company rests on *his shoulders*.
   (f) The prime minister has a serious situation on *his hands*.
   (g) The musician's name is on *the tip of my tongue*. (about to say or recall something)
   (h) Allu Arjun's name is on *everyone's lips* after the success of `Pushpa'. (widely spoken or frequently mentioned)
   (i) The worker deftly balanced the bricks on *his head*.
   (j) I am unable to put *my finger* on the problem. (inability to identify or define the issue precisely)
   (k) The coach gave the player a pat on *his back*. (show encouragement or praise)
2. Use of "for" - Natural ability, talent, or special sensitivity toward something.
   (a) The artist has an *eye* for *detail*.
   ("Eye" is used figuratively for visual perception or awareness. The phrase means that the artist notices fine elements like shapes, textures, or patterns. In other words, the artist is highly observant.)
   (b) Even as an infant, she had an *ear* for *music*.
   ("Ear" symbolises a sensitivity to sound. The phrase means she could naturally recognise rhythm and melody from a young age.)
   (c) The journalist has a *nose* for *news* and always reaches the scene before anyone else.
   ("Nose" stands for intuition or instinct. It means that the journalist is naturally good at sensing important or newsworthy events.)
3. Use of "in" – often used with body parts to suggest something internal, contained or deeply felt.
   (a) Music is in *her blood,* and her family has many singers. (A natural part of someone, something instinctive or inherited)
   (b) In *her heart,* she knew she was wrong. (Refers to deep emotion or inner conviction)
   (c) He had a melody stuck in *his head* all day. (A recurring mental loop)
   (d) In *his eyes,* she could do no wrong. (Refers to someone's personal view)
   (e) He had a mischievous glint in *his eyes*. (Refers to visible harmless playfulness)
   (f) She keeps her memories in *her heart*.
   (g) I can feel the storm coming in *my bones*. (To suggest a strong, instinctive feeling)
   (h) Sometimes the problem is just in *our heads*. (Refers to psychological or imagined experiences)
4. Use of "at" – Used to indicate a specific location, position, or point of focus, often on or near a part of the body. It may be used literally (physical location) or figuratively (emotional or mental focus).
   (a) His pet dog Casper lay at *his feet*. (Physical position)
   (c) He keeps his colleagues at *arm's length*. (To describe emotional or professional distance)
   (d) The two politicians were at *each other's throats*. (Intense rivalry or verbal conflict)
   (e) It was always at *the back of her mind* that she might fail. (lingering thought or worry)
5. Use of "by" – Used to show who performs an action, how something is done, the position near someone, or to express support or means
   (a) The robber grabbed him by *the arm*.
   (b) My dog walked by *my side*.
   (c) His wife always *stands* by *him*. (To mean emotional or moral support)
   (d) My mother *swears* by herbal medication for curing common cold (Trust or strongly believe in)
   (e) I was *touched* by my neighbour's gesture. (emotionally affected in a kind, positive way)
   (f) Do not judge a book by *its cover* or a person by *his clothes*. (To mean superficial judgements)
   (g) He escaped an accident by *the skin of his teeth*. (Barely managed to avoid)
6. Use of "with" – To show how an action is done, especially when a body part is the tool or means.
   (a) He saw it with *his own eyes*.
   (b) She ate with *her fingers*.
   (c) The child clapped with *his hands*.

(d) Manhar writes **with** *his left hand.*
(e) I welcomed my nephew **with** *open arms.* (warm and lovingly)
(f) The teacher looked at the student **with** *raised eyebrows.* (Facial expression, often indicating surprise)
(g) His mother stared at him **with** *wide eyes.* (Facial expression of shock or disbelief)

7. Use of "**from**" – To show origin or source or in a figurative sense.
(a) Blood was oozing **from** *his nose.*
(b) She spoke **from** *her heart.* (Being sincere)
(c) He was grinning **from** *ear to ear.* (Expresses a very wide, joyful smile)

8. Use of "**under**" – To indicate position, also used figuratively.
(a) The accident left a scar **under** *his right eye.*
(b) Infants suffer rashes **under** *the chin* during summer.
(c) The factory manager had the workers **under** *his thumb.* (Total control)
(d) The thief stole the wallet right under the guard's nose. (In plain sight, but not found)
(e) His constant boasting was beginning to get under my skin. (Irritating or bothersome)

9. Use of "**around**" – Indicating surrounding or encircling a body part.
(a) She put her arm around the baby's neck.
(b) He wrapped a towel around his waist.
(c) The nurse tied a bandage around his injured wrist. (Using "on" in this context would mean placed on top)
(d) The party rallied **around** *the Prime Minister*, promising full support. (Showing unity or loyalty)

10. Use of "**across**" – Indicates position from one side to another.
(a) He wore a sling across his shoulder. (Suggesting stretched diagonally, from one side to the other. Using "on" would mean resting on top of the shoulder.)
(b) A look of disappointment passed **across** *her face.* (Refers to a quick, noticeable change in expression, like a wave of emotion)

11. Use of "**through**" - Indicating movement from one end or side of something to the other.
(a) The bullet went **through** *the soldier's arm.*
(b) An idea flashed **through** *his mind.* (To show a thought suddenly occurring or passing quickly)

12. Use of "**up**" – Indicates upward movement, emotional strength, or recovery
(a) She *looked* **up** at the sky. (Moving the face and eyes upwards)
(b) Tears welled **up** in her *eyes.* (Eyes filled up with tears)
(c) His father told him to *stand* **up** *for himself.* (To defend oneself confidently)
(d) It is important to *keep your chin* **up** during difficult times. (To stay positive in tough times)
(e) It is not always easy to *pick yourself* **up** after a setback. (To recover after a failure or a difficult situation)
(f) They gained a leg **up** after the rival team suffered injuries. (To have an advantage over someone)

13. Use of "**above**" – To indicate a location higher than or superior to.
(a) The bowler suffered a bruise **above** *his knee.*
(b) She held her *head* **above** *water.* (Literally to stay afloat, figuratively, to survive under pressure)
(c) She is *head and shoulders* **above** the rest of the class in math. (Far superior to others)

14. Use of "**to**" – To indicates closeness, direction, or figurative response
(a) She held the child close **to** *her chest.*
(b) This information is music **to** *my ears.* (Something pleasing or welcome to hear)
(c) The official was *deaf* **to** the protesters' demands. (Used figuratively to mean ignored them entirely)
(d) When in doubt, *listen* **to** *your heart.* (Follow your instincts or emotions)
(e) The Indian team *stood shoulder* **to** *shoulder* in support of their young captain. (Staying united and supportive)

15. Use of "**off**" – Indicates removal, detachment, or emotional release
(a) I shook the water **off** *my hands.* (Removed from the surface)
(b) I needed to get this **off** *my chest.* (To express something that has been bothering or weighing emotionally)
(c) The manager *shrugged* **off** the criticism. (To dismiss or ignore)
(d) The student *laughed his head* **off**. (To laugh uncontrollably)

16. Use of "out" – Indicates extension or intensity
   (a) The mountaineer screamed his *lungs* out on top of Mount Kanchenjunga. (To show extreme effort or intensity)
   (b) He held his *hand* out for a handshake. (Extended away from the body)
   (c) The child stuck out *his tongue* for the doctor to examine.
17. Use of "down" – To indicate downward movement, firmness or emotional release
   (a) A tear rolled down *her cheek*. (To show downward motion)
   (b) Once your exams are over, you can *let your hair* down. (To relax and enjoy)
   (c) *Put your foot* down and do not tolerate indiscipline. (To take a firm stand)
   (d) A chill ran down *her spine*. (To describe a sudden feeling of fear)
18. Use of "of" – To show belonging, quality, or association
   (a) The colour of *the cat's eyes* was mesmerising.
   (b) He is *hard* of *hearing*.
   (c) He has the eyes of a hawk. (Sharp eyesight and observation)
   (d) The colonel *became the face* of the army operation. (represented or was identified with)

4. Fixed Prepositional Phrases

Let us now look at expressions that are commonly used with specific prepositions. These are fixed phrases where the preposition and the accompanying word(s) typically occur together in usage.

Now, let us look at common patterns where specific prepositions follow certain **verbs**, **adjectives**, or **nouns**. These combinations are fixed and must be used together correctly.

1. Expressions with "in"

- In advance
- In my opinion
- In a hurry
- In cash
- In general
- In a soup
- In a car
- In a helicopter
- In the bedroom
- In the library
- In detail
- In good faith
- In high spirits
- In general
- In disguise
- In debt
- In danger
- In anticipation of
- In fact
- In good condition

2. Expressions with "on"

- On business
- On work
- On holiday
- On purpose
- On the train
- On foot
- On the phone
- On TV
- On the radio
- On the whole
- On a trip
- On strike
- On a spending spree
- On watch
- On a large scale
- On behalf of
- On business
- On a journey
- On oath

3. Expressions with "by"

- By cheque
- By mistake
- By chance
- By air
- By train
- By bus
- By sea
- By rail
- By accident
- By design
- By definition
- By all means
- By chance
- By air
- By all accounts
- By no means
- By birth
- By appointment

4. Expressions with "at"

- At length
- At peace
- At the rate of
- At all costs
- At a distance
- At one time
- At the outset
- At high speed

5. Prepositions of Movement and Location

Certain prepositions that indicate movement, direction, or location are typically followed by place-related nouns.

1. I am walking along the river.
2. I am walking up / down the stairs.

3. I am walking across the bridge.
4. I am walking on the pavement.
5. I am walking towards the exit.

Word + Preposition Patterns

Some nouns, verbs and adjectives are followed or preceded by specific prepositions. These combinations are grammatically fixed or idiomatic.

1. Words followed by "with"

- Careful with
- Dispense with
- Pleased with
- Honest with
- Agree with
- Angry with
- Associated with
- Satisfied with
- Familiar with
- Good with
- Busy with
- Involved with
- Done with
- Fed up with
- Friendly with
- Patient with
- Struggle with
- Fight with
- Acquaint with
- Afflict with
- Annoyed with

2. Words followed by "to"

- Dedicated to
- Committed to
- Attachment to
- Partial to
- Access to
- Married to (not with)
- Alternative to
- Adhere to
- Antidote to
- Addicted to
- Superior to
- Kind to
- Similar to
- Allergic to
- Faithful to
- Exposed to
- Opposed to
- Indifferent to
- Used to
- Attracted to
- Accustomed to
- Grateful to
- Introduce to

3. Words followed by "for"

- Responsible for
- Notorious for
- Known for
- Famous for
- Prepared for
- Ready for
- Zest for
- Thankful for
- Grateful for
- Sorry for
- Appetite for

4. Words followed by "of"

- Jealous of
- Ashamed of
- Scared of
- Proud of
- Bereft of
- Nice of
- Kind of
- Conscious of
- Approve of
- Afraid of
- Deprived of
- Dispose of (not *off*)

5. Words followed by "about"

- Nervous about
- Excited about
- Upset about
- Concerned about
- Glad about
- Mad about (Extremely fond of someone or something)
- Serious about
- Enthusiastic about
- Worried about
- Careful about

6. Words followed by "into"

- Admission into (Also used with *to*)
- Break into (To enter by force)
- Run into (To meet someone unexpectedly)
- Get into (To enter or become interested in something)
- Look into (To investigate)
- Turn into
- Translate into
- Crash into
- Fall into
- Change into
- Burst into (to suddenly begin, usually tears, laughter, flames, etc.)
- Pour into

7. **Words followed by "on / upon"**
- Authority on
- Attack on
- Impress on/upon
- Encroach on
- Revenge on
- Rely on
- Based on
- Decide on
- Comment on
- Lecture on
- Influence on

8. **Words followed by "at"**
- Work at
- Shout at
- Scream at
- Mad at
- Shocked at
- Smile at
- Stare at
- Surprised at
- Good at
- Horrified at
- Look at
- Arrive at
- Laugh at
- Point at
- Hint at
- Arrive at

9. **Words followed by "from"**
- Free from
- Recover from
- Suffer from
- Hide from
- Escape from
- Learn from
- Borrow from
- Resign from
- Depart from
- Receive from
- Steal from
- Grab from
- Exempted from

10. **Words followed by "against"**
- Lean against
- Fight against
- Protect against
- Rebel against
- Defend against
- Discriminate against
- Warn against
- Complain against
- Vote against

11. **Words followed by "towards"**
- Respectful towards
- Run towards
- Turn towards
- Drive towards
- March towards

12. **Words followed by "off"**
- Get off
- Cut off
- Take off
- Jump off
- Pay off
- Walk off
- Show off
- Turn off
- Keep off
- Send off
- Set off
- Lift off

13. **Words followed by "in"**
- Get in
- Believe in
- Hold in (high esteem - to respect or admire someone or something greatly)
- Employed in
- Participate in
- Succeed in
- Skilled in
- Result in
- Trust in
- Fail in
- Clothed in
- Born in
- Interested in
- Trust in
- Invest in
- Specialise in

Chapter 3: Phrasal Verbs

What is a Phrasal Verb?

A phrasal verb is formed when a verb is combined with one or more short words called *particles*. These particles are usually adverbs (e.g., up, out, away) or prepositions (e.g., on, over, into), and sometimes both.

A simple verb such as *run*, *take*, or *live* has its own meaning. However, when it is combined with a particle, its meaning may change entirely.

For example, *live on, live down* and *live off* all have different meanings. In short, adding a particle can change the meaning of the base verb.

This list contains commonly used phrasal verbs. In addition, a few other verb forms are included because they are important for fluent communication, even though they are not strictly phrasal verbs. These include prepositional verbs and verb + object + preposition.

Understanding the Difference Between Phrasal Verbs and Related Forms

Not every verb + word combination is a "true" phrasal verb. It is therefore helpful to know the difference:

Type	Structure	Example	Key Point
Phrasal Verb	verb + adverb (sometimes + preposition)	*give up, run into, put up with*	Meaning is often idiomatic and cannot be guessed from the words alone.
Prepositional Verb	verb + preposition (object comes after the preposition)	*look at, believe in, wait for*	Meaning is usually closer to the base verb; the preposition is fixed.
Verb + Object + Preposition	verb + object + preposition	*remind someone of, deprive someone of, thank someone for*	These are ordinary verbs that need both an object and a preposition to make sense.

A – Phrasal Verbs

Most of these follow *verb + preposition/adverb* or both, where the combined meaning is sometimes idiomatic and not always evident from the individual words.

S. No	Phrasal Verb	Meaning	Example
1.	account for	(a) To form the total of something (b) To explain or justify something	(a) Girls now account for over 48% of students in Indian schools. (b) He could not account for the missing documents.
2.	act on	To take action based on information or advice	The police acted on a tip-off and caught the thieves.
3.	act out	(a) To demonstrate something by acting (b) To express emotions (often negative) through actions or behaviour	(a) The director acted out the part for his crew. (b) The child acted out because he was upset.
4.	act up	To behave badly or not function properly	His laptop is acting up again.
5.	add up	To make sense, be logical	The accused's alibi in court did not add up.
6.	add up to	To total or result in	The bills for the party added up to Rs 5000.
7.	aim at	To target or intend to achieve something	This campaign aims at raising awareness.
8.	allow for	To take into account	You should allow for unexpected traffic delays.
9.	answer back	To reply in a rude manner	Instead of answering back, one should calmly explain one's point of view.

S. No	Phrasal Verb	Meaning	Example
10.	answer for	To take responsibility for	The employee will have to answer for his behaviour.
11.	ask after	To inquire about someone's well-being	He asked after my grandparents at the party.
12.	ask around	To ask many people the same question	He asked around for directions to the shop.
13.	ask for	(a) To request something (b) To inquire if someone is around	(a) I asked my neighbour for a first aid kit. (b) The visitor asked for Satish at the office reception.
14.	ask out	To invite someone to join you for an activity	She asked her friend out for a game of badminton after school.
15.	amount to	(a) To convey the total of something (b) Result or achievement	(a) Our monthly electricity bill amounts to over ₹ 2000. (b) His insincere apology does not amount to much.
16.	ache for	To want someone or something very much	He was homesick and ached for his family.
17.	attend to	To deal with or manage something	Please attend to this task immediately.
18.	argue over	To quarrel about something	Do not argue over petty things.
19.	argue with	To disagree or discuss opposing views	I sometimes argue with my cousin about which cricket team is the best.
20.	arrive at	(a) To reach a place (b) To reach a conclusion	(a) He arrived at the auditorium in a fancy car. (b) The party arrived at a compromise.
21.	associate with	To connect or link with someone or something	My father is associated with the company as a consultant.

A — Related Verbs

These are not strictly phrasal verbs. These include prepositional verbs (*verb + fixed preposition*) or *verb + object + preposition* structures. The meaning often remains close to the literal sense of the verb.

S. No	Related Verb	Meaning	Example
1.	abide by	To follow and act according to a rule or law	Employees are expected to abide by the rules of the company.
2.	adhere to	To stick to rules or plans	You have to adhere to the rules of the organisation.
3.	accompany on	To join someone and provide support, especially in music or travel	The musician was accompanied on the *tabla* by Ustad Nazir Khan.
4.	assure of	To remove doubt or give confidence about something	The bank manager assured me of all help.
5.	agree to	To give permission or consent to something	The government agreed to all the demands.
6.	agree with	To have the same opinion as someone	The principal agreed with the idea of improving the library.
7.	agree upon	To reach a mutual decision after discussion	The two companies agreed upon the terms of the contract.
8.	apply to	To state where a request or application is sent	I applied to the bank for a loan.
9.	apply for	To make a formal request for something	He applied for a job at the bank.
10.	appoint to	To assign someone to a specific position or post	He was appointed to the post of general manager.

S. No	Related Verb	Meaning	Example
11.	appoint for	To assign someone for a particular purpose or period	He was appointed for a period of five years.
12.	avail of	To take advantage of something	I availed of my leave before the end of the year.
13.	authority on	An expert on a subject	He is an authority on Shakespeare.
14.	approve of	To have a favourable opinion about something	My parents approve of my decision to learn music.

B – Phrasal Verbs

S. No.	Phrasal Verb	Meaning	Example
1.	back away	To move backwards in fear or dislike	She backed away when the dog barked loudly.
2.	back down	To withdraw from a position or give up in an argument or confrontation	The government finally backed down after public protests.
3.	back off	To move away or stop being aggressive or interfering	The police told the protestors to back off from the area
4.	back out	To withdraw from a commitment or agreement.	He backed out of the agreement at the last minute.
5.	back up	To support someone /something; make a copy	My colleagues backed me up during the discussion.
6.	bear with	To be patient with someone or something	Please bear with me while I explain the details.
7.	beat up	To hurt someone badly by hitting them	They beat up the thief before handing him over to the police.
8.	beef up	To strengthen or improve	The airport beefed up its security for the minister's arrival.
9.	bite off	To take on a difficult task; to remove something using teeth	He bit off more than he could chew by taking on four assignments.
10.	black out	To faint or lose consciousness	He was dehydrated and blacked out.
11.	blow away	(a) To defeat completely (b) To impress greatly (c) To be moved away (by wind)	(a) Our team blew away the opponents in the final match. (b) Her singing performance blew me away. (c) The papers blew away in the strong breeze.
12.	blow off	To ignore or dismiss	He blew off the meeting to go hiking.
13.	blow out	To extinguish	Reena blew out the candles on her birthday cake.
14.	blow up	(a) To enlarge (b) To explode (c) To inflate (d) To get very angry	(a) Blow up the photograph for framing. (b) The balloon blew up and popped with a loud bang. (c) Please blow up the balloons for the party. (d) The teacher blew up at the students for being late.
15.	boil down to	Be essentially about	Success boils down to hard work and patience.
16.	break away	To escape or leave suddenly; separate	Four legislators broke away from the political party.
17.	break down	(a) To stop working (b) To collapse emotionally	(a) His car broke down on the highway. (b) She broke down after hearing the bad news.

S. No.	Phrasal Verb	Meaning	Example
18.	break even	Neither profit nor loss (covering costs without making a profit)	A year after starting his business, he finally **broke even**.
19.	break into	To enter by force	Burglars **broke into** the house last night.
20.	break out	Begin suddenly	A fire **broke out** in the market.
21.	break up	To end a relationship or gathering	The meeting **broke up** at midnight.
22.	break with	To end a connection or relationship	India **broke with** its colonial past in 1947.
23	bring about	To cause something to happen	The new policy **brought about** many reforms.
24.	bring down	To cause something to be lower or to make someone unhappy	The news **brought** him **down**.
25.	bring in	To introduce	The government plans to **bring in** an ordinance.
26.	bring on	Lead to or to cause something	Vitamin D deficiency **brings on** ailments.
27.	bring out	To publish or make clear	We managed to **bring out** the magazine.
28.	bring up	Mention a topic; raise a child	The poet **brought up** an interesting topic.
29.	brush up on	To revise or improve knowledge	You need to **brush up** on your grammar.
30.	bump into	To meet someone by chance	I **bumped into** my relative at the theatre.
31.	burn out	To become exhausted from overwork	Studying 10 hours daily will **burn** you **out**.
32.	burst into	Begin suddenly (tears, laughter, flames)	We **burst into** laughter hearing his joke.
33.	buy out	To purchase someone's share in a business	The company **bought out** a minority shareholder.
34.	buy up	To buy large amounts of something	Fearing a power cut, residents **bought up** all the candles at the store.

B — Related Verbs

S. No.	Related Verb	Meaning	Example
1.	beg for	To request something earnestly	He **begged for** mercy.
2.	begin at	Indicate a time or place	The concert will **begin at** 8 pm.
3.	begin in	To show a starting time like month, year, season, or location	The project **began in** 2023.
4.	begin with	To start with something	The movie **begins with** a thrilling scene.
5.	believe in	To trust or have faith in	She **believes in** hard work.
6.	bent on	To be very determined	He was **bent on** finishing the homework quickly.
7.	bet on	To be sure about something	I can **bet on** Siraj doing well in this match.
8.	blind in	To have sight deficiency in one eye	He is **blind in** one eye.
9.	blind to	To ignore or fail to notice something; to lack awareness or judgement	The mother was **blind to** her son's faults.
10.	born into	To enter the world as a member of a group/class	He was **born into** wealth.
11.	born of	To be the result of something	The idea was **born of** necessity.
12.	born to	To have as parents	She was **born to** a family of musicians.
13.	born with	To have from birth	She was **born with** a rare talent.

Important Notes:

- **Back off vs Back away vs Back down:**
  - Back off: stop being involved or retreat
  - Back away: physically move back
  - Back down: admit defeat or withdraw from a position or argument
- **Blow away vs Blow off:**
  - Blow away: carried off by wind; defeat; impress greatly;
  - Blow off: moved from a fixed position by wind.
  - Blow out: extinguish (a flame, light, etc.)
  - Blow up: enlarge; explode; inflate; get very angry
- **Bite vs Bite off:**
  - Bite: sink teeth into something, but not necessarily removing a piece
  - Bite off: remove a piece by biting; Figuratively, it means to take on more than one can handle
- **Born into vs Born of vs Born to vs Born with:**
  - Born into: enter the world as a member of a group or class
  - Born of: result of something
  - Born to: have as parents
  - Born with: have from birth
- *Born into, born of, born to, and born with* all convey different shades of meaning about origin, family, ability, or destiny.

C – Phrasal Verbs

S. No	Phrasal Verb	Meaning	Example
1	Call back	To return a phone call	I will call you back after my morning prayer.
2	Call off	To cancel something	The cricket match was called off due to rain.
3	Call on	To visit someone or ask them to speak	The Prime Minister called on the President. The principal called on the Chief Guest to address the gathering.
4	Call out	(a) To shout (b) To challenge someone (c) To expose	(a) He called out for help. (b) The boxer called out his opponent for a fight. (c) The worker called out unsafe conditions in the factory.
5	Call for	To need something; to ask for or demand	Mahatma Gandhi called for India's independence. He called for an emergency meeting of the association.
6	Call in	To summon	The technician was called in to repair the computer.
7	Call up	To contact, usually over the phone	I called up my friend to clear my doubts.
8	Call upon	To urge or request with energy to get people to do something	Mahatma Gandhi called upon fellow Indians to come together.
9	Calm down	To become or make someone calmer	My uncle calmed down after hearing that the thief had been caught.
10	Carry on	To continue doing something	Please carry on with your work.
11	Carry out	To perform or complete a task; to implement	The ministers carried out the PM's orders.
12	Carry away	To be swept away physically or emotionally	The floods carried away much of the standing crop.
13	Catch on	To understand or become popular	The new song by Arijit Singh has caught on.
14	Catch up	To reach the same level as others	He walked fast to catch up with the other mountain hikers.

S. No	Phrasal Verb	Meaning	Example
15	Check in	To register at a hotel or airport	Most hotels allow guests to check in only at noon.
16	Check out	(a) To leave a hotel (b) To examine something	(a) I decided to check out of the hotel early. (b) Let's check out the new bookshop.
17	Cheer up	To become or make someone happier	Going to an amusement park may cheer you up.
18	Chip in	To contribute money or effort	We all chipped in to help the disaster victims.
19	Clear up	To clarify or make something clean	The sky cleared up after the storm.
20	Cling to	To hold tightly physically or emotionally	(a) The baby clung to her mother. (b) She still clings to the hope that her lost dog will be found.
21	Close down	To shut a business permanently	The iron and steel unit closed down last year.
22	Come across	(a) To find by chance (b) To give an impression	(a) I came across my old photos in the attic. (b) She comes across as an upright person.
23	Come apart	To break into pieces	The old toy came apart.
24	Come back	To return	I came back from Kerala last week.
25	Come by	(a) To obtain (b) To pass by	(a) Fresh fruits are easy to come by in summer. (b) I saw your friend come by our house this morning.
26	Come down	To reduce	Prices have come down in the real estate sector.
27	Come down with	To become ill with something	He came down with a cold last night.
28	Come in	To enter	I asked him to come in.
29	Come of	To happen as a result of something	Nothing good will come of cheating in an exam.
30	Come off	To succeed or to detach	The plan did not come off as expected.
31	Come out	(a) To be revealed (b) To be published or released	(a) The truth finally came out during the meeting. (b) The results came out today.
32	Come over	To visit someone's place	I asked my friend to come over in the evening.
33	Come to	(a) To regain consciousness (b) To total an amount (c) To reach a decision (d) To reach the point of realising something	(a) She came to after fainting in the heat. (b) The bill came to ₹500. (c) They came to an agreement quickly. (d) He came to realise the importance of honesty.
34	Come up	(a) To appear or arise (b) To be mentioned or or talked about in conversation (c) To approach or move towards someone (d) To be happening soon or approaching	(a) The exhibition will come up next week. (b) Her name came up in conversation. (c) The child came up to his teacher. (d) My exams are coming up soon.
35	Come up with	To think of an idea or plan	He came up with a brilliant solution.
36	Come around	To change one's opinion or agree after initial resistance	He came around to our idea of going on a picnic.
37	Count on	To rely or depend on someone	I knew I could count on my sister in difficult times.
38	Crack down on	To take strict action	The police cracked down on anti-social elements in the city.
39	Cross out	To draw a line through something	The teacher crossed out all the incorrect answers.
40	Cut back on	To reduce usage or expenses	The residents were asked to cut back on water usage.

S. No	Phrasal Verb	Meaning	Example
41	Cut down	To reduce or shorten	I have cut down on sugar.
42	Cut in	To interrupt	He asked his colleague not to cut in while he was speaking.
43	Cut off	To stop or isolate	The villages were cut off after the floods.
44	Cut out	(a) To remove (b) To eliminate (c) To be suited for something	(a) He cut out a picture. (b) We must cut out bad habits early. (c) I think he is cut out for city life.
45	Cut up	To be unhappy	He is very cut up with you.

C – Related Verbs

S. No	Related Verb	Meaning	Example
1	Condemn to	To declare that someone must suffer a particular fate	The judge condemned the accused to life imprisonment.
2	Confine to	To restrict or limit to a place or activity	The sick child was confined to bed for a few days.
3	Commit to	To promise or dedicate oneself to something	She committed to finishing her homework before dinner.
4	Care for	(a) To take care of (b) To like or want (in negative or questions)	(a) She cares for her pets. (b) I do not really care for spicy food. (c) Would you care for some tea?
5	Careful of	To be cautious about danger or harm	Be careful of that ferocious dog.
6	Careful about	To be cautious about actions or decisions	Be careful about crossing the road during rush hour.
7	Careful with	To be cautious in handling objects	Be careful with that glass object.
8	Charge with	To accuse of something	The player was charged with breaking the rules of the game.
9	Complain to	To direct a complaint to someone	We complained to the manager.
10	Complain about	To express dissatisfaction generally	We complained about the noise next door.
11	Comply with	To obey	Even cyclists must comply with traffic signals.
12	Congratulate on	To congratulate someone for a specific achievement or event	I congratulated him on his promotion.
13	Congratulate for	To congratulate someone for their effort, behaviour, or contribution leading to an achievement	I congratulate your team for their hard work.
14	Courteous to	To be polite or respectful toward someone	We should be courteous to everyone.
15	Cause for	A reason to have/do something, usually with a reaction	There was no cause for alarm.
16	Cause of	The source or reason something happened (often negative)	Smoking is a major cause of lung cancer.

D – Phrasal Verbs

S. No	Phrasal Verb	Meaning	Example
1	Dash off	To do something quickly	She dashed off an email before leaving for work.
2	Die down	To become less intense	The sound of firecrackers died down after midnight.
3	Dig in	To start eating enthusiastically	Let us dig in before the food gets cold.

S. No	Phrasal Verb	Meaning	Example
4	Dig up	To uncover something, literally or figuratively	The reporter **dug up** hidden facts.
5	Double back	To return in the direction you came from	We **doubled back** after missing the turn.
6	Double down	To increase effort or commitment despite criticism	The team **doubled down** on their practice after losing the match.
7	Double up (as)	To take on two roles	My study **doubles up** as a meditation room.
8	Do away with	(a) To get rid of or abolish something (b) To kill someone (informal)	(a) The committee decided to **do away** with the rule. (b) The villain tried to **do away with** the hero.
9	Do without	To manage without something	During the floods, families had to **do without** electricity.
10	Drag on	To last longer than expected	The meeting **dragged on** for hours.
11	Draw a blank	(a) To fail to find anything (b) To be unsuccessful	(a) Investigators **drew a blank** at the site. (b) I tried to solve the puzzle but **drew a blank**.
12	Draw back	To retreat or move away, usually due to fear or surprise	I **drew back** when the dog growled.
13	Draw down	(a) To reduce military presence (b) To take money from reserves	(a) The army was **drawn down**. (b) We **drew down** on the loan.
14	Draw even	To come in equal in a race	The athletes **drew even** at the finish line.
15	Draw from	(a) To take or use something as a source (b) To use as inspiration	(a) He **drew** water **from** the well. (b) The author **drew from** his childhood memories to write the novel.
16	Draw in	(a) To involve someone (b) To arrive and stop (train/vehicle) (c) Shortening of time or daylight (d) Breathing in	(a) The teacher drew in the backbenchers by asking them questions. (b) The evenings are **drawing in**. (c) The train has **drawn in** at the station. (d) He **drew in** a deep breath.
17	Draw into	To involve someone in a situation	I was **drawn into** the discussion.
18	Draw near	To approach or come closer in time or space	The exams are **drawing near**.
19	Draw on	(a) To use something as a supply, source or reserve (often money, energy, strength) (b) To make use of experience, knowledge or skills	(a) He **drew on** his savings to pay for the medical bills. (b) She **drew on** her experience to solve the problem.
20	Draw out	(a) To induce someone to speak/act (b) To make something last longer / prolong (c) To withdraw money	(a) The teacher asked gentle questions to **draw** the shy student **out**. (b) The meeting was **drawn out** for hours. (c) He **drew out** ₹5000 from the ATM.
21	Draw up	(a) To prepare a document or plan (b) When a vehicle comes and stops (c) To pull a chair	(a) The lawyer **drew up** a contract. (b) The taxi **drew up** outside. (c) **Draw up** a chair and join us.

S. No	Phrasal Verb	Meaning	Example
22	Dress down	(a) To wear casual clothes (b) To scold	(a) It is fine to dress down on Fridays. (b) The coach dressed down the players for being late to practice.
23	Dress up	To wear formal/fancy clothes	Everyone dressed up for the party.
24	Drift apart	To slowly become less close to someone over time (similar to *grow apart*)	Minu and her best friend drifted apart after moving to different cities.
25	Drum up	To actively increase support	The volunteers drummed up donations for the relief fund.
26	Drop by	To stop briefly, often on the way somewhere	Do drop by when you are in town.
27	Drop in	To arrive casually/unexpectedly for a short time	Feel free to drop in anytime.
28	Drop off	(a) To fall asleep (b) To deliver someone or something (c) To reduce	(a) He dropped off during the lecture. (b) Please drop me off at the station. (c) Interest rates have dropped off.
29	Drop out	To quit school/college/activity before completion	She dropped out of engineering college and pursued medicine.
30	Dry up	(a) To stop being available (supply ends) (b) To lose water (become dry) (c) To stop speaking (often suddenly, because nervous or forgetting)	(a) His savings dried up. Job opportunities dried up during the pandemic (b) The river dried up. (c) She dried up in the middle of his presentation.
31	Dumb down	To make something simpler, often too simple	The teacher dumbed down the lesson.
32	Dive in	(a) To jump into water (b) To begin eagerly	(a) He dived into the pool. (b) She dived in without reading the instructions.
33	Dive into	To start doing something with enthusiasm	She dove into her new project.
34	Dwell on	To think or talk about something for too long (often negative)	Do not dwell on the past.

D — Related Verbs

S. No	Related Verb	Meaning	Example
1	Dawn on	To suddenly realise	It dawned on her that she had left her keys behind.
2	Deal in	To be involved in buying/selling something	The shop deals in imported cars.
3	Deal with	To handle or address a problem or person	The teacher dealt with the situation calmly.
4	Deliver on	To complete successfully; to keep a promise	He delivered on his promises.
5	Die from	Used for external causes/events leading to death	He died from a gunshot wound.
6	Die of	Used for internal causes of death (illness, condition, emotion)	He died of a heart attack.

S. No	Related Verb	Meaning	Example
7	Differ from	To be different in nature or characteristics	This design differs from the previous one.
8	Differ with	To disagree with someone	I differ with you on that point.
9	Dispose of	To discard	We disposed of the old car and bought a new one.
10	Draw on	To mention passing or approaching time (usually seasons, parts of the day, or old age) – (less commonly used)	As summer draws on, it gets uncomfortable. He grew weaker as old age drew on.

Important Notes:

- **Die of** vs **Die from**
  - Die of → internal causes (illness, emotions, conditions).
  - Die from → external causes (injuries, accidents, exposure).
- **Draw on** vs **Draw from**
  - Draw from → source of inspiration/ideas (where it comes from).
  - Draw on → application of inspiration/ideas (how it is used).

Rule: If talking about inspiration, use draw from. If talking about application, use draw on.

- **Drop in** vs **Drop by**
  - Drop in → more casual, often unexpected.
  - Drop by → slightly more intentional, brief stop.
- **Draw in**
  - 'Pull in' and 'Come in' mean the same as 'Draw in'.
- **Draw in (breathing sense)**
  - 'Take in' means the same.
- **Draw up**
  - 'Pull up' also means the same.
- **Draw out (money)**
  - 'Withdraw' is more commonly used in this context.
- **Drop out**
  - A 'drop-out' is someone who leaves school or college without finishing the course.
- **Dispose of**
  - It is used with 'of', not 'off'.

E – Phrasal Verbs

S. No	Phrasal Verb	Meaning	Example
1	Earmark for	To set aside for a specific purpose, usually by authority	The land was earmarked for building a new hospital.
2	Ease off	To become slower or less intense	The rain eased off by noon.
3	Ease up	To relax, become less strict, or reduce effort intentionally	You need to ease up and take a break.
4	Eat away	To gradually destroy or erode	Rust has eaten away parts of the old gate.
5	Eat into	To gradually reduce resources like time or money	Unexpected medical bills ate into their savings.
6	Eat out	To have a meal at a restaurant	We decided to eat out on Friday night.
7	Eat in	To have a meal at home (opposite of *eat out*)	We will cook dinner and eat in tonight.
8	Eat up	To consume or destroy completely (resources or emotions)	The project is eating up a lot of time.

S. No	Phrasal Verb	Meaning	Example
9	Edit out	To remove parts of a film or writing	The director **edited out** two scenes to shorten the film.
10	Egg on	To encourage or urge someone, often to do something foolish or risky	His friends **egged him** on to jump into the freezing lake.
11	Eke out	To make something last longer or manage to survive with difficulty	They **eked out** a living by working part-time jobs.
12	Edge out	To narrowly defeat or replace someone	She **edged out** her rival to win the scholarship.
13	Elaborate on/upon	To give more details or explain more clearly	The teacher **elaborated on** the main points of the lesson.
14	Empty out	To remove contents or evacuate	He **emptied out** his bag when he got home.
15	Embark on/upon	To begin a journey, project, or new phase	After her graduation, she **embarked on** a career in law.
16	Encroach on	To gradually take or intrude	The weeds **encroached on** the vegetable garden.
17	End up	To finally be in a situation, often unintended	After taking the wrong bus, he **ended up** far from home.
18	Endow with	To be given a particular talent or quality	She is **endowed with** great musical ability.
19	Engage in	To take part in an activity	The students **engaged in** a lively discussion.
20	Expand on (same as *Enlarge on/ upon*)	To give more details about something	The speaker **expanded on** her ideas in the second part of the talk.
21	Enter into	To begin formally, especially an agreement or relationship	The two companies **entered into** a partnership.
22	Even out	To make or become balanced, smooth, or equal	The new policy will help even out differences in pay.
23	Explain away	To justify or make excuses for something bad	He tried to **explain away** his absence by saying he was unwell.

E – Related Verbs

S. No	Related Verb	Meaning	Example
1	Enlarge on/upon	To give more details or expand (same as *Expand on*)	The author **enlarged on** the themes in her book.

Important Notes:

- **Ease off vs Ease up:**
  - Ease off → when intensity reduces naturally (rain, traffic).
  - Ease up → when effort, pressure, or strictness is reduced intentionally.
- **Eat away vs Eat into vs Eat up:**
  - Eat away → gradual destruction/erosion (rust, corruption).
  - Eat into → gradual reduction of resources (time, money).
  - Eat up → complete consumption (resources, emotions, land).
- **Eat out vs Eat in:**
  - Direct opposites (restaurant vs home).

Egg on vs Egg on the face:
- Egg on → urge someone (often toward reckless action).
- Egg on the face → embarrassment.

- **Expand on vs Enlarge on/upon:**
  - Both mean 'to give more details.'
  - Enlarge on/upon → old-fashioned, formal, not used much today.
  - Expand on → modern, standard, used in everyday speech and writing.

***Examples*:**
- o Old style: The teacher enlarged upon the lesson with examples.
- o Common today: The teacher expanded on the lesson with examples.

F – Phrasal Verbs

S. No	Phrasal Verb	Meaning	Example
1	Face up to	To accept, acknowledge and deal with something difficult or unpleasant	It is time you faced up to the truth.
2	Face off	To confront someone in a direct or competitive situation	The ruling party and opposition members faced off over the controversial bill in Parliament.
3	Fade away	To gradually disappear, become less important, frequent, or intense	His voice faded away as he walked into the distance.
4	Fade out	To gradually reduce to silence or darkness	The editor made sure the music faded out at the end of the scene.
5	Fall apart	(a) To break into pieces (b) To become emotionally unstable (c) To stop working well / fail (plans, systems, organisations)	(a) His old bicycle fell apart due to years of disuse. (b) He fell apart after losing the final match. (c) The meeting fell apart because no one was prepared
6	Fall back	To move backward or retreat, especially in the face of danger or pressure	The soldiers were ordered to fall back as the enemy advanced.
7	Fall back on	To rely on something as a backup	When his business failed, he had to fall back on his mother's savings.
8	Fall behind	To fail to keep up with progress or schedule	He fell behind in his studies due to prolonged illness.
9	Fall for	(a) To fall in love with someone or something you care about a lot (b) To be tricked	(a) She fell for the kitten's big blue eyes. (b) I advised my mother not to fall for online scams.
10	Fall out	To have a disagreement or quarrel, or to stop being friendly	The two friends fell out over a game.
11	Fall on/upon	(a) To suddenly notice or see something (b) To take responsibility for something	(a) The detective's eyes fell upon a note in the dustbin. (b) The duty of looking after the dog fell upon her.
12	Fall through	To fail before being completed, usually referring to a plan or arrangement	His plan to book a chartered flight fell through.
13	Fall under	To belong to a group or type	Mathematics falls under the subject of science.
14	Fan out	To spread out in different directions	The soldiers fanned out in different directions.
15	Fear for	To be worried because someone may be in danger	With a leopard on the prowl, the farmer feared for his cattle.

S. No	Phrasal Verb	Meaning	Example
16	Feel for	To have sympathy for someone	I feel for the puppy; it looks so hungry.
17	Fend off	To prevent or avoid something (attack, questions, problems)	The minister fended off tough questions from journalists.
18	Figure out	To understand or solve something	She could not figure out why the remote was not working.
19	Fight back	To resist something strongly	She fought back her fear before going on stage.
20	Fight off	To get rid of something unpleasant; to resist successfully and keep something harmful away	The administration needs help to fight off the hyenas wandering into the village.
21	Factor in	To include something in a calculation, decision or plan	The company failed to factor in the rising cost of coal.
22	Fill in	(a) To complete a form (b) To substitute temporarily	(a) The students filled in their details in the form. (b) The nurse filled in for the senior doctor for a short time.
23	Fill out	To complete a form fully, in detail	Students need to fill out this application form completely.
24	Fill up	To make something full	I decided to fill up the petrol tank before leaving.
25	Find out	To discover or learn something new	They were delighted to find out about their daughter's award.
26	Finish up	To complete a routine task	The employee will finish up this report before leaving.
27	Finish off	To complete or eliminate something with intensity	I finished off the dessert in one bite.
28	Fish for	To try to get praise or information indirectly	She is always fishing for compliments.
29	Flesh out	To add more details	The editor asked the reporter to flesh out his article.
30	Fit into	(a) To be suitable for or adjust to a place/ group (b) To be the right size or shape to go into something	(a) He quickly fit into the new school and made new friends. (b) The toys could not fit into the small box.
31	Fool around	To waste time	If you fool around, you will fail the exam.
32	Frown on/ upon	To disapprove of something	Spitting in public places is frowned upon in many countries.
33	Fizzle out	To end weakly or disappointingly	The workers' strike fizzled out in a day.
34	Fix up	To arrange or repair something	The technician fixed up the microwave.
35	Follow through	To continue with a plan until completion	He promised to clear the files but failed to follow through.
36	Follow up	To take further action on something already started	The doctor advised me to follow up after two weeks.
37	Flirt with	To consider an idea without commitment	He flirted with the idea of studying law.
38	Freak out	To become very anxious, upset, or angry	The tourist freaked out when he lost his passport.
39	Fly into	To suddenly become very angry	The neighbour flew into a temper over the parking issue.
40	Foist on	To force someone to accept something	The politician foisted his views on the people.

S. No	Phrasal Verb	Meaning	Example
41	Fold up	To close or shut down	The eatery folded up in six months due to low footfalls.
42	Force into	To compel someone into doing something against their will	He was forced into joining the game even though he was tired.
43	Forge ahead	To continue making progress	The team forged ahead with their project despite the power cut.
44	Freeze up	(a) To be covered with ice (b) To stop moving due to fear	(a) The river froze up during the cold winter. (b) He froze up when he saw a spider on his desk.
45	Freshen up	To wash and tidy oneself	I will go to my room to freshen up.
46	Frighten away/off	To scare someone/something so they leave or do not approach	His dog frightened off the burglar.
47	Fritter away	To waste in a foolish manner	The team frittered away its lead by careless play.
48	Fuss over	To pay too much attention, showing concern	Her mother fussed over her dog's health.

G – Phrasal Verbs

S. No	Phrasal Verb	Meaning	Example
1	Gang up	To form a group or unite against someone	The team ganged up to solve the puzzle quickly.
2	Gather around	To come together in a group and surround someone	As children, we would gather around our grandmother to listen to stories.
3	Gear up	To prepare yourself for an event or activity	The mountaineering team is gearing up for the expedition.
4	Get across	To communicate an idea effectively	I was able to get across my point to the audience.
5	Get after	To try to catch, punish or make someone take action, especially if they have done something wrong	The teacher got after the students who did not submit their homework.
6	Get ahead	To make progress and be successful	Being tech-savvy will help him get ahead in his career.
7	Get along (with)	To have a friendly relationship (informal)	The neighbours get along with each other.
8	Get around/round	(a) To move from place to place (b) To avoid or to bypass (c) To spread news	(a) It will be easy to get around Delhi by Metro rail. (b) She got around the problem by asking her friend for help. (c) Word got around/round that Mayank was going to be promoted soon.
9	Get at	(a) To criticise repeatedly (usually in a nagging or fault-finding way) (b) To imply or suggest indirectly (c) To reach or obtain (something hard to access)	(a) The coach kept getting at the players for not following the strategy. (b) What exactly are you getting at by quoting those statistics? (c) The reporters were desperate to get at the minister for a quick comment.

S. No	Phrasal Verb	Meaning	Example
10	Get away	(a) To escape from a place or situation (b) To go on a short holiday / take a break (c) To succeed in doing something unnoticed (slip away quietly)	(a) The intruders **got away** before the landlady arrived. (b) We are hoping to **get away** to Goa during the summer holidays. (c) The actor managed to **get away** without being recognised by fans.
11	Get away from	(a) To distance oneself from a style, habit, idea, or association (b) To stop being influenced by something	(a) It is difficult to **get away from** social media once you are hooked on it. (b) The school is trying to **get away from** rote learning and focus on creativity.
12	Get away with	To avoid punishment despite doing something wrong	The motorist **got away with** jumping the red traffic light.
13	Get back	(a) To return to a place (b) To regain something	(a) I will **get back** by 3 pm. (b) He hopes he can **get back** his stolen mobile.
14	Get back at	To take revenge or retaliate	She **got back at** her brother by eating the last piece of cake.
15	Get back into	To restart or re-engage in an earlier activity	It is time for him to **get back into** the stock market.
16	Get by	To manage or cope (usually financially)	He **got by** with help from his childhood friends.
17	Get down	(a) To move lower (physically) (b) To start doing something seriously (c) To feel sad	(a) The cat **got down** from the tree. (b) Let us **get down** to solving the problem before the deadline. (c) Rainy days always **get** me **down**.
18	Get in	(a) To enter (a vehicle, building, room, etc.) (b) To arrive at a place (often home, office, or travel destination)	(a) I **got in** the car and drove off. (b) Do you know what time the chemistry professor will **get in**?
19	Get into	(a) To enter a place (b) To become involved (often in trouble or an activity) (c) To be accepted (usually into a school, college, or group)	(a) He **got into** the classroom quietly. (b) He **got into** trouble at school. (c) Tejaswini **is working hard to get into** XLRI, Jamshedpur.
20	Get off	(a) To leave a vehicle (b) To avoid punishment or criticism	(a) Vibhuti **got off** at the wrong railway station. (b) She **got off** with a warning for being late.
21	Get on	(a) To board (b) To progress (c) To continue (d) To have a good relationship	(a) Yamuna **got on** the bus just in time. (b) Sandeep is **getting on** well with his new job. (c) **Get on** with your painting. (d) Does he **get on** with his colleagues?
22	Get out	(a) To leave or exit a place (b) To become known / revealed	(a) We need to **get out** of the house before it starts raining. (b) Despite their best efforts, the news of the deal **got out** quickly.

S. No	Phrasal Verb	Meaning	Example
23	Get out of	To avoid doing something	Vikas tried to get out of doing the errand.
24	Get over	To recover or accept and move on	It took Manish a week to get over the viral flu.
25	Get through	(a) To survive or endure (b) To establish contact (c) To complete	(a) She got through the surgery successfully. (b) I tried calling several times but could not get through to her. (c) He got through the paperwork quickly.
26	Get to	(a) To affect emotionally (positively or negatively) (b) To reach / uncover the real cause, truth, or heart of something	(a) Her heartfelt speech really got to me. (b) The committee is trying to get to the root of the problem.
27	Get together	To meet socially	The residents decided to get together for the festivities.
28	Get up	To rise from bed or a seated position	I get up at 5 am every day.
29	Give away	(a) To reveal (b) To donate	(a) Her accent gave away the fact that she was from the US. (b) My friend decided to give away her old clothes.
30	Give up	To quit or stop doing something	The doctor advised him to give up junk food.
31	Give in	To surrender or agree after persuasion	The management finally gave in to the workers' demands.
32	Give out	To distribute	The class teacher gave out the question papers.
33	Give off	To emit smell, light, or heat	The lilies gave off a lovely fragrance.
34	Give back	To return something	I gave back his book yesterday.
35	Give over	To hand something over formally	The retiring principal gave over his responsibilities to the new head.
36	Give way	(a) To collapse (b) To yield to someone	(a) The dam gave way during the floods. (b) Drivers must give way to pedestrians at crossings.
37	Give up on	To stop trying (abandon)	He will never give up on cinema.
38	Gloss over	To ignore, conceal, or treat a problem/ error superficially	The article glossed over the main problem.
39	Go about	(a) To deal with a task (b) To continue in the usual way	(a) The team went about preparing the hall for the event. (b) The fishermen went about their daily chores.
40	Go after	To chase	She decided to go after her dream of becoming a scientist.
41	Go against	To contradict	The verdict went against the association.
42	Go ahead	To proceed; to begin	The host was asked to go ahead and announce the winners.
43	Go on	To continue	Please go on with your presentation.
44	Go off	(a) To explode or make noise (b) To get spoiled	(a) The fire alarm went off in our hostel. (b) The milk has gone off; don't drink it.

S. No	Phrasal Verb	Meaning	Example
45	Go over	To review or examine something	Let us **go over** the answers before submitting them.
46	Go down	(a) To decrease or sink (b) To be received in a certain way (reaction) (c) To be remembered or recorded (d) To lose or be defeated	(a) (a) The temperature **went down** after the rain. (b) His speech did not **go down** well with the audience. (c) This battle will **go down** in history. (d) The team did not **go down** without a fight.
47	Go through	To experience or undergo something	The students **went through** an exciting science exhibition that sparked their curiosity.
48	Go with	To match or suit	This pair of jeans **goes with** your shirt.
49	Go under	(a) To fail financially (b) To sink	(a) The textile company **went under** last year. (b) The Titanic **went under** after striking an iceberg.
50	Go without	To manage despite not having something	They had to **go without** water for three days.
51	Go by	(a) To rely on / base judgment on (b) To pass the time	(a) You should never **go by** appearances alone. (b) As the years **went by**, their friendship became stronger.
52	Go along with	To support a decision or idea	Neelima will **go along with** whatever Garima decides.
53	Goad on	To encourage or push someone (often against their better judgement)	The boys **goaded** him **into climbing** the tall tree.
54	Gobble down	To eat quickly and greedily, especially by swallowing large amounts at a time (informal)	The hungry dog **gobbled** the meat **down** in seconds.
55	Grapple with	To try hard to solve a problem	The scientists **grappled with** the new virus strain.
56	Grow apart	To develop different interests (similar to *Drift apart*)	The two friends **grew apart** over time.
57	Grow on	To start liking something gradually	Her cheerful personality slowly **grew on** everyone in the office.
58	Guard against	To avoid risks, problems, or dangers before they happen	A healthy diet helps **guard against** many ailments.
59	Gun for	(a) To make a great effort to win or obtain something (b) To aggressively target someone, often with the intention of harming or defeating them	(a) Rohan is **gunning for** the top position in his class. (b) The opposition team is **gunning for** our star player.
60	Gun down	To shoot or eliminate a target decisively, often when the target cannot defend itself (Can be literal or figurative)	(a) The hunters **gunned down** the dangerous animal to protect the villagers. (b) She **gunned down** all the zombies in the video game to clear the level.

Important Notes:

- **Get in** vs **Get into:**
  - 'Got into the car' stresses the action of moving inside, while 'Got in the car' stresses the state of being inside.

- **Give over** vs **Hand over:**
    - In modern usage, 'hand over' is commonly used.
- **Grow apart** vs **Drift apart:**
    - Interchangeable, but 'grow apart' is more common in everyday English.

H – Phrasal Verbs

S. No	Phrasal Verb	Meaning	Example
1	Hack down	To remove something by cutting it down (usually a tree)	The tree in front of the building was hacked down.
2	Hack off	To cut something in a rough and violent way (*Chop off* means the same)	The woodcutter hacked off the top branches.
3	Hail from	To be born in or live in a place	I hail from Palakkad.
4	Hand down	To pass to the next generation	The exquisite artefact was handed down to her by her grandfather.
5	Hand in	To submit something	The minister handed in his resignation yesterday.
6	Hand out	To distribute to a group	The volunteers handed out food packets to the flood victims.
7	Hand over	To give control or responsibility	The chief architect handed over the project to his assistant.
8	Hand round	To pass something within a group	The chef handed round the pastries.
9	Hang on	(a) Wait briefly (b) Hold tightly	(a) Hang on a minute, I will finish lunch. (b) Mayank hung on to the tree branch until help arrived.
10	Hang around	To stay without purpose	The two friends hung around the shopping mall, chatting.
11	Hang out	To socialise or relax	The children love to hang out at the beach.
12	Hang up	To end a phone call	He hung up before I could say goodbye.
13	Hanker after	To desire greatly	It is not good to hanker after money all the time.
14	Harp on	To keep talking about a subject	My neighbour kept harping on the overflowing garbage bin.
15	Haul up	To be forced to appear in court	The shopkeeper was hauled up in court for not paying taxes.
16	Head back	To return to a place	Since it is getting dark, let us head back home.
17	Head for	(a) To move towards a specific place (b) To move towards a likely result	(a) The children headed for the playground after school. (b) She is headed for success with all her hard work.
18	Head off	(a) To leave or start a journey (b) Prevent something	(a) We headed off early to beat traffic. (b) Quick police action headed off a major riot.
19	Head towards	(a) To move nearer to a place (b) To move towards a likely result	(a) The train is heading towards Kolkata. (b) India is heading towards the General Election.
20	Heap on	To shower praise or criticism	The teacher heaped praise on the students for their hard work.
21	Hear about	To get news/details	Did you hear about the new science teacher?

S. No	Phrasal Verb	Meaning	Example
22	Hear of	To learn something exists	Have you heard of Athirapally waterfalls?
23	Hear out	To listen until finished	Please hear me out before deciding.
24	Heat up	(a) To make hot (b) To become intense	(a) I will heat up your dinner. (b) The argument started to heat up.
25	Help out	To do a favour	The association helped out the disaster victims financially.
26	Herd together	To gather a group	The staff herded the passengers together to board the bus.
27	Hide behind	To use as an excuse	He hid behind his busy schedule to avoid helping.
28	Hinge on	To depend entirely on	The success of the picnic hinges on good weather.
29	Hint at	To suggest indirectly	He hinted at wanting a new bicycle for his birthday.
30	Hit back	To criticise or retaliate	The actor hit back at the media for spreading lies.
31	Hit off	To like each other and become friends	Anil and Aman hit it off right away because they both love cricket.
32	Hit on/upon	To think of an idea or solution	The engineers hit upon the idea to execute the project.
33	Hit out	To attack or criticise strongly, especially in speech or writing	The player hit out at the referee's decision.
34	Hold against	To blame or resent someone	They argued yesterday, but they did not hold it against each other today.
35	Hold back	(a) To restrain (b) To keep hidden	(a) She held back her tears. (b) They held back the name of the winner until the end of the event.
36	Hold on	(a) To wait briefly (b) To grip	(a) Will you hold on while I fetch your file? (b) Hold on to the pole while the bus is running.
37	Hold forth	To talk at length, often boringly	The writer held forth on filmmaking techniques.
38	Hold up	(a) To delay (b) To rob	(a) Bad weather held up the cricket match. (b) A jewellery shop was held up last night.
39	Hook up	(a) To connect devices (b) To meet someone (informal, often just meaning 'to meet/catch up')	(a) Can you hook up the speaker to your phone? (b) They hooked up during the college reunion.
40	Huddle together	To sit or stand close (often for warmth, safety, or comfort or simply being in a close group)	The family huddled together at the hill station.
41	Hunt down	(a) To succeed in finding (b) To find and capture	(a) After weeks of searching, Kavya hunted down a rare book in a small shop. (b) The police hunted down the escaped prisoner.
42	Hurry up	To do something faster	Hurry up, or we will miss the train.
43	Hush up	To prevent public knowledge	The government hushed up the details of the investigation.

I – Phrasal Verbs

S. No	Phrasal Verb	Meaning	Example
1	Idle away	To spend time doing nothing or in a relaxed way	On Sunday, he idled away watching a movie.
2	Inform on	To secretly report someone's wrongdoing to the authorities	He informed on the student who was copying during the exam.
3	Insist on	To demand something firmly or repeatedly	She insisted on completing the puzzle before dinner.
4	Interfere with	To hinder or get in the way of something	The barking dog interfered with my sleep.
5	Iron out	To resolve problems or disagreements	The neighbours ironed out their differences over the boundary wall.
6	Invite over	To ask someone to come to your house	The Indian High Commissioner invited the team over for dinner.
7	Invest in	To put time, money, or effort into something expecting benefit	The veteran industrialist has invested in several start-up companies.
8	Impress upon	To make someone understand the importance of something	I try to impress upon students that they should understand the entire chapter.
9	Impress with	To cause admiration by using something specific	The students impressed me with their out-of-the-box thinking.
10	Influence over	To have control or power over someone	The teacher has a positive influence over her students.
11	Influence with	To persuade someone because of a relationship or position	She has a lot of influence with the committee members.
12	Inquire into	To investigate or examine	The inspector is inquiring into the case.
13	Inquire of	To ask someone a question (formal)	He inquired of the librarian about the book.
14	Identify with	To feel a strong connection with someone or something	I identify with the character in the story who never gives up.

Important Notes:

- **Inquire of:**
  - 'Inquire of' is a formal English.
    - In everyday English, people say 'inquire with' or 'ask'.
    - Formal/old-fashioned →He inquired of the librarian about the book.
    - Modern/common →He inquired with the librarian about the book.
    - Everyday English → He asked the librarian about the book.

J – Phrasal Verbs

S. No	Phrasal Verb	Meaning	Example
1	Jack up	(a) To lift with a jack (b) To increase prices or levels sharply (informal)	(a) The mechanic jacked up the car to change the tyre. (b) Many shopkeepers jack up the prices before festivals.
2	Jam up	(a) To be stuck or blocked (b) To cause a blockage or stoppage	(a) The printer jammed up in the middle of the work. (b) Traffic jammed up on the narrow road for over an hour.

S. No	Phrasal Verb	Meaning	Example
3	Jazz up	To make something more interesting, lively, or exciting	(a) She jazzed up her room with colourful posters. (b) He jazzed up his speech with a few funny stories.
4	Jot down	To write something briefly and quickly	The manager jotted down his phone number on a paper napkin.
5	Jump at	To accept an opportunity or offer eagerly	He jumped at the chance to be part of the Indian cricket team.
6	Jump in	To enter a conversation suddenly or enthusiastically	During the discussion, Arun jumped in with an idea.
7	Jump on	To criticise verbally or attack physically	The coach jumped on the team's weak performance.
8	Jump over	To leap across something	The athlete jumped over the hurdles with ease during the race.
9	Jump to	To make a quick judgement or assumption, often without enough thought	Do not jump to conclusions before hearing the whole story.
10	Join in	To take part in an activity or discussion with others	The children joined in the game happily.
11	Jut out	To protrude	The bridge juts out into the harbour.

K – Phrasal Verbs

S. No	Phrasal Verb	Meaning	Example
1	Keep at	To continue doing something, especially something difficult	If he continued to keep at fast bowling, he would only get better.
2	Keep away (from)	(a) To stay at a distance (b) To avoid something	(a) He kept away from work because he had a fever. (b) We were told to keep away from chocolates to protect our teeth.
3	Keep back	(a) To maintain a distance (b) To withhold something	(a) The police asked the crowd to keep back. (b) She kept back her excitement until the surprise was revealed.
4	Keep down	(a) To prevent something from increasing or growing (b) To lower the level of sound or noise	(a) Farmers try to keep down weeds using natural methods. (b) Keep your voice down in the library.
5	Keep off	(a) To avoid something (b) Prevent something from touching	(a) The doctor advised him to keep off oily foods. (b) The gardener asked the children to keep off the grass.
6	Keep on	To continue doing something	He kept on practising the song until she got it right.
7	Keep out (of)	(a) Stay outside or not enter (b) To not become involved	(a) The sign warned people to keep out of the construction site. (b) I prefer to keep out of any arguments.

S. No	Phrasal Verb	Meaning	Example
8	Keep to	(a) To stick to a plan, rule, path or topic (b) To restrict oneself or be reserved	(a) Participants were asked to **keep to** the time limit. (b) During the party, she **kept to** herself and did not join the games.
9	Keep up	To maintain a particular standard or pace	I cannot **keep up** with your walking.
10	Keep up with	To stay at the same level or follow developments	It is hard to **keep up with** new developments in the world of Artificial Intelligence.
11	Kick off	To begin something (informal, often sports)	The World Cup will **kick off** with a match between India and Australia.
12	Kick out	To force someone to leave	The miscreant was **kicked out** of the auditorium.
13	Knock down	To demolish	The Municipal Corporation decided to **knock down** the dilapidated structure.
14	Knock out	(a) To make someone unconscious (b) To eliminate in a competition	(a) The boxer **knocked out** his opponent in the second round. (b) Our team was **knocked out** of the tournament in the semifinals.
15	Knuckle down	To start working seriously	You should **knuckle down** and prepare for your board exams.
16	Key to	Something crucial or essential for success	Persistence and discipline are **keys to** success.
17	Key in	To write on a computer or enter details	I will **key in** the report this evening.
18	Knock on	To tap or strike a surface (usually a door) to get attention	There was a loud **knock on** the door.
19	Knock at	To tap or strike a surface, like a door	Someone is **knocking at** the door.
20	Knock over	To hit or push something, causing it to fall	She accidentally **knocked over** the vase.
21	Keep from	To prevent someone from doing something or to stop oneself from doing something	He **kept** himself **from** eating too much chocolate.

Important Notes:

- **Knock on vs Knock at**
  - Knock on → on a surface (door, table, etc.)
    - E.g. She knocked on the door before entering.
  - Knock at → at a door or entrance
    - E.g. Someone is knocking at the front gate.

L – Phrasal Verbs

S. No	Phrasal Verb	Meaning	Example
1	Lack in	To be deficient or not have enough of something	He **lacks in** confidence when speaking in public.
2	Lack of	Not having something at all	There is a **lack of** water in the village.

S. No	Phrasal Verb	Meaning	Example
3	Lay off	To stop employing someone, to terminate from service	The company **laid off** several employees after it posted losses.
4	Lay out	(a) To explain something clearly (b) To arrange something neatly	(a) I **laid out** the seating plan for the guests at the wedding. (b) She laid out the clothes on the bed.
5	Leak out	To become known accidentally	The news of the secret deal between the two countries **leaked out**.
6	Leave out	To not include someone or something	The student has left out an important point in her answer.
7	Let down	To disappoint someone	By not turning up for the wedding, you **let down** your friend.
8	Let in (on)	To allow someone to know a secret	My neighbour **let** me **in** *on* his plan to foil the corporator's bid.
9	Let off	To excuse someone from punishment or a duty	The traffic inspector **let** him **off** with a stern warning.
10	Let out	(a) To release or allow to leave (b) To give on rent	(a) He **let out** a scream when he spotted the crocodile. (b) He has decided to **let out** the room on the terrace.
11	Lie down	To rest by placing your body flat	He was tired and decided to **lie down** for a while.
12	Light up	(a) To become visibly happy (b) To illuminate a place	(a) His face **lit up** when he saw the surprise gift. (b) Fireworks **lit up** the city sky after India's victory.
13	Line up	To form a line or be arranged in a line	The students are expected to **line up** for the morning assembly by 8 am.
14	Live up to	To meet expectations or standards	The latest movie did not **live up to** the hype.
15	Look after	To take care of someone or something	He **looks after** his aged parents.
16	Look ahead	To think about and plan for the future	The team **looked ahead** to next year's competition.
17	Look back (on)	To think about something that happened in the past	At the reunion, we **looked back on** our school days with nostalgia.
18	Look down on	To think of someone as inferior	It is insensitive to **look down on** anyone.
19	Look for	To search for something	I am **looking for** my physics textbook.
20	Look forward to	To feel excited about something that is going to happen	He is **looking forward to** the summer vacation.
21	Look into	To investigate or examine	The association is **looking into** the complaint of gas leakage.
22	Look on	To watch something without participating	He **looked on** while his sister baked a cake.
23	Look out (for)	To be careful or to watch for something	**Look out** for cars when crossing the road.

S. No	Phrasal Verb	Meaning	Example
24	Look over	To quickly examine or review	The lawyer looked over the affidavit before it was submitted to the court.
25	Look through	(a) To examine or read something quickly or carefully (b) To ignore someone, as if they are not there	(a) I looked through my notes to prepare for the exam. (b) Sometimes we accidentally look through people when we are busy.
26	Look to	(a) To rely on someone for help or advice (b) To plan or aim to do something	(a) The cadre looked to the leader for inspiration. (b) The company looks to expand next year.
27	Look up	(a) To search for information (b) To improve	(a) Please look up the word in the dictionary. (b) Things are finally looking up for my friend.
28	Look up to	To admire or respect someone	I look up to my older brother because he is kind and helpful.
29	Lay aside	(a) To store or reserve for future use (b) To stop doing or thinking about something (usually for a short time) (c) To abandon or reject (emotion, plan, or idea)	(a) He lays aside some money every month for his retirement. (b) He laid aside his book and went to have dinner. (c) She laid aside her fears and tried the Ferris wheel.
30	Lay down	(a) To sacrifice or give up something important (b) To put or place something carefully (c) To set rules	(a) He laid down his life for the sake of his country. (b) He laid down the tools after finishing the work. (c) They laid down clear guidelines for the contest.
31	Lay up	To confine someone to bed due to illness or injury	He has been laid up with viral fever for over a week.
32	Lead on	To deceive or mislead (especially about feelings or intentions)	She was led on to think she had won the game.
33	Lean on	To rely on or depend on someone emotionally or for support	I can always lean on my friend during difficult times.
34	Listen in (on)	To secretly overhear a conversation	The children listened in on their parents talking about the holiday plans.
35	Load up	(a) To fill or pack heavily (b) To stock up	(a) They loaded up the truck with essential supplies. (b) Before leaving for work, my mother loaded up the refrigerator.

M – Phrasal Verbs

S. No	Phrasal Verb	Meaning	Example
1	Make after	To chase (slightly uncommon, more British)	(a) The police made after the thief. (b) The fielder made after the ball as it raced to the boundary.
2	Make away with	To steal	The burglars made away with all the diamonds.

S. No	Phrasal Verb	Meaning	Example
3	Make for	(a) To move towards (b) To make something possible	(a) The children **made for** the playground as soon as school ended. (b) Constant arguments do not **make for** a happy atmosphere.
4	Make into	To change something into another form / to convert	They **made** the old textile mill **into** a TV studio in Mumbai.
5	Make of	To understand or think about something	What do you **make of** his rather weird behaviour?
6	Make off	To leave quickly, often to escape	The robbers **made off** before the police arrived.
7	Make out	(a) To understand, see, or hear clearly	(a) The mike was malfunctioning, so I could not **make out** what the anchor was saying. (b) I could **make out** the figure of a tall man in the darkness.
8	Make over	(a) To transfer ownership (b) To change appearance, renovate	(a) He **made over** the property to his son. (b) She **made over** her old attic into a study room.
9	Make up	(a) To reconcile after a quarrel or disagreement (b) To convey a decision or resolve (c) To invent, often an excuse or a story (d) To complete something missed or unfinished	(a) The two friends **made up** after the argument. (b) I have **made up** my mind to pursue art. (c) Sandeep **made up** an excuse to avoid the dinner party. (d) She **made up** the lessons she skipped last week.
10	Make up for	To compensate for something lost, missed, or done wrong	He worked extra hours to **make up for** being late.
11	Mix up	(a) To confuse someone or something (b) To combine things (c) To get involved in trouble or a difficult situation (d) To disorganise or disorder something	(a) People always **mix me up** with my sister. (b) He **mixed up** the flour, sugar, and eggs to bake a cake. (c) He got **mixed up** with the wrong crowd. (d) Someone has **mixed up** all the application forms.
12	Move in	To start living in a new place	The new neighbours **moved in** during the Dussehra vacation.
13	Move out	To leave your home to live elsewhere	They **moved out** after the lease ended.
14	Mess up	To make a mistake or cause a problem	He **messed up** the presentation by forgetting the main points.
15	Mop up	(a) To clean (b) To complete the last part of a task	(a) She **mopped up** the spilt water. (b) We stayed late to **mop up** the last bit of paperwork.
16	Move to	(a) To change position or location (b) To indicate a change of mood	(a) I **moved to** Lucknow from Patna. (b) I was **moved to** tears on hearing his story.

S. No	Phrasal Verb	Meaning	Example
17	Move on	(a) To go on to a different place, subject, activity, job, topic, stage, etc. (b) To stop thinking about something upsetting	(a) The crowd moved on after the meeting ended. (b) She lost the first game, but she moved on and won the next one.
18	Map out	To plan in detail	We mapped out our vacation itinerary.
19	Monkey around	To act silly	The children monkeyed around the whole day.
20	Marry off	To arrange for someone (esp. a son/daughter) to get married	In the old days, families often married off their daughters at a young age.
21	Measure up	To be as good as something else or as good as expected (usually used in negative sentences and questions)	(a) The movie did not measure up to the hype. (b) Can the bakery's cake measure up to Mom's homemade one?

Important Notes:

- **Make up vs Make up for**
  - Make up → complete something missed or lost
    - Focuses on finishing or doing something that was missed.
      - o E.g. I will make up the homework I missed yesterday. Here, it is about completing a task.
- Make up for → compensate
  - Focuses on correcting a loss, mistake, or something wrong.
    - o E.g. I will make up for being late by working extra hard. Here, it is about compensation or balancing out.

N – Phrasal Verbs

S. No	Phrasal Verb	Meaning	Example
1	Narrow down	To reduce or limit the number of possibilities	(a) He narrowed down his choice of engineering colleges to two.
2	Nod off	To fall asleep, especially unintentionally	She nodded off during the lecture.
3	Note down	To write something so that you remember it	Please note down your homework in your diary.
4	Name after	To give someone the same name as another person	The baby was named after her grandmother.
5	Nail down	(a) To finalise or agree on something clearly (b) To determine or identify something clearly and precisely	(a) We need to nail down the date for the school trip. (b) Scientists worked hard to nail down the exact cause of COVID-19.
6	Nibble away at	To gradually reduce or erode something	Rising inflation is nibbling away at our savings.
7	Nose around	To look for something, often in a secretive way	The reporter was nosing around for more details.
8	Notch up	To achieve something, especially a score or success	Gukesh notched up his fifth win of the season.

N – Related Expressions (not true phrasal verbs)

S. No	Expression	Meaning	Example
1	Need of	To indicate that something is lacking or required	I am in need of money right now.
2	Need for	To show the requirement or necessity of something	There is a need for stricter safety rules.
3	Necessary to	To show that an action is required (used before a verb)	It is necessary to wear a seat belt while driving.
4	Necessary for	To show that something is essential for a person or thing (used before a noun/pronoun)	It is necessary for a sailor to learn swimming.

O – Phrasal Verbs

S. No	Phrasal Verb	Meaning	Example
1	Object to	To express disapproval or disagreement	They objected to playing loud music at night.
2	Occur to	To suddenly come into someone's mind	It did not occur to me to check the weather forecast before stepping out.
3	Open up	(a) To become more communicative and willing to share feelings (b) To make something accessible or available	(a) The actor opened up about his struggles in his early years. (b) The new mall will open up many job opportunities.
4	Open to	To be willing to consider, accept, or be influenced by something	Politicians should always be open to constructive criticism from the public.
5	Opt for	To choose or select something	She opted for juice instead of milk.
6	Opt out	To decide not to take part in something	Vivan opted out of the music competition as he had a sore throat.
7	Own up	To admit or confess something, usually a mistake or misdeed	The children owned up to breaking the vase.
8	Offend by	To feel hurt or insulted by something (usually used in the passive)	My friend was offended by the joke.

P – Phrasal Verbs

S. No	Phrasal Verb	Meaning	Example
1	Pack up	(a) To stop doing something or finish an activity (b) To put things into bags or boxes to carry or store	(a) Let us pack up and go home; it is getting dark. (b) The children packed up their toys before dinner.
2	Pack in	To do a lot in a short time	My boss packs a lot in a day.
3	Pass away	To die (euphemism, polite use in formal or informal settings)	His grandfather passed away peacefully last night.

S. No	Phrasal Verb	Meaning	Example
4	Pass off	(a) To happen or be received in a certain way (b) To give a false identity	(a) The event passed off without any trouble. (b) The fake painting was passed off as a masterpiece.
5	Pass out	To faint or lose consciousness	She passed out from exhaustion.
6	Pay back	To return borrowed money	I will pay you back next week.
7	Pay off	To finish paying a debt	He finally paid off his car loan.
8	Pick on	To treat someone unfairly or bully them	It is not right to pick on someone.
9	Pick out	To choose or select	She picked out a dress for the party.
10	Pick up	(a) To lift something (b) To learn something new	(a) He picked up his bag. (b) He picked up Spanish during his trip to Mexico.
11	Pile up	To accumulate	The work piled up while I was on leave.
12	Play along	To pretend to agree or cooperate	I decided to play along with his joke.
13	Play down	To make something seem less important	She played down her role in the success of the project.
14	Point out	To draw attention to something	The teacher pointed out areas for improvement in my essay.
15	Pull ahead	To move in front of others	Our team pulled ahead in the final lap.
16	Pull down	To demolish	They pulled down the old building.
17	Pull off	To succeed in doing something difficult	She pulled off a surprise victory.
18	Pull out	(a) To withdraw or remove oneself from an activity, event, or situation (b) To drive a vehicle onto a road or away from a place (c) To take something out from inside	(a) The company pulled out of the deal. (b) The bus pulled out of the station on time. (c) The magician pulled out a rabbit from the hat.
19	Pull over	To move a vehicle to the side of the road and stop	He pulled over to answer the phone.
20	Put across	To explain clearly	He put across his ideas very well.
21	Put aside	To save or reserve something	She puts aside some money every month.
22	Put away	To store or tidy something	Please put away your books.
23	Put down	(a) To place something on a surface (b) To write something (c) To criticise, belittle, or devalue someone	(a) She put down her glass on the table. (b) She put down her thoughts in a diary. (c) Never put yourself down by saying you are not good enough
24	Put forward	To suggest or propose	She put forward a new plan for the project.
25	Put off	To postpone or discourage	The wedding was put off due to the pandemic.

S. No	Phrasal Verb	Meaning	Example
26	Put on	(a) To wear clothes (b) To organise an event (c) To pretend or fake (d) To gain weight	(a) He put on his coat before going out. (b) The school put on a play. (c) She put on a smile even though she was sad. (d) He has put on much weight this year
27	Put out	(a) To extinguish (b) To inconvenience someone	(a) Put out the candle. (b) The delay really put me out.
28	Put up	(a) To accommodate (b) To display (c) To tolerate	(a) They put up guests in their spare room. (b) Posters were put up all over the city. (c) We had to put up with the hot sun during the match.
29	Pipe down	To quieten down	I am working, will all of you please pipe down a bit?
30	Play up	To make something seem more important	The shop played up the discounts to attract customers.
31	Pull up	(a) To scold or criticise someone (often in passive form) (b) To stop a vehicle or someone (c) To move something closer (often a chair/seat) (d) To improve one's situation or recover	(a) He was pulled up by the manager for being late. (b) He was pulled up by the police for speeding. (c) She pulled up a chair and sat next to me. (d) The company was struggling at first, but soon pulled up.
32	Put by	To lay aside something for future use	Vinita had put money by, and that came in handy now.
33	Polish off	To finish something completely and quickly, especially food (informal)	The puppy polished off his bowl of milk in seconds.
34	Pass by	To go past something en route	I passed by Mathura on my way to Delhi.
35	Pass for	To be accepted as something or someone else	Her English accent is so fluent that she could pass for a native speaker.
36	Pass on	(a) To decline (b) To die (euphemism) (c) To give or transfer something	(a) I passed on the job offer. (b) The mayor passed on yesterday. (c) Could you pass the book on to me when you are finished?
37	Pass through	To travel across or go through a place without staying long	We passed through Jaipur on our way to Udaipur.
38	Prey on	(a) To hunt (b) To exploit someone vulnerable	(a) Lions prey on deer. (b) Scammers usually prey on the elderly by tricking them into giving money.
39	Pitch in	To contribute, usually effort, help, or money	Everyone pitched in to clean up the park.
40	Press for	To insistently demand something	The workers pressed for better wages and working conditions.
41	Press on	To continue doing something despite difficulties	Even though it was late, they pressed on with their journey.

P – Related Verbs

S. No	Related Verb	Meaning	Example
1	Present with	To give someone something formally or unexpectedly	She was **presented with** an award for her outstanding performance.
2	Present to	To formally give or introduce something to someone (often in a ceremony)	The chief minister **presented** the trophy **to** the Indian captain.
3	Proceed with	To continue doing something	Despite the rain, they **proceeded with** the outdoor ceremony.
4	Proceed against	To start legal action against someone	The company decided to **proceed against** the supplier for breach of contract.
5	Protest against	To express strong disagreement with something	The students **protested against** the fee hike.
6	Part with	To give up or let go of something you value	He refused to **part with** his grandfather's watch.
7	Part from	To separate from someone	It was hard for her to **part from** her childhood friends.
8	Pity on	To feel compassion or sympathy for someone *(usually occurs in "take pity on")*	She took **pity on** the stray dog and gave it food.
10	Pity for	The feeling of compassion or sympathy itself	I felt deep **pity for** the victims of the flood.

Q – Phrasal Verbs

S. No	Phrasal Verb	Meaning	Example
1	Queue up	To wait in line for something	Fans **queued up** to meet the cricketer.
2	Quiet down	To become or make someone quieter	The children were asked to **quiet down** during dinner.

Q – Related Verbs

S. No	Related Verb	Meaning	Example
1	Quarrel with	To argue or disagree with someone	I **quarrelled with** my sister.

R – Phrasal Verbs

S. No	Phrasal Verb	Meaning	Example
1	Rack up	To accumulate or achieve something, often in large amounts	He **racked up** several awards during his career.
2	Rattle off	To say or recite something quickly and easily, often without much effort	She **rattled off** the names of all the states in India.
3	Rake in	To earn or bring in large amounts	The company **raked in** huge profits last year.

S. No	Phrasal Verb	Meaning	Example
4	Rake up	To revive or bring up unpleasant memories or past issues	We should not rake up past quarrels when things are peaceful now.
5	Reach out	To try to communicate or help	The NGO reached out to the flood victims.
6	Read out	To read aloud	The teacher read out the names of the winners.
7	Read over	To check by reading carefully	Please read over your work before submitting it.
8	Rally around	To gather and help	After the earthquake, everyone rallied around to rebuild the town.
9	Reel off	To list quickly	He reeled off the names of the students in no time.
10	Reduce to	To worsen, make smaller, weaker, or lesser in amount	After typhoid, he was reduced to skin and bones.
11	Ramble on	To talk or write continuously and aimlessly	The man rambled on about his childhood for hours.
12	Rein in	To restrain or control	The teacher had to rein in the noisy class.
13	Reason out	To find a logical answer	We reasoned out a solution to the problem.
14	Rule out	To eliminate a possibility	The police have ruled out theft as a motive.
15	Rent out	To allow someone to use something in exchange for money	They rented out their house during the summer holidays.
16	Reconcile with	To make up with someone	I want you to reconcile with your friend.
17	Ride out	To survive despite difficulties	The fishermen rode out in the storm.
18	Rip off	To overcharge, cheat or swindle	The shopkeeper tried to rip me off by charging double.
19	Root for	To support with enthusiasm	The fans rooted for their team loudly.
20	Rough up	To hurt or attack physically	The players roughed each other up during practice.
21	Revel in	To enjoy something very much	She revelled in her role as a pilot.
22	Rope in	To persuade or involve someone	We roped in our friends to help with the fair.
23	Roll out	To introduce or launch	The company rolled out its newest SUV in July.
24	Roll back	To withdraw or reduce	The minister rolled back the new tax after protests.
25	Run into	(a) To meet unexpectedly (b) To experience a problem (c) To reach an amount (d) To crash into	(a) I ran into my teacher at the theatre. (b) He ran into trouble with his policy. (c) The costs ran into millions. (d) The truck ran into a car.
26	Run across	To find by chance	I ran across an old friend in the market.
27	Run after	To chase	The dog ran after the ball.
28	Run against	To compete with	She is running against a strong opponent in the election.

S. No	Phrasal Verb	Meaning	Example
29	Run along	To leave (informal, often said to children)	The teacher told the children to run along after class.
30	Run away	To leave quickly or escape	The prisoners ran away from jail.
31	Run down	(a) To lose power and stop (a machine or battery) (b) To criticise (c) In poor condition (d) To knock down	(a) My phone battery has run down. (b) She ran down her colleague in public. (c) The building is run down. (d) The driver almost ran down a pedestrian.
32	Run for	To campaign for an elected position	He decided to run for president of the club.
33	Run off	To leave suddenly	The thief ran off with her handbag.
34	Run out	(a) To use up or finish a supply of something; to have nothing left (b) To flow out suddenly (c) To come to an end (time, supply, contract, etc.)	(a) We ran out of milk this morning. / My phone has run out of charge. (b) Tears ran out of her eyes. (c) My lease for my house runs out next month.
35	Run over	(a) Overflow for spill (b) To hit with a vehicle (c) To exceed time or limit	(a) Turn off the tap; the bucket is running over. (b) The car nearly ran over a dog. (c) The lecture ran over by an hour.
36	Run through	(a) To rehearse or review (b) To move/spread through	(a) Let us run through the plan once more. (b) A wave of excitement ran through the crowd.
37	Run up	To incur or accumulate (usually debts or bills)	He ran up a huge medical bill.
38	Run in	To rush in quickly	She ran in through the main gate.
39	Run around	To go to different places for a purpose	I ran around all day looking for work.
40	Run past	To tell someone about an idea to get their reaction	I would like to run this idea past you.
41	Run on	To operate using a certain fuel or system	Most buses in Delhi run on CNG.
42	Run to	To total or add up to	The manuscript ran to 500 pages.
43	Run short of	To have less than needed	We are running short of time.

R — Related Expressions

S. No	Expression	Meaning	Example
1	Regard for	To respect	I have great regard for your father.
2	Responsible for	To be accountable	Who is responsible for the delay?
3	Rejoice at	To be extremely happy about something	He rejoiced at his daughter's success.
4	Run-in *(noun)*	A quarrel or argument	He had a run-in with his manager.

S – Phrasal Verbs

S. No	Phrasal Verb	Meaning	Example
1	Saddle with	To burden with something difficult or unpleasant	Sreedhar was saddled with too much work.
2	Sail through	To complete something easily and successfully	My sister sailed through her exams with distinction.
3	Save up	To accumulate money for a purpose	Manish is saving up to buy a new mobile phone.
4	Scale down	To reduce in size, amount, or extent	We decided to scale down the literary conference due to a lack of funds.
5	Scare away / Scare off	To frighten someone so that they leave	I tried to scare away an aggressive dog with a stick.
6	Scout round/ around	To go to different places looking for something	I spent time at the Sunday Book Market scouting round for quality novels.
7	Scrape through	To barely succeed with difficulty (often exams)	He was lucky to scrape through the exam.
8	Scrub off	To remove dirt or stains by rubbing hard	My mother scrubbed off the turmeric stain on my shirt.
9	Scrub out	To clean thoroughly (same as *clean out*)	He agreed to scrub out the hostel dormitory for Rs 800.
10	Seal off	To block all entry or exit points	The police sealed off the entrance to the conference venue.
11	See off	(a) To say goodbye at a departure place (b) To get rid of someone or defeat them	(a) I went to the airport to see off my aunt. (b) Our team saw off the challenge and completed the project ahead of time.
12	See through	To understand the true nature of something	I saw through his false promises.
13	Set about	To begin doing something determinedly	I set about writing my novel during the summer holidays.
14	Set aside	To reserve for a particular purpose	I set aside time to teach my neighbour's son.
15	Set in	When something begins and seems likely to continue	This year, the monsoon set in early.
16	Set off	(a) To start a journey (b) To trigger something	(a) The Saxenas set off for Delhi. (b) The news of the gas leak set off a wave of panic.
17	Set out	To start a purposeful journey, task, plan or goal	He set out to explore Himalayan herbs.
18	Set up	To establish something, such as a business	Laxman set up his own startup on organic seeds.
19	Show off	To boastfully display something	He showed off his new bicycle to his friends.
20	Show up	To appear or arrive, often unexpectedly or late	The chief guest showed up an hour late.
21	Shut down	To stop operating	The factory was shut down due to safety violations.

S. No	Phrasal Verb	Meaning	Example
22	Shut out	To exclude or block completely	Raksha decided to **shut out** all distractions and prepare for her exams.
23	Single out	To choose one from a group for special attention	The coach **singled out** the fastest runner for extra training.
24	Sit back	To relax and do nothing	You cannot just **sit back** and expect success.
25	Sit out	To not participate in an activity	My friend **sat out** the cricket match due to an injury.
26	Sleep on	To delay a decision until the next day	I advised my friend to **sleep on** it and decide tomorrow.
27	Slip away	To leave quietly and slowly in a way that is hardly noticed	Feeling bored at the event, I **slipped away** without anyone noticing.
28	Slip out	(a) To be said unintentionally (b) To leave quickly and quietly, often for a short while (c) To fall out accidentally	(a) The truth **slipped out** during the argument. (b) She **slipped out** for a few minutes during the meeting. (c) The coin **slipped out** of his pocket.
29	Sort out	To resolve or organise	The two friends decided to **sort out** their differences.
30	Speak out	To express an opinion publicly and clearly	The voters **spoke out** against the MLA's arrogance.
31	Stand by	To support or be ready	My parents always **stand by** me.
32	Stand out	To be noticeable or exceptional	Her video documentary on education **stood out** for its emotional appeal.
33	Stand up for	To defend or support	A true friend will always **stand up for** you.
34	Stand up to	To confront boldly	You must learn to **stand up** to bullies.
35	Step down	To resign from a position	The CEO **stepped down** to enjoy retirement.
36	Step in	To become involved, usually to help	The Prime Minister **stepped in** to resolve the dispute.
37	Stick to	To continue consistently	**Stick to** a regular exercise routine and a healthy diet.
38	Stick up for	To defend or support someone, especially when criticised	She **stuck up for** her team when people criticised their work.
39	Send for	To request someone to come	She **sent for** the mechanic.
40	Set on	(a) To attack (b) To firmly decide on or be determined about something	(a) The dogs were **set on** the intruders. (b) He is **set on** becoming an astronaut.
41	Spell out	To explain in detail	I want you to **spell out** your tour plan.
42	Stash away	To secretly store or hide something (same as *squirrel away*)	Mom **stashed away** the cookies so we would not eat them all.
43	See to	To ensure completion of a task	Our hosts **saw to** it that we were comfortable.
44	Shoot down	To reject an idea or proposal	The committee **shot down** her idea.
45	Snack on	To eat a small quantity	I **snacked on** dry fruits during my field trip.
46	Size up	To assess carefully	I **sized up** the situation before speaking.

S – Related Verbs

S. No	Related Verb	Meaning	Example
1	Satisfy with	To feel content or pleased with an outcome	I am satisfied with your designs.
2	Succumb to	(a) To fail to resist or give in to something (often temptation, pressure, or desire) (b) To die of something	(a) He succumbed to peer pressure and joined the party. (b) Many people succumbed to COVID-19.
3	Smack of	(a) To give the impression of something, often a particular quality (usually negative)	His attitude smacks of arrogance.

Important Points:

- **Set off** vs **Set out**
  - Set off → To start a journey
    - is more general, often used for journeys or triggering events.
      - o E.g. The Saxenas set off for Delhi.
  - Set out → To start a purposeful journey, task, plan or goal
    - is more purposeful and goal-directed.
      - o E.g. He set out to explore Himalayan herbs.

T – Phrasal Verbs

S. No	Phrasal Verb	Meaning	Example
1	Take after	To resemble a family member in appearance or behaviour	She takes after her mother in her love for music.
2	Take apart	To dismantle something	The mechanic took apart the engine to find the fault.
3	Take back	To withdraw a statement or reclaim something	I take back my words about him.
4	Take down	(a) To note or write (b) To pull something down, remove or dismantle	(a) Please take down notes while I teach. (b) The workers took down the old signboard.
5	Take in	(a) To absorb information (b) To shelter someone	(a) The arts student took in every detail of the painting. (b) The family took in a tiny kitten found on the street.
6	Take off	(a)To remove or to take something away from the body (b) To depart, especially an aircraft (c) To suddenly become successful or popular (d) To leave suddenly	(a) She took off her shoes before entering the house. (b) The flight to Indore took off on time. (c) Her singing career took off after she appeared on the reality show. (d) He took off without saying a proper goodbye.
7	Take on	To accept responsibility or challenge	He took on the role of coordinator during the crisis.
8	Take out	(a) To remove or extract something (b) To invite someone (usually socially, for a meal, etc.)	(a) He took out his lunchbox and offered us the food. (b) He took his parents out on a trip to Goa.

S. No	Phrasal Verb	Meaning	Example
9	Take over	(a) To gain control (b) To assume responsibility	(a) The company was taken over by a powerful multinational corporation. (b) She took over as the new captain of the team.
10	Take stock of	To review or evaluate carefully	The management took stock of the situation.
11	Take to	To begin to like someone or something	She took to music like a fish to water.
12	Take up	(a) To start a hobby or activity (b) To occupy space	(a) He decided to take up the job. (b) This cupboard is taking up too much space in my study.
13	Take for	To mistake someone for another	My father looks so young that people often take him for my elder brother.
14	Talk into	To persuade someone	He talked me into seeing the play.
15	Talk over	(a) To discuss thoroughly (b) To drown someone's voice	(a) We decided to talk over the plan. (b) The TV anchor kept talking over the guest.
16	Tear down	To demolish	Bulldozers will tear down the dilapidated structure.
17	Tear up	To rip into small pieces	He tore up the letter in anger.
18	Tear into	To criticise severely	The opposition leader tore into the government in the parliament.
19	Think over	To consider carefully	Could you think over my offer?
20	Throw away	To discard	Please do not throw away my old magazines.
21	Throw up	To vomit; to abandon or unexpectedly produce	The child threw up after eating street food.
22	Try on	To test clothing for fit	It is best to try on footwear before buying.
23	Turn around	To change direction or improve a situation	The new management turned around the company.
24	Turn down	(a) To reduce volume (b) To reject	(a) Can you please turn down the volume of the TV? (b) She turned down the job offer.
25	Turn in	(a) To surrender (b) To submit work (c) To go to bed / retire for the night	(a) The thief turned himself in to the police. (b) I turned in my assignment yesterday. (c) I usually turn in early on weekdays.
26	Turn off	(a) To switch off a device or light (b) To dislike	(a) Please turn off the lights. (b) His rude behaviour turned me off.
27	Turn on	(a) To switch on a device or light (b) To suddenly attack or become hostile	(a) I turned on the TV to watch the bulletin. (b) He felt let down when his friends turned on him.

S. No	Phrasal Verb	Meaning	Example
28	Turn out	(a) To happen or end up in a certain way (b) To attend an event (c) To produce, especially in large numbers	(a) The party turned out better than expected. (b) The entire team turned out at his farewell function. (c) The factory turns out hundreds of garments every day.
29	Turn up	(a) To increase volume (b) To appear unexpectedly	(a) Can you turn up the volume? (b) He turned up late to the meeting.
30	Turn against	To oppose or become hostile towards someone	The people turned against the corrupt leader.
31	Turn back	(a) To return to a previous place or reverse direction (b) To be unhelpful or refuse assistance, to not support (c) To cause someone or something to stop or retreat (d) To revert to an earlier state or undo	(a) We had to turn back halfway due to bad weather. (b) When she needed help, everyone turned their back on her. (c) The army turned back the invaders at the border. (d) We cannot turn back time, but we can learn from our mistakes.
32	Turn away	(a) To refuse entry or service (b) To avert one's face or eyes (c) To reject or refuse help	(a) The hotel turned away guests because it was fully booked. (b) She turned away when the scene was too violent. (c) The charity never turns away anyone in need.
33	Tag along	To accompany	He tagged along with me on the trip.
34	Tap into	To access and use a resource, skill or feeling	The campaign tapped into people's desire for change.
35	Taste for	A liking or preference for something	He has a taste for classical music.
36	Tip off	To warn or give a clue	The neighbour tipped off the police.
37	Tone down	To make something less harsh or intense	Tone down the language of your letter.
38	Try out	To test something	You should try out this recipe.

T – Related Verbs

S. No	Related Verb	Meaning	Example
1	Tired of	To be bored with or exhausted	I am tired of watching basketball.
2	True to	To be faithful or loyal to	He remained true to his word.

Important Points:

☞ **Try on** vs **Try out**

- Try on → test clothing/accessories for fit
  - o E.g. She tried on the dress before buying it.
- Try out → test a product, skill, or idea
  - o E.g. Let us try out this new recipe.

- **Turn back** vs **Turn away**
  - Turn back → To be unhelpful or refuse assistance, to not support
    - *Focuses on attitude or inaction rather than formally denying entry or service*
    - *Often implies someone could help but chooses not to*
      - o E.g. When she needed help, everyone turned their back on her.
  - Turn away → To reject or refuse help
    - *Focuses on active refusal or denial*
    - *Often involves a formal action or decision.*
      - o E.g. The shelter turned away people because it was full.

U – Phrasal Verbs

S. No	Phrasal Verb	Meaning	Example
1	Urge on	To encourage someone to do something	The coach urged the team on despite the tough match conditions.
2	Urge upon	To strongly recommend (formal; often found in speeches or official contexts)	The teacher urged the value of discipline upon her students.
3	Use up	To consume completely	The cook used up the entire carton of milk while making rice pudding.
4	Usher in	To mark the beginning of something (formal)	The Green Revolution in India ushered in an age of self-reliance.
5	Use against	To utilise something as a weapon or argument	Anything you say may be used against you in court.
6	Uphold against	To defend or support someone or something against opposition	The minister upheld his decision against all criticism.
7	Unwind from	To relax and recover from stress or pressure	He took a vacation to unwind from the work pressure.

U – Related Verbs

S. No	Related Verb	Meaning	Example
1	Useful to	Focuses on the recipient of benefit	My book is useful to students preparing for the English exam.
2	Useful for	Focuses on purpose, activity, or function	This manure is useful for growing healthy plants.
3	Use for	To apply something for a specific purpose.	I use this knife only for cutting jackfruit.

V – Phrasal Verbs

S. No	Phrasal Verb	Meaning	Example
1	Varnish over	To hide unpleasant aspects of a situation (similar to gloss over or paper over)	She varnished over her disappointment with a forced smile.

S. No	Phrasal Verb	Meaning	Example
2	Vouch for	To guarantee or speak in support of someone or something	I can vouch for his honesty and integrity.
3	Verge on	To be very close to something (usually a quality, state, or extreme behaviour) (less common in everyday speech)	His obsession with his car verged on madness.
4	Vie with	To compete hard to obtain something	Many companies are vying with each other to win the government order.
5	Vote down	To reject something by voting against it	The proposal was voted down by the committee.
6	Vote in	To elect someone to a position by voting	They voted in a new municipal corporator yesterday.
7	Vote out	To remove someone from a position by voting	The residents decided to vote out the building secretary.
8	Vanish into	To disappear completely	The pickpocket vanished into the crowd before anyone noticed.
9	Venture out	To go out somewhere despite risk or discomfort	The volunteers ventured out in the heavy rain to help flood victims.

V – Related Verbs

S. No	Related Verb	Meaning	Example
1	Volunteer for	To willingly offer to do something (followed by a noun)	He volunteered for the role of team captain.
2	Volunteer to	To willingly offer to do something (followed by a verb)	He volunteered to clean the park.

W – Phrasal Verbs

S. No	Phrasal Verb	Meaning	Example
1	Wake up	To stop sleeping or become alert	I wake up at 5 a.m. every day.
2	Walk out	To leave a place angrily or abruptly	The opposition walked out of the parliament.
3	Walk off	To leave a place or situation, often to calm down or avoid conflict	He walked off without saying a word.
4	Walk in on	To enter unexpectedly and catch someone doing something private	The security guard walked in on the cashier stealing money.
5	Walk away from	To leave a situation without being affected, or to avoid responsibility	The racing driver walked away from the car crash without a scratch.
6	Wash away	To be carried off by water	The flash floods washed away the bridge across the river.
7	Watch out	To be careful or alert	Watch out for sharp bends on this hill road.
8	Wear out	To become damaged or exhausted from use	These iron pipes are completely rusted and worn out.

S. No	Phrasal Verb	Meaning	Example
9	Wear off	To gradually disappear, especially of effects	The excitement of adopting a pet wore off after a month.
10	Work out	(a) To exercise (b) To find a solution	(a) He works out at the gym every evening. (b) We worked out a solution to the dog menace.
11	Work on	To spend time improving or developing something	I am working on my voice modulation to improve my speaking skills.
12	Wind up	To end or conclude something	We decided to wind up the party before midnight.
13	Wipe out	To destroy or remove completely	The fire wiped out the honey bee population in that forest.
14	Write down	To make a written note	Please write down what I say.
15	Write off	(a) To cancel a debt (b) To treat something as a loss or failure	(a) The bank wrote off the bad loan. (b) Do not write him off as an actor too soon.
16	Wrap up	To finish or conclude something	The morning yoga session will be wrapped up by 7 a.m.

Y – Phrasal Verbs

S. No	Phrasal Verb	Meaning	Example
1	Yell out	To shout loudly, often so that others can hear it from a distance	I yelled out his name so that he could hear me in the din.

Y – Related Verbs

S. No	Related Verb	Meaning	Example
1	Yield to	To give in or surrender	She finally yielded to temptation and ate the cake.

Z – Phrasal Verbs

S. No	Phrasal Verb	Meaning	Example
1	Zoom in on	To focus on something very closely, either with a camera or figuratively	The documentary on the Discovery Channel zoomed in on the life of the tribes in the Andamans.
2	Zoom out	To pull back to a broader view	The Chairman asked us to zoom out and look at the macro picture.

Chapter 4: Join the Sentences

Ready to level up your writing? Discover how to connect sentences smoothly using simple techniques that will make your teachers think you suddenly became a writing genius.

Rules for Joining Sentences without using And, But, So

Rule 1: Use of participles

Let us first understand what a participle is.

A **participle** is a verb form that functions as an adjective in a sentence. It describes or modifies a noun or pronoun.

Examples:

1. Seeing the police, the thief ran away.
2. Hearing the commotion, Manas woke up.

Here, 'seeing' or 'hearing' are verb forms, but they also give us more information about the thief or Manas, just like adjectives do. A word formed from a verb and used as an adjective or a noun is called a participle.

Deeper Explanation: The word 'seeing' is not just a verb; it is a present participle.
`Seeing' is the present participle form of the verb `see'. In this sentence, it does not act as the main verb. Instead, it introduces a participle phrase (seeing the police) that gives more information about why the thief ran away.
It functions like an adjective, describing the thief (the subject of the sentence) and tells us what he was doing when he ran away.

If the sentence is rewritten as:

When the thief saw the police, he ran away.

Then `saw' is a simple past verb.

Type of Participles

(a) Present Participle: ends in *-ing* and shows an action that is ongoing or happening at the same time as another action. It can also express the cause or reason for the main action in the sentence.

Examples:

1. Eating *idlis*, the child smiled at Amma. (ongoing action)
2. Reading the newspaper, Grandpa smiled quietly. (describing an action during another)
3. Walking down the busy street, he thought to himself. (simultaneous action)
4. Feeling cold, Rani shut the window. (showing cause or reason)

(b) Past Participle: shows a completed action and is often used to describe a noun or pronoun. It usually ends in *-ed*, *-d*, *-t*, *-n*, or *-en*)

Examples:

1. Praised by her parents, Niharika felt confident.
2. Driven by greed, he stole the money.

(c) Perfect Participle: is formed using "having" + *past participle*. It shows that one action was completed before another began.

Examples:

1. Having *eaten* lunch, we resumed our music session.
2. Having *painted* a portrait, Deepa put it up for sale.

(d) Participial Phrase with "Being": is formed using "being" + *adjective* or *past participle*. It describes a state, condition, or reason that exists at the time of the main action.

Examples:

1. The sea being smooth, I went boating.
2. Being tired, Kishore went to bed early.

Let us examine some additional examples of how two sentences can be joined using participial phrases.

We can use 'having' to show a completed action, and 'being' to describe a condition or state.

Examples:

1. I lost all my money. I went home.
   Answer: Having *lost* all my money, I went home.
2. Anil finished the homework. He watched TV.
   Answer: Having *finished* the homework, Anil watched TV.
3. The weather was fine. We enjoyed the picnic.
   Answer: The weather being *fine*, we enjoyed the picnic.
4. The field was wet. The match was called off.
   Answer: The field being *wet*, the match was called off.

Rule 2: Use of 'as soon as'

As soon as is a conjunction used to join two actions when the second one happens immediately after the first.

Let us see how two related sentences can be combined using as soon as.

Example:

Ramana saw Prashansa. He stopped talking on the phone immediately.
As soon as Ramana saw Prashansa, he stopped talking on the phone.

Note: As soon as is followed by a subject and a verb. It introduces a complete clause. It means the same as *immediately*, so avoid using both in the same sentence.

× Incorrect: As soon as he reached, the event began immediately.

✓ Correct: As soon as he reached, the event began.

Rule 3: Use of "no sooner... than"

No sooner... than is a formal expression used to join two actions when the second happens immediately after the first.

It has the same meaning as "as soon as". However, it is more commonly used for dramatic or literary effect rather than in everyday speech.

***Structure 1*:**

No sooner + *did* + subject + base verb + than + subject + past verb

This is used when both actions are in the simple past tense.

***Example*:**

The minister entered the office. The meeting began.

No sooner *did* the minister enter the office than the meeting began.

Structure 2:
No sooner + *had* + subject + past participle + than + subject + past verb
This is used when the first action was completed before the second, that is, when the first action is in the past perfect tense.

Example:
The police had reached the scene. The robbers fled.
No sooner *had* the police reached the scene than the robbers fled.

Structure 3:
No sooner + *does* + subject + base verb + than + subject + present tense verb
This is used when the sentence is in the present tense.

Example:
He opens the door. The dog jumps out.
No sooner *does* he open the door than the dog jumps out.

Important Points to Remember:

(a) No sooner already means '*immediately*', so do not use the word 'immediately' in the same sentence.
× Incorrect: No sooner did the delegates arrive than the meeting started immediately.
✓ Correct: No sooner did the delegates arrive than the meeting started.

(b) The phrase no sooner is always followed by the word than, not 'then.'
× Incorrect: No sooner... then
✓ Correct: No sooner... than

(c) Never use a comma after no sooner.
× Incorrect: No sooner had he entered, than the lights went off.
✓ Correct: No sooner had he entered than the lights went off.

(d) When a sentence begins with No sooner, always place the helping verb (*did/had/does*) before the subject, just like in questions. This is called **inversion**.
× Incorrect: No sooner Rakesh did eat than he felt sleepy.
✓ Correct: No sooner did Rakesh eat than he felt sleepy.

Rule 4: Use of 'hardly' and 'scarcely'

We use hardly and scarcely to show that one action happened just before another, with very little time in between.

Structure: Hardly / Scarcely + *had* + subject + past participle + *when* + subject + past tense verb

Examples:

1. He reached the office. The power failed.
Hardly had he reached the office *when* the power failed.

2. I had stepped out of school. It started raining.
Scarcely had I stepped out of school *when* it started raining.

Note: When using "hardly" or "scarcely " to show two past actions, use 'had' after the subject, and follow with 'when' — not 'than'.

Rule 5: Use of "not only... but also"

"Not only... but also" is a correlative conjunction. This pair of words is used to present two related ideas, both of which are true and carry equal importance in the sentence. It is often used to add emphasis. It connects grammatically equal parts of a sentence, such as two nouns, two verbs, two adjectives or two clauses.

Structure: Not only + [part 1] + but also + [part 2]

Important Points to Remember:

(a) Both parts should be parallel. That is, the words or phrases joined must be of the same grammatical type (e.g. noun+-noun, verb+verb, clause + clause).

× Incorrect: He not only reads fiction but also writing blogs.
✓ Correct: He not only reads fiction but also writes blogs.

Examples:

1. The CM was present. The officers were present.
   Not only the CM but also the officers were present. (both nouns)
2. He sings well. He paints nicely.
   He not only sings well but also paints nicely. (both verbs)
3. He is sensible. He is kind.
   He is not only sensible but also kind. (both adjectives)

(b) If a sentence begins with "Not only" and is followed by a full clause (a group of words containing both a subject and a verb), the word order is flipped, just like in a question. This means that the helping verb comes before the subject. This inversion adds emphasis and formality.

Structure: Not only + auxiliary verb + subject + main verb + but also...

Example: She cracked NEET. She secured a seat at IIT Mumbai.
Not only *did* she crack NEET, but she also secured a seat at IIT Mumbai.

However, if "not only" is followed by a noun, verb, or adjective - and not a complete clause - then inversion is NOT needed.

Example:
The CM was present. The officers were present.
Not only the CM but also the officers were present. (no inversion)

Rule 6: Use of "as well as"

"As well as" means '*in addition to*', and is similar in meaning to '*besides*'. It is used to add extra information about a person or thing. While it conveys addition, it is NOT the same as 'and'.

Examples:

1. He lost his ticket. He lost his luggage.
   He lost his ticket as well as his luggage.
2. The hotel offers a subsidised breakfast. It offers free wi-fi.
   The hotel offers a subsidised breakfast as well as free wi-fi.

Important Points to Remember:

(a) When "as well as" joins two subjects, the verb agrees with the first subject (not both).

Example:
The teacher, as well as the students, is attending the seminar. (The verb "is" agrees with the subject "teacher", the first subject, which is singular)

(b) The words or phrases connected by "as well as" must be grammatically similar.

Example:
She enjoys painting as well as singing. (both are ***-ing*** verbs)

Rule 7: Use of prepositional phrases and adverb clauses

(a) Prepositions like "after", "before", "despite", "in spite of", "due to", and "because of" can join sentences and show time, reason, or contrast.

Examples:

1. He was unwell. He went to the office.
   Despite being unwell, he went to the office.

2. I finished cooking. I went to the market.
   After finishing cooking, I went to the market.
3. He is talented. He is hardworking.
   Besides being talented, he is hardworking.

(b) Adverb clauses introduced by words like "although", "if", and "when" show contrast, condition, or reason.

Examples:

1. The landlord is wealthy. He is miserly.
   Although the landlord is wealthy, he is miserly.
2. It rained heavily. The match continued.
   Although it rained heavily, the match continued.
3. Keep your mobile phone away. You will be able to focus.
   If you keep your mobile phone away, you will be able to focus.
4. Play well. You will win the match.
   Unless you play well, you will not win the match.
   (**Note:** "Unless" means "*if not*", so the second part must show what will happen if the condition is not met.)
5. The bell rang. The children ran out of the classroom.
   When the bell rang, the children ran out of the classroom.

Rule 8: Use of "neither... nor"

This pair of correlative conjunctions is used to join two negative ideas, indicating that both parts are not true. It means "*not this and not that*". It is used to link and negate two related parts of a sentence, such as subjects, actions, or qualities.

Structure: Neither + [part 1] + nor + [part 2]

Example:
Anil is not intelligent. He is not hardworking.
Anil is neither intelligent nor hardworking.

Important Points to Remember:

(a) When "neither... nor" joins two subjects, the verb agrees with the subject closer to it (the second one).

Examples:

1. Neither the teacher nor the students *were* present. (Verb "were" agrees with "students", which is plural)
2. Neither the students nor the teacher *was* present. (Verb "was" agrees with "teacher", which is singular)

(b) The two parts joined by "neither... nor" should be grammatically similar (both should be nouns, verbs, adjectives, etc.)

Examples:

1. We neither *sang* nor *danced*. (Both *sang* and *danced* are verbs.)
2. The washroom is neither *clean* nor *large*. (Both *clean* and *large* are adjectives.)

(c) "Neither... nor" already conveys a negative meaning. So, avoid adding another negative word, such as *not* or *don't* in the same sentence.

× Incorrect: He does not neither sings nor dances. (double negative)

✓ Correct: He neither sings nor dances.

Rule 9: Use of "either... or"

"Either... or" is a pair of correlative conjunctions used to show a choice between two possibilities. It means only one of the two options will happen or is true, not both.

Structure: Either + [part 1] + or + [part 2]

> *Example*: I may complete the work. I may ask my sister to do it.
> Either I may complete the work or ask my sister to do it.

Important Points to Remember:

(a) When "either... or" joins two subjects, the verb agrees with the second subject (the one closer to the verb).

> *Examples:*
> 1. Either the teacher or the students *are* coming. (Verb "are" agrees with "students" – the second subject)
> 2. Either the students or the teacher *is* coming. (Verb "is" agrees with the "teacher" – the second subject)

(b) "Either... or" is used to emphasise choice, especially in instructions or warnings.

> *Example*:
> You apologise. You leave my class.
> Either you apologise or you leave my class.

Rule 10: Use of "while" and "whereas"

"While" and "whereas" are conjunctions used to join two clauses. They are commonly used to contrast two ideas and illustrate how they are different. In some cases, "while" can also indicate two actions happening simultaneously.

(a) "While" can be used to join two contrasting facts or opinions. In such cases, it has the same meaning as "whereas".

Structure: While + Clause 1, Clause 2

OR

Clause 1 + while + Clause 2.

> *Example*:
> He loves cricket. His brother prefers badminton.
> While he loves cricket, his brother prefers badminton.
> OR
> He loves cricket while his brother prefers badminton.

(b) "While" can be used to link two actions happening at the same time.

Structure: Action 1 + while + Action 2

OR

While + Action 1, Action 2

> *Examples:*
> 1. My brother was studying. I was watching TV.
> My brother was studying while I was watching TV.
> OR
> While my brother was studying, I was watching TV.

(c) "Whereas" is used only for contrast and is considered more formal than "while".

Structure: Clause 1 + whereas + clause 2.

> *Example*:
> Casper is obedient. Tommy is naughty.
> Casper is obedient, whereas Tommy is naughty.

Rule 11: Use of relative pronouns (who, whom, whose, which, that, where)

Relative pronouns connect two sentences by referring back to a noun in the first sentence and adding more information about it.

They help form relative clauses — the part of a sentence that begins with a relative pronoun like "who", "which", "that", etc.

(a) "Who" – used when referring to people (as the subject)

Examples:

1. This is my classmate. He won the prize.
   This is my classmate who won the prize.
2. These are the boys. They saved Shalini from the goons.
   These are the boys who saved Shalini from the goons.

(b) "Whom" – used when referring to people (as the object)

Example:
That is the boy. I met him yesterday.
That is the boy whom I met yesterday.

Note: While "whom" is still used in formal writing or academic contexts, "who" is often used instead of "whom" in everyday speech and casual writing, in modern English.

(c) "Whose" – used to show possession.

Example:
I know the man. His son won the race.
I know the man whose son won the race.

(d) "Which" – used for things or animals (to add extra, non-essential information)

Example:
I bought a novel. It is very interesting.
I bought a novel which is very interesting.

(e) "That" – used for people or things (to give essential information)

Example:
This is the birth certificate. You need to submit it.
This is the birth certificate that you need to submit.

(f) "Where" – used to refer to a place

Example:
This is the school. I studied here.
This is the school where I studied.

Chapter 5: Rules for Transformation of Sentences

Rule 1:

'Too...to' is converted to 'So...that'

Explanation:

When transforming sentences that use 'too...to' into 'so... that', ensure that the negative form 'cannot' (expressing inability) is used instead of 'will not' (which expresses reluctance or refusal).

Example 1:

Original Sentence: The box is too heavy to lift.

Transformed Sentence: The box is so heavy that it cannot be lifted.

Explanation:

- 'Too heavy to lift' is converted to 'so heavy that it cannot be lifted.'
- 'Cannot' indicates the inability to lift the box, not a refusal to do so.

Example 2:

Original Sentence: The road was too slippery to drive on.

Transformed Sentence: The road was so slippery that one could not drive on it.

Explanation:

- 'Too slippery to drive on' becomes 'so slippery that one could not drive on it.'
- Here, 'could not' expresses the inability to drive on the road, not reluctance.

Example 3:

Original Sentence: The cake is too delicious to resist.

Transformed Sentence: The cake is so delicious that one cannot resist it.

Explanation:

- The phrase 'too delicious to resist' changes to 'so delicious that one cannot resist it.'
- 'Cannot' indicates that it is impossible to resist the cake.

Example 4:

Original Sentence: The task is too complicated for me to understand.

Transformed Sentence: The task is so complicated that I cannot understand it.

Example 5:

Original Sentence: She is too young to drive a car.

Transformed Sentence: She is so young that she cannot drive a car.

Rule 2:

'Besides' means 'in addition to'

Explanation:

- The word 'besides' is used to indicate addition or further information. It carries the meaning of 'in addition to', so it is not necessary to repeat this meaning with words like 'also' or 'always'.

- The phrase following 'besides' typically starts with a gerund (verb + ing) and is followed by a comma.

Example 1:
Original Sentence: Virat Kohli is a good batsman and is also athletic.
Transformed Sentence: Besides being a good batsman, Virat Kohli is athletic.

Explanation:
- 'Besides being a good batsman' conveys the idea of 'in addition to being a good batsman', so there is no need to add 'also'.
- The sentence is shortened and restructured for clarity, using 'besides being' followed by a comma.

Example 2:
Original Sentence: Not only did Sunder score 65 runs, but he also took five wickets.
Transformation: Besides scoring 65 runs, Sunder took five wickets.

Explanation:
- The sentence is restructured with 'besides scoring', which means 'in addition to scoring 65 runs.'
- The comma follows 'besides' to separate the clauses.

Example 3:
Original Sentence: The movie is entertaining and also informative.
Transformation: Besides being entertaining, the movie is informative.

Example 4:
Original Sentence: She is a talented artist and is always cheerful.
Transformation: Besides being a talented artist, she is cheerful.

Example 5:
Original Sentence: Veda not only sings but also plays the guitar.
Transformation: Besides singing, Veda plays the guitar.

Rule 3:

'But for' is used to introduce the reason something did not happen.

Explanation:
- 'But for' is often used to indicate that without a certain condition, the outcome would have been different.
- When transforming sentences, replace 'If it were not for ...' or 'If it had not been for ...' with 'But for ...', that is, remove the word 'not' from the condition and begin the sentence with `But for'.
- 'But for' typically introduces a noun phrase (the reason or condition).

Example 1:
Original Sentence: If it were not for the power cut, we would have finished the project by now.
Transformation: But for the power cut, we would have finished the project by now.

Explanation:
- The condition 'If it were not for the power cut' is converted to 'But for the power cut.'
- The phrase now directly indicates the reason the project was delayed, without mentioning the negative condition.
- 'Not' is removed after 'but for'.

Example 2:
Original Sentence: If it were not for the ISRO Chairman's dedication, the team would have failed.

Transformation: But for the ISRO Chairman's dedication, the team would have failed.

Explanation:
- The sentence 'If it were not for the ISRO Chairman's dedication' becomes 'But for the ISRO Chairman's dedication'.
- The cause of the team's success is the dedication of the ISRO Chairman.

Example 3:
Original Sentence: If it had not been for the late arrival of the guests, the party would have started on time.
Transformation: But for the late arrival of the guests, the party would have started on time.

Explanation:
- The phrase If it had not been for' is shortened to 'But for', while removing 'not'.
- The cause of the delay (late arrival of guests) is now clearly stated.

Example 4:
Original Sentence: If it were not for his quick thinking, the situation would have worsened.
Transformation: But for his quick thinking, the situation would have worsened.

Rule 4:

'Little did I know' is used to express unawareness of something that occurred or was to occur later.

Explanation:
The phrase 'Little did I know' emphasises that you were completely unaware or had no clue about the outcome or event at a past time.

When transforming sentences:
- Begin the sentences with 'Little did I know'.
- Follow it with the fact or event that was not anticipated.
- The transformation typically reorders the sentence.

Example 1:
Original Sentence: I did not know that this journey would change my life.
Transformed Sentence: Little did I know that this journey would change my life.

Explanation:
The phrase 'I did not know' is replaced by 'Little did I know', emphasising the speaker's unawareness of the significant impact the journey would have.

Example 2:
Original Sentence: I did not know that meeting him would lead to such a wonderful friendship.
Transformed Sentence: Little did I know that meeting him would lead to such a wonderful friendship.

Example 3:
Original Sentence: I was unaware that the storm would cause such widespread damage.
Transformed Sentence: Little did I know that the storm would cause such widespread damage.

Example 4:
Original Sentence: I had no idea that 'Baahubali' would become a blockbuster.
Transformed Sentence: Little did I know that 'Baahubali' would become a blockbuster.

***Example 5*:**
Original Sentence: I did not realise that this opportunity would open so many doors for me.
Transformed Sentence: Little did I know that this opportunity would open so many doors for me.

Rule 5:

'Not only... but also' is used to connect and emphasise two elements (words or phrases) in the same position in a sentence.

***Explanation*:**
- It adds emphasis to the second element.
- Ensure the elements connected by this structure are grammatically parallel (such as two adverbs, two adjectives, two verbs, or two nouns).

Sentence Structures with Examples

***Pattern 1*:**
Subject + Verb + Not Only + Adverb + But Also + Adverb

***Example 1*:**
Sneha sings not only melodiously but also passionately.

***Explanation*:**
The adverbs' melodiously' and 'passionately' are connected to emphasise how Sneha sings.

***Example 2*:**
Aman works not only diligently but also quickly.

***Explanation*:**
The adverbs 'diligently' and 'quickly' describe Aman's work style.

***Pattern 2*:**
Subject + Verb + Not Only + Adjective + But Also + Adjective

***Example 1*:**
Ravi is not only intelligent but also creative.

***Explanation*:**
The adjectives' intelligent' and 'creative' are connected to describe Ravi.

***Example 2*:**
The dress is not only beautiful but also affordable.

***Explanation*:**
The adjectives' beautiful' and 'affordable' highlight two qualities of the dress.

***Pattern 3*:**
Subject + Not Only + Verb + But Also + Verb

***Example 1*:**
Aparna not only studies hard but also excels in sports.

***Explanation*:**
The verbs' studies' and 'excels' are connected to emphasise Aparna's well-rounded abilities.

***Example 2*:**
They not only visited the museum but also explored the art gallery.

***Explanation*:**
The verbs 'visited' and 'explored' show their activities.

Pattern 4:
Subject + Verb + Not Only + Noun + But Also + Noun

Example 1:
I like not only coffee but also tea.

Explanation:
The nouns' coffee' and 'tea' are connected to describe the speaker's preferences.

Example 2:
She bought not only flowers but also chocolates for the celebration.

Explanation:
The nouns 'flowers' and 'chocolates' highlight what she bought.

Important Notes:

- Emphasis: This structure is used to add emphasis to the second element while highlighting both.
- Placement: 'Not only' is followed immediately by the first element, and 'but also' introduces the second.
- Parallelism: The two elements connected by 'not only... but also' must be of the same grammatical type (e.g., two adverbs, two adjectives, two verbs, or two nouns).
  ✓ He is not only tall but also strong (both adjectives).
  × He is not only tall but also runs fast (mixing an adjective and a verb).

Starting a Sentence with 'Not Only'

When a sentence starts with 'Not only', the sentence structure changes slightly because it requires **inversion** in the first clause.

Inversion means the subject and auxiliary verb swap places, creating a question-like structure. However, it remains a statement, not a question.

Starting with 'Not only + Inverted Structure

Example 1 (present simple):
Original Sentence: He plays the guitar and also composes songs.
Transformed Sentence: Not only does he play the guitar, but he also composes songs.

Explanation:
When starting with 'Not only', the auxiliary verb 'does' comes before the subject 'he' due to **inversion**.

Example 2 (present simple – verb 'to be'):
Original Sentence: She is talented and kind-hearted.
Transformed Sentence: Not only is she talented, but she is also kind-hearted.

Explanation:
The auxiliary verb 'is' comes before the subject 'she' because the sentence begins with 'Not only'.

Example 3 (past perfect):
Original Sentence: They had visited Rome and also travelled to Paris.
Transformed Sentence: Not only had they visited Rome, but they had also travelled to Paris.

Example 4 (modal verb)
Original Sentence: We can solve the problem and also help others.
Transformed Sentence: Not only can we solve the problem, but we can also help others.

Let's Revise:

What changes when we begin a sentence with "Not Only'?

1. Inversion: The subject and auxiliary verb switch places in the first clause (e.g. does he, is she, had they, can we).

2. Emphasis: Beginning with `Not only' adds more emphasis to the sentence, making it sound formal or dramatic.
3. Formality: Sentences starting with `Not only' are often more formal and are commonly used in written English rather than casual speech.
4. Conciseness: In the second clause, the repeated subject and verb can be removed to make the sentence concise.

Rule 6:

How to use 'Lest'

Explanation:

- 'Lest' is a conjunction that means 'to avoid the risk of' or 'for fear that'.
- When using 'lest', the auxiliary verb 'should' traditionally follows, and the clause describes a possible undesirable outcome.
- This use of 'should' is somewhat old-fashioned, giving the sentence a formal or literary tone.
- In modern English, 'should' is often omitted, and the verb after 'lest' is used in its base form. However, both forms are grammatically correct.

Pattern 1: Using 'Lest' with 'Should' (Traditional Usage)

Example:
Original Sentence: Cover the food or it may get spoiled.
Transformed Sentence: Cover the food lest it should get spoiled.

Explanation:
Here, 'Lest' is followed by the auxiliary verb 'should' to indicate the precaution.

Pattern 2: Using 'Lest' Without 'Should' (Modern Usage)

Example:
Original Sentence: Lock the door or someone may break in.
Transformed Sentence: Lock the door lest someone break in.

Explanation:
The auxiliary verb 'should' is omitted in this variation, and the verb 'break' remains in its base form while still conveying the same meaning. Even if 'should' is included, the verb after it remains in its base form (e.g. break, without *-s*, *-ed*, or *-ing*).

More Examples:

Example 1:
Original Sentence: Write down the instructions. You may forget them.
With 'Should': Write down the instructions lest you should forget them.
Without 'Should': Write down the instructions lest you forget them.

Example 2:
Original Sentence: Speak softly. The baby might wake up.
With 'Should': Speak softly lest the baby should wake up.
Without 'Should': Speak softly lest the baby wake up.

Example 3:
Original Sentence: Take your umbrella. It might rain.
With 'Should': Take your umbrella lest it should rain.

Without 'Should': Take your umbrella lest it rain.

Example 4:

Original Sentence: She explained carefully. The students might not understand.

With 'Should': She explained carefully lest the students should not understand.

Without 'Should': She explained carefully lest the students not understand.

Example 5:

Original Sentence: Hurry up, we may miss the bus.

With 'Should': Hurry up lest we should miss the bus.

Without 'Should': Hurry up lest we miss the bus.

Important Points to Remember

1. Old-fashioned vs Modern Usage:
   - Traditional: 'should' after 'lest'
     - E.g. Lest it should rain.
   - Modern: 'should' omitted for simplicity.
     - E.g. Lest it rain.
2. No double negatives with 'lest':
   - × Lest it does not happen.
   - ✓ Lest it happen.
3. Tone:
   - Using 'lest' creates a formal or literary tone, so it is less common in casual speech.

Rule 7:

'Provided (that)' means 'on condition that'

Explanation:

- The conjunction 'provided (that)' introduces a condition that must be fulfilled for the main clause to occur.
- It works like 'if' in conditional sentences, but gives a slightly formal tone.
- The word 'that' after 'provided' is optional.
- Both 'provided' and 'provided that' are correct.

Example

Original Sentence: If you complete your homework, you can go out to play.

Transformed Sentence: Provided (that) you complete your homework, you can go out to play.

Explanation: Completing homework is the condition for being allowed to play. 'Provided that' expresses this condition formally.

Example 2

Original Sentence: If you keep it a secret, I will tell you the plan.

Transformed Sentence: Provided (that) you keep it a secret, I will tell you the plan.

Explanation: Keeping it a secret is the condition for revealing the plan.

Example 3

Original Sentence: If they submit their forms on time, they can attend the workshop.

Transformed Sentence: Provided (that) they submit their forms on time, they can attend the workshop.

Explanation: Submitting forms on time is the condition for attending the workshop.

Important Notes

1. Placement: Like 'if', 'provided' can appear at the start of a sentence or before the second clause.
   - Beginning: Provided you follow the rules, you can enter.
   - Middle: You can enter, provided you follow the rules.
2. Formality: Using 'provided (that)' sounds slightly more formal than 'if'.

Rule 8:

Transforming 'Despite' or 'In Spite of' into 'Though or 'Although'

Despite / In Spite of + Noun Phrase / Gerund → Though / Although + Subject + Verb

Explanation:

- 'Despite' and 'In spite of' are prepositions, and must be followed by a noun, pronoun, or gerund (e.g. despite the rain; in spite of feeling tired).
- 'Though' or 'although' are subordinating conjunctions and must be followed by a clause (subject + verb) (e.g. although it was raining; though she was tired).
- When transforming a sentence that begins with 'despite' or 'in spite of', convert the noun phrase or gerund into a clause with an appropriate subject and verb.

Example 1

Original Sentence: In spite of her hard work, she failed the exam.

Transformed Sentence: Though/Although she worked hard, she failed the exam.

Explanation: 'In spite of her hard work' changes to 'Though/Although she worked hard', maintaining the same meaning.

Example 2

Original Sentence: Despite the rain, we went for a walk.

Transformed Sentence: Though/Although it was raining, we went for a walk.

Explanation: 'Despite the rain' changes to 'Though/Although it was raining', converting the noun phrase into a dependent clause.

Example 3

Original Sentence: In spite of feeling tired, she continued working.

Transformed Sentence: Though/Although she was tired, she continued working.

Example 4

Original Sentence: In spite of his injury, he finished the race.

Transformed Sentence: Though/Although he was injured, he finished the race.

Explanation: The noun' his injury' is converted into a clause 'he was injured'.

Example 5

Original Sentence: Despite their warnings, she went ahead with the plan.

Transformed Sentence: Though/Although they warned her, she went ahead with the plan.

Explanation: The phrase' their warnings' is transformed into the clause 'they warned her'.

Important Points to Remember

1. Interchangeability:
   - 'Despite' and 'In Spite of' are interchangeable in meaning and usage. So are 'though' and 'although'.
   - Though' is slightly less formal than 'although', but either can be used without changing the meaning.

2. Punctuation:
   - When a contrast phrase or clause (*though, although, despite, in spite of*) comes before the main clause, a comma is placed after it. E.g.:
     - o Although she was tired, she continued.
     - o Despite the rain, we went out.
   - If it comes after the main clause, a comma is usually not needed. E.g.:
     - o She continued, although she was tired.
     - o We went out despite the rain.
3. Structure:
   - 'Despite/In spite of' → followed by a noun or gerund
     - o E.g.: Despite the rain, In spite of being tired.
   - 'Though/Although' → followed by a subject and verb
     - o E.g. Though it was raining, Although she was tired.
4. Do not use 'yet' with 'though/although' in the same clause, because these words already express contrast:
   - × Although it rained yet we went out.
   - ✓ Although it rained, we went out. [or] It rained, yet we went out.

Rule 9:

Using Absolute Phrases Like 'Having' and 'Being'

Explanation:
- Absolute phrases are participial phrases that give background information or context for the main clause, without using conjunctions like 'and', 'so', or 'because' while maintaining the original meaning of the sentence.
- Use 'having' for actions completed before the main verb
- Use 'being' to describe a state or condition.

Example 1
Original Sentence: He finished his homework and went to play. (Remove 'and')
Transformed Sentence: Having finished his homework, he went to play.

Explanation: 'Having finished his homework' provides the reason or context for the action that follows.

Example 2
Original Sentence: The room was messy, so I cleaned it. (Remove 'so')
Transformed Sentence: The room being messy, I cleaned it.

Explanation: 'The room being messy' describes the condition that led to the action.

Example 3
Original Sentence: I passed the test and celebrated with my friends. (Remove 'and')
Transformed Sentence: Having passed the test, I celebrated with my friends.

Explanation: 'Having passed the test' shows an earlier action that preceded the celebration.

Example 4
Original Sentence: She completed her presentation and left the office. (Remove 'and')
Transformed Sentence: Having completed her presentation, she left the office.

Explanation: 'Having completed her presentation' gives the background for her departure.

Important Points to Remember

1. *Use 'Having' for past actions:*
   - o Having finished the report, he took a break.
     - Indicates that the finishing happened before the main event (the break).
2. *Use 'Being' for descriptions, ongoing conditions or existing situations:*
   - o The weather being cold, we stayed indoors.
     - Describes the condition (cold weather) why the main action (staying indoors) happened.
   - o The lights being off, we used candles.
     - Shows the existing situation that led to the action.

Rule 10:

Using 'Unless' to Indicate 'Except if'

Explanation:

- 'Unless' is used to indicate a condition that must be met for the main clause to happen, functioning like 'except if'.
- When transforming 'if + negative verb' changes to 'unless + affirmative verb', the meaning remains the same, but the sentence becomes more concise.
- Unless' already implies a negative condition, so the verb following it must be affirmative.

Transformation Pattern:

- If it does not rain → Unless it rains
- If he does not invite me → Unless he invites me

Example 1

Original Sentence: We will go for a picnic tomorrow if it does not rain.

Transformed Sentence: Unless it rains, we will go for a picnic tomorrow.

Example 2

Original Sentence: I shall go if he invites me.

Transformed Sentence: Unless he invites me, I shall not go.

Example 3

Original Sentence: She will call you if she is free.

Transformed Sentence: Unless she is free, she will not call you.

Example 4

Original Sentence: You will not pass the test if you do not study.

Transformed Sentence: Unless you study, you will not pass the test.

Example 5

Original Sentence: I will be happy if I get a promotion.

Transformed Sentence: Unless I get a promotion, I will not be happy.

Important Points to Remember:

- Using 'unless' usually means the main part of the sentence becomes negative when the original sentence is positive, as shown in Examples 2, 3, and 5.
- Sentences with *if* + negative verb become more direct and natural with 'unless'.
- Do not use negatives after 'unless':
  - × Unless I will not get a promotion
  - ✓ Unless I get a promotion

Rule 11:

Using 'Under No Circumstances'

Explanation:

- Under no circumstances' means 'regardless of the situation or event', or 'never.'
- When transforming sentences that contain 'must never' or similar modals plus 'never', the structure changes to" Under no circumstances + auxiliary/modal verb + subject + verb.'
- The word 'never' is omitted because 'Under no circumstances' already expresses the idea of 'never.'

Example 1

Original Sentence: You must never lie.

Transformed Sentence: Under no circumstances must you lie.

Explanation: 'Never' is removed and replaced with 'Under no circumstances' to emphasise the absolute prohibition.

Example 2

Original Sentence: One must never take medicines on an empty stomach.

Transformed Sentence: Under no circumstances must one take medicines on an empty stomach.

Example 3

Original Sentence: You must never be late for an important meeting.

Transformed Sentence: Under no circumstances must you be late for an important meeting.

Example 4

Original Sentence: One should never ignore the safety rules.

Transformed Sentence: Under no circumstances should one ignore the safety rules.

Important Points to Remember:

- After 'Under no circumstances', invert the auxiliary/modal verb and the subject:
  - × Under no circumstances *you must tell* a lie.
  - ✓ Under no circumstances *must you tell* a lie.
- 'Under no circumstances' is a formal phrase used for strong emphasis.

Rule 12:

Use of 'As soon as' and 'No sooner...than'

Explanation: 'As soon as' conveys a sense of immediacy. It means something happens immediately after another event. 'No sooner...than' has the same meaning as 'as soon as', but is more formal and requires inversion of the auxiliary / modal verb.

The word 'immediately' should not be used with either structure, as they both already convey immediacy.

Example 1

Original Sentence: When Kanishka saw Nupur, he stopped talking on the phone immediately.

Transformed Sentence: As soon as Kanishka saw Nupur, he stopped talking on the phone.

Explanation: 'Immediately' is omitted as 'as soon as' already shows immediacy.

Example 2

Original Sentence: As soon as the delegates arrived, the meeting started.

Transformed Sentence: No sooner did the delegates arrive than the meeting started.

Explanation: 'No sooner' replaces 'As soon as', and the auxiliary verb 'did' is used for past tense inversion, followed by 'than'.

Example 3
Original Sentence: He completed the project, and the boss approved it immediately.
Transformed Sentence: As soon as he completed the project, the boss approved it.

Example 4
Original Sentence: The moment the rain stopped, the children ran outside.
Transformed Sentence: No sooner did the rain stop than the children ran outside.

Example 5
Original Sentence: As soon as she saw the message, she called back.
Transformed Sentence: No sooner did she see the message than she called back.

Explanation: 'No sooner' is used for immediacy, and 'did' helps invert the subject and the verb.

Important Points to Remember

- *Auxiliary verb rule:*
  - If there is no auxiliary verb (*was, has, have, had*), then use 'did' for past tense and 'do' or 'does' for present tense.
    - ✓ No sooner did the delegates arrive than the meeting started.
    - × No sooner had the delegates arrived than the meeting started. (Incorrect here—because the original is simple past, not past perfect.)
- *Using 'had' for past perfect tense:*
  - Use 'had' when one action was fully completed before the next.
    - o No sooner had the train left the platform than it started raining. (The train departure was fully completed before the rain began.)
- *Using 'did for simple past tense:*
  - Use 'did' when the two actions are immediate and sequential or seen as happening almost simultaneously.
    - o No sooner did the train leave the platform than it started raining. (Focus on immediacy, not completion.)

Rule 13:

Use of 'Hardly When' (Also similar to 'Scarcely when' and 'Barely when')

Explanation:

- 'Hardly' when used with 'when' conveys a meaning almost similar to 'No sooner... than' and 'As soon as.'
- It expresses that one event happens immediately after another, often with the implication of something happening almost simultaneously or with minimal delay.
- 'Hardly' is followed by the auxiliary verb 'had' in past tense sentences, and the structure 'when' is used to connect the two actions.

Example 1
Original Sentence: As soon as I reached the school, the assembly began.
Transformed Sentence: Hardly had I reached the school when the assembly began.

Explanation: 'Hardly' is used with the inversion 'had' to convey that the assembly began immediately after I reached the school.

Example 2
Original Sentence: No sooner did the bell ring than the students ran out of the class.
Transformed Sentence: Hardly had the bell rung when the students ran out of the class.

Explanation: The structure 'Hardly had' is used to show the immediacy between the bell ringing and the students running out.

Example 3
Original Sentence: As soon as the guests arrived, the party started.
Transformed Sentence: Hardly had the guests arrived when the party started.

Example 4
Original Sentence: As soon as the sun set, the temperature dropped.
Transformed Sentence: Hardly had the sun set when the temperature dropped.

Example 5
Original Sentence: As soon as she opened the door, the dog ran out.
Transformed Sentence: Hardly had she opened the door when the dog ran out.

Explanation: 'Hardly had' is used to show the immediate connection between opening the door and the dog running out.

Example 6
Original Sentence: As soon as I finished my meal, my friend called me.
Transformed Sentence: Scarcely had I finished my meal when my friend called me.

Explanation: The transformation shows that the call from my friend came right after I finished my meal, with 'scarcely' emphasising the brief time between the two events.

Example 7
Original Sentence: No sooner had the teacher entered the classroom than the students became silent.
Transformed Sentence: Barely had the teacher entered the classroom when the students became silent.

Explanation: 'Barely' conveys the immediacy, suggesting that the students became silent almost the moment the teacher entered.

Rule 14:

Use of 'Only' at the Beginning of a Sentence for Rhetorical Effect

Explanation:
- When 'Only' is placed at the beginning of a sentence for rhetorical effect, it often requires the inversion of the subject and auxiliary verb.
- This inversion adds emphasis or urgency to the statement.
- However, inversion is not needed when 'only' is followed directly by the subject.

Examples with Inversion:

Example 1
Original Sentence: If you do not come, I will not go out.
Transformed Sentence: Only if you come will I go out.

Explanation: The subject 'I' and auxiliary verb 'will' are inverted after 'Only if' to emphasise the condition.

Example 2
Original Sentence: You can only play after you finish your homework.
Transformed Sentence: Only after finishing your homework can you play.

Explanation: The auxiliary verb 'can' is inverted with the subject 'you' after 'Only after' for emphasis.

Example 3
Original Sentence: He called me only when he needed some help.
Transformed Sentence: Only when he needed some help did he call me.

Explanation: The auxiliary verb 'did' is inverted with the subject 'he' to emphasise the condition under which he called.

Examples with No Inversion (when 'Only' is directly followed by the subject):

Example 4
Original Sentence: No one else can understand.
Transformed Sentence: Only you can understand.

Explanation: There is no inversion because 'only' is directly followed by the subject 'you'.

Important Points to Remember:

- If 'only' is followed by an adverbial phrase or clause at the start, inversion is required.
- If 'only' is followed immediately by the subject, no inversion is needed.
- Inversion in this structure is common in formal or emphatic writing.

Rule 15:

Special Transformations – Using 'In all likelihood' and 'In all probability'

Explanation:

- When a sentence expresses an assumption or a likelihood about something happening, 'In all likelihood' or 'In all probability' can be used to begin the sentence.
- These expressions:
  - Add emphasis to the degree of certainty
  - Are often used for making predictions or assumptions.
  - Work with both present, past and future events.

Example 1
Original Sentence: Shikhar has most likely forgotten your birthday.
Transformed Sentence: In all likelihood, Shikhar has forgotten your birthday.

Explanation: 'In all likelihood' is used to express the high probability of Shikhar forgetting the birthday, and the sentence structure is rearranged for emphasis.

Example 2
Original Sentence: Vikas has probably misplaced his exam admit card.
Transformed Sentence: In all probability, Vikas has misplaced his exam admit card.

Explanation: 'In all probability' is used to convey the likelihood that Vikas misplaced the admit card, emphasising the assumption.

Example 3
Original Sentence: She is most likely to be late for the meeting.
Transformed Sentence: In all likelihood, she will be late for the meeting.

Example 4
Original Sentence: The weather will probably be bad tomorrow.
Transformed Sentence: In all probability, the weather will be bad tomorrow.

> ***Example 5***
> Original Sentence: They are most likely to arrive late at the airport.
> Transformed Sentence: In all likelihood, they will arrive late at the airport.

Rule 16:

Use of 'Rather' for Transformation

> ***Explanation***:
> - The word 'rather' can be used to express a preference or a contrast.
> - It is often used to replace phrases like 'instead', 'preferably', or 'more than' in a transformed sentence.
> - It can also be used to emphasise a specific choice or to show the comparative relationship between options.

Common Uses of 'Rather' in Transformations:

1. *To Express Preference:*
   When 'rather' is used to show a preference, it typically replaces a choice or preference expression in the original sentence.

> ***Example 1***
> Original Sentence: I would prefer to go to the beach rather than stay at home.
> Transformed Sentence: I would rather go to the beach than stay at home.

> ***Explanation***: The transformation simplifies the sentence by using 'rather' in place of 'prefer to' and keeps the comparative phrase 'than'.

2. *To Show a Contrast:*
   'Rather' can also emphasise a contrast between two choices or possibilities.

> ***Example 2***:
> Original Sentence: She is not interested in a vacation but would prefer to focus on her work.
> Transformed Sentence: She would rather focus on her work than go on a vacation.

> ***Explanation***: 'Rather' highlights her preference for focusing on work over taking a vacation, showing a clear contrast.

3. *In Negative Statements ('rather than'):*
   When expressing a preference in a negative sentence, 'rather than' can show an alternative or choice.

> ***Example 3***
> Original Sentence: I do not want to go to the party. I prefer to stay at home.
> Transformed Sentence: I would rather stay at home than go to the party.

> ***Explanation***: 'Rather' replaces the expression 'prefer to', and 'than' highlights the contrast between the two actions.

Change Sentences Without Changing Their Meaning

Transforming Affirmative Sentences to Negative and Vice Versa

An affirmative sentence states a positive idea.

A negative sentence expresses denial, prohibition, absence, or refusal — in short, it conveys a 'no'.

Note: The meaning of the original sentence must remain the same even when converting.

To form a negative sentence, we often use negative words such as *no, never, not, neither, nor, nothing, none*.

However, using these words directly can sometimes alter the tone or the meaning. To avoid this, we can use negative prefixes such as *-un-, dis-, im-* or suffixes such as *-less*.

***Examples*:**

uncomfortable, impossible, unable, disobey, careless, fearless

Affirmative: Janhavi is polite.

Negative: Janhavi is not impolite.

Affirmative: Sameer always obeys his parents.

Negative: Sameer never disobeys his parents.

Common affirmative-negative word pairs:

- always ↔ never
- everywhere ↔ nowhere
- ever ↔ never
- anyone ↔ no one
- somebody ↔nobody

Sometimes, 'not' can be replaced with phrases such as *refrain from, avoid,* or *abstain from.*

***Example*:**

Avoid making mistakes ⇔ Do not make mistakes ⇔ Refrain from making mistakes

Rules for transforming sentences

1. If a sentence contains 'only' or 'alone', transform it using one of the following structures:

- only (thing) → not more than / nothing but
- only (persons) / alone (persons) → none but
- only (time, number) → not more than (for upper limit, especially with quantities)
- only (time, number) → not less than (for lower limits or emphasis)

***Examples*:**

(a) I need only 30 minutes of rest.
I do not need more than 30 minutes of rest.
I need nothing but 30 minutes of rest.

(b) Only a responsible person can do this.
None but a responsible person can do this.

(c) The hardworking alone deserve the award.
None but the hardworking deserve the award.

(d) I need only a cup of tea now.
I need nothing but a cup of tea now.

(e) He ran only five kilometres.
He ran not less than five kilometres.

2. 'And' / 'Both' changes to not only ... but also

***Examples*:**

(a) Debashree played tennis and badminton.
Debashree played not only tennis but also badminton.

(b) We visited both the zoo and the museum.
We visited not only the zoo but also the museum.

3. 'Too...to' change to 'so...that + not' (to show something cannot happen)

When something is "too [adjective] to [verb]," it means it cannot happen because of excess.
We can change it using "so...that" + 'cannot' / 'will not' to keep the same meaning.

***Examples*:**

(a) The news is too good to be true.
The news is so good that it cannot be true.

(b) The patient is too weak to climb the stairs.
The patient is so weak that he cannot climb the stairs.
('Cannot' means inability. 'Will not' means reluctance or refusal.)
Sometimes we reverse the transformation, but the meaning must still be the same:

(c) I am so thirsty that I can finish the entire bottle of water.
✓ I am too thirsty not to finish the entire bottle of water.
× I am too thirsty to finish the entire bottle of water. (Changes meaning)

4. 'The most...' changes to 'No other...as...as'

Example:
Mumbai is the most crowded city in India.
No other city in India is as crowded as Mumbai.

5. Use of Antonyms

To change a sentence, use the opposite (antonym) of a word along with *not, never,* or *nobody*.
Important: The meaning must stay the same.

Examples:
(a) He is sometimes foolish.
He is not always wise.
(b) Everybody will admit that he did his best.
Nobody will deny that he did his best.
(c) He passed the exam.
He did not fail the exam.

6. Use of Degrees of Comparison (Positive ↔ Comparative)

An affirmative comparative sentence can be changed to a negative sentence using "not as...as" in the positive degree.

Example:
(a) You are richer than I.
I am not as rich as you are.
(b) This room is bigger than that one.
That room is not as big as this one.

7. Use of 'No sooner...than'

When one action happens immediately after another, we can start the sentence with "No sooner... than".

Important: This structure requires inversion (placing the auxiliary verb before the subject).

Note: If the original sentence does not contain an auxiliary verb (was, were, has, have, had), use 'did' for past tense and 'do / does' for present tense during transformation.

Examples:
(a) As soon as we got the money, we bought the television set.
No sooner did we get the money than we bought the television set.
(b) As soon as he arrived home, he washed his clothes.
No sooner did he arrive home than he washed his clothes.
(c) Hardly had I reached school when the bell rang.
No sooner had I reached school than the bell rang.
As soon as I reached school, the bell rang.

8. Universal Truths

When converting universal truth sentences from affirmative to negative form (without changing their meaning), often interrogative-negative questions, such as 'doesn't it', 'isn't it', are used.

Examples:

(a) The sun rises in the east.
Doesn't the sun rise in the east?

(b) Honesty is the best policy.
Isn't honesty the best policy?

9. As + adjective + as changes to not less + adjective + than

Example:

(a) Rahman is as *talented* in music as Harris.
Rahman is not less *talented* in music than Harris.

10. Changing Interrogative Sentences to Assertive

Some questions are actually statements in disguise. These are often rhetorical or emphatic questions that express strong opinions or facts.

To convert an interrogative sentence to an assertive:

- Change the question sentence into a statement.
- Place the subject before the verb.
- Remove the question mark.
- Make sure the tense remains the same.
- If the question uses *do* / *does* / *did*, replace it with the correct tense of the verb.

A. *Yes/No Type Questions*

(a) Interrogative: Does he like to play video games?
Assertive: He likes to play video games.

(b) Interrogative: Did they cheat in the exam?
Assertive: They cheated in the exam.

(c) Interrogative: Is he brave?
Assertive: He is brave.

B. *Emphatic or Rhetorical Questions*

These are not real questions. They express a strong opinion or fact, so the sentence should be changed accordingly.

Example:

(a) Interrogative: Who can beat PV Sindhu on the badminton court?
Assertive: No one can beat PV Sindhu on the badminton court.
(This is not asking for names of those who can beat PV Sindhu; rather, it is saying Sindhu is unbeatable.)

(b) Interrogative: Is blood not thicker than water?
Assertive: Blood is thicker than water.

(c) Interrogative: Is there anything tastier than masala dosa?
Assertive: There is nothing tastier than masala dosa.

11. Changing Assertive to Interrogative

To change an assertive sentence into a question:

- Change the statement into a question sentence.
- Move the helping verb (is, was, can, etc.) before the subject.
- If there is no helping verb, use 'do / does / did' based on the tense and subject.
- In negative sentences, place the helping verb + not before the subject.

A. With Helping Verb

Assertive: He is cooking a meal.
Interrogative: Is he cooking a meal?

B. Without Helping Verb:

Assertive: He plays the piano.
Interrogative: Does he play the piano?

Assertive: They drove to the theatre.
Interrogative: Did they drive to the theatre?

C. Negative Sentences
Assertive: She is not financially literate.
Interrogative: Is she not financially literate?

More examples:

(a) Assertive: There is nothing better than an afternoon nap.
Interrogative: Is there anything better than an afternoon nap?

(b) Assertive: We can never forget our 1983 World Cup victory.
Interrogative: Can we ever forget our 1983 World Cup victory?

(c) Assertive: Everyone has heard of Netaji Subhas Chandra Bose.
Interrogative: Who has not heard of Netaji Subhas Chandra Bose?

(d) Assertive: We did not come here to relax.
Interrogative: Did we come here to relax?

12. Changing Exclamatory Sentences to Assertive

An exclamatory sentence expresses strong emotion such as happiness, sadness, surprise, or shock. It always ends with an exclamation mark (!)

Common Structure:

What + a/an + adjective + subject + verb!
[OR]
How + adjective + subject + verb!

Examples:
What a beautiful car it is!
How lovely the weather is!
Other forms of exclamatory sentences:

Example:
If only I had stayed longer at your home! (used instead of "I wish...")

How is an Assertive Sentence written?

- It states a fact without any strong emotion.
- It ends with a full stop.

Structure:
Subject + Verb + rest of the sentence

Examples:
The weather is very lovely.
The car is very beautiful.

To change an exclamatory sentence into an assertive:

- Replace emotional words like "what," "how," "alas," "oh" with neutral words such as "very," "extremely," or "it is sad that."
- Change the punctuation mark (!) to a full stop.
- Convert any emotional or wishful phrasing into factual or declarative statements.

Examples:

(a) How sweet the song is!
The song is very sweet.

(b) Oh, for a prize! (the expression is that of wishing)
I wish I had won a prize.

(c) Oh, that I had the grace of a tiger!
I wish I had the grace of a tiger.

(d) How gracefully the Indian captain bats! (Emotion is admiration)
The Indian captain bats very gracefully.
(e) Alas! We lost the game!
It is sad that we lost the game.
(f) What a grand celebration!
It was a grand celebration.

Tip: Identify the emotion (joy, surprise, sadness) in the sentence and express it in neutral or factual language.

13. Changing Assertive to Exclamatory

Rules for transformation:

☞ If the assertive sentence follows this structure:
- o Subject (It/This) + linking verb (is/was) + noun phrase or adjective,

Then, the exclamatory structure becomes:
- o What + (a/an) + noun phrase + subject + linking verb + !
- o How + adjective + subject + linking verb + !

☞ If the assertive sentence expresses a wish, it can become an exclamatory sentence using:
- o 'Oh that...!' or 'If only...!'

Examples:
(a) It was a terrible accident.
What a terrible accident it was!
(b) The weather is charming indeed.
How charming the weather is!
(c) It is very silly of me to forget your name.
How silly of me to forget your name!
(d) This is an extremely innovative experiment.
What an innovative experiment this is!
(e) I wish that we could travel again.
Oh, that we could travel again!

QUESTION TAGS

What are Question Tags?

Question tags are short questions added at the end of a statement. They are used to:
- check information
- seek agreement
- encourage a response
- add emphasis to what is being said

In other words, question tags help confirm what is said, especially when the speaker is unsure, wants affirmation or wishes to make a strong point.

Let us understand this better with the help of some examples.
- It is very cold today, isn't it? (Used to check information)
- That was an outstanding performance, wasn't it? (Used to seek agreement)
- You know the answer, don't you? (Used to encourage a reply)

☞ In terms of structure, a question tag usually mirrors the *helping verb* or *modal verb* in the main sentence and matches the tense and subject of the sentence.

☞ A question tag must always be followed by a question mark.

Rules to Remember

(a) The sentence and question tag must be in the same tense.
(b) For a negative question tag, use the contracted form of a helping verb + not (such as, isn't, won't)
(c) If the sentence is positive, the question tag must be negative and vice versa.
(d) Always use a pronoun in the question tag.
(e) Sentences with negative adverbs such as *hardly*, *rarely*, *barely*, *scarcely*, *seldom* take positive question tags.

Example:
He *hardly* eats anything, does he?
(The auxiliary verb "does" is used because the main verb "eats" is in the present tense.)

(f) If a sentence begins with "there", the question tag will also have "there" in place of the pronoun.

Example:
There are no good hotels in this town, are there?

(g) The question tag should match the main clause of the sentence and not the introductory phrases.

Example:
I think he is wise, isn't he? (Here, "he is wise" is the main clause of the sentence.)

(h) "Aren't I" is the contracted question tag for "I am", not "ain't."

Example:
I am fine, aren't I?

(i) Words like *every, each, everyone, everybody, no one, none, nobody* are treated as singular and take a singular verb, pronoun or adjective. However, their question tag uses "they" and plural verbs.

Examples:
Everyone has arrived, haven't they? ✓
Everyone has arrived, hasn't he? ✗
None of your friends play cricket, do they? ✓

(j) If the sentence starts with "Let us" or "Let's", then "shall we?" is used as a question tag.

Example:
Let us go to play football today, shall we?

(k) Collective nouns take singular verbs and singular pronouns in the question tags.

Example:
The jury has given its verdict, hasn't it?

(l) For Imperative sentences (instructions, requests or commands), use:
- won't you (for polite invitation)
- will you or won't you (for neutral or polite request)

Examples:
Come in, won't you?
Pour the water, would you?
Open the window, would you?

(m) The negative tag "won't you?" can be used to express a persuasive tone.

Example:
Have some snacks, won't you?

(n) "A few" and "A little" are positive in meaning and take negative tags.

Examples:
A few children played in the pond, didn't they?
Only a few people have turned up to the event, haven't they?
The officer gave us a little time to fill out the forms, didn't he?

(o) "Few" and "little" are negative in meaning. These take positive tags.

Examples:

He has little interest in geopolitics, does he? (It means he hardly cares about geopolitics.)

Few people know this rule, do they? (This means hardly anyone knows.)

(p) If the subject of the sentence is *nothing*, *everything*, *anything*, or *something*, then the question tag used will be "it".

Examples:

Something good will materialise, won't it?

Everything has been arranged, hasn't it?

Nothing is vegetarian here, is it?

Note: *Nothing* is a negative word, so the question tag is positive.

(q) If the subject includes phrases such as, *all of us*, *some of us*, *any of us*, *none of us*, *most of us*, *either of us*, or *neither of us* (and their "you" variants), the question tag must match the pronoun used:

- Use "we" when the subject includes us
- Use "you" when the subject includes you

Examples:

All of us are ready, aren't we?

Neither of you can drive a car, can you?

(r) With "need" and "dare", the tag depends on their use.

- As a modal verb without "to", the question tag is formed directly from "need" and "dare".

Examples:

We needn't go now, need we?

The workers dare not go on strike, dare they?

- As a regular verb with "to", "do", "did", and "does" are used in the question tag.

Examples:

She needs to rest more, doesn't she?

He dares to object, doesn't he?

Practice Questions - Add a Question Tag

1. You are coming to the party, ____________________.
2. The sun sets in the west, ____________________.
3. She hasn't finished her homework yet, ____________________.
4. They will help us with the project, ____________________.
5. He doesn't like ice cream, ____________________.
6. She can play the piano well, ____________________.
7. We shouldn't waste water, ____________________.
8. You haven't seen this movie before, ____________________.
9. He was late to the meeting, ____________________.
10. They are not coming to the picnic, ____________________.
11. I didn't scold you, ____________________.
12. Tea isn't prepared yet, ____________________.
13. Everything is free here, ____________________.
14. These students seldom visit the library, ____________________.
15. The Patels will go to India soon, ____________________.

Answer Key

1. You are coming to the party, <u>aren't you?</u>
2. The sun sets in the west, <u>doesn't it?</u>

3. She hasn't finished her homework yet, <u>has she?</u>
4. They will help us with the project, <u>won't they?</u>
5. He doesn't like ice cream, <u>does he?</u>
6. She can play the piano well, <u>can't she?</u>
7. We shouldn't waste water, <u>should we?</u>
8. You haven't seen this movie before, <u>have you?</u>
9. He was late to the meeting, <u>wasn't he?</u>
10. They are not coming to the picnic, <u>are they?</u>
11. I didn't scold you, <u>did I?</u>
12. Tea isn't prepared yet, <u>is it?</u>
13. Everything is free here, <u>isn't it?</u>
14. These students seldom visit the library, <u>do they?</u>
15. The Patels will go to India soon, <u>won't they?</u>

Active and Passive Voice

What is the difference between Active and Passive Voice?

In the *active voice*, the subject of the sentence performs the action and the object receives it.

Example: Mohit cleaned his cupboard.
(*Mohit* is the subject, *cleaned* is the verb, and *cupboard* is the object.)
In *passive voice*, the subject receives the action.

Example: The cupboard was cleaned by Mohit.
(Now, *the cupboard* becomes the subject and receives the action, while Mohit is the agent performing the action)
That is, the *object* of the *active sentence* becomes the *subject* in the *passive sentence*.

Rules for conversion (Active to Passive)

To change a sentence from active to passive voice:

1. Identify the **subject**, **verb**, and **object**.
2. Move the **object** of the active sentence to the **subject** position.
3. Change the verb form: use the appropriate tense of "**to be**" + **past participle (V3)** of the main verb.
4. Add "**by** + **agent**" (the original subject), if/as needed.
   - If the agent is clear and important, include it.
   - Omit agent if unknown, obvious, or unimportant.

Let us look at examples across tenses.

1. **Simple Present**
   Structure (Active): Subject + base verb (+ object)
   Structure (Passive): Object + is/am/are + past participle (+ by + agent)

Example:
Active: Nishant washes clothes.
Passive: Clothes are washed by Nishant.

2. **Simple Past**
   Structure (Active): Subject + past tense verb
   Structure (Passive): Object + was/were + past participle (+ by + agent)

Example:
Active: Nishant washed the clothes.
Passive: The clothes were washed by Nishant.

3. **Simple Future**
   Structure (Active): Subject + will/shall + base verb
   Structure (Passive): Object + will/shall + be + past participle (+ by + agent)

Example:

Active: Nishant will wash the clothes.

Passive: The clothes will be washed by Nishant.

4. Present Continuous

Structure (Active): Subject + is/am/are + verb (-ing)

Structure (Passive): Object + is/am/are + being + past participle (+ by + agent)

Example:

Active: Nishant is washing the clothes.

Passive: The clothes are being washed by Nishant.

5. Past Continuous

Structure (Active): Subject + was/were + verb (-ing)

Structure (Passive): Object + was/were + being + past participle (+ by + agent)

Example:

Active: Nishant was washing the clothes.

Passive: The clothes were being washed by Nishant.

6. Present Perfect

Structure (Active): Subject + has/have + past participle

Structure (Passive): Object + has/have + been + past participle (+ by + agent)

Example:

Active: Nishant has washed the clothes.

Passive: The clothes have been washed by Nishant.

7. Past Perfect

Structure (Active): Subject + had + past participle

Structure (Passive): Object + had + been + past participle (+ by + agent)

Example:

Active: Nishant had washed the clothes.

Passive: The clothes had been washed by Nishant.

8. Modal Verbs

Structure (Active): Subject + modal (can, could, may, might, should, etc.) + base verb

Structure (Passive): Object + modal + be + past participle (+ by + agent)

Example:

Active: Nishant can wash the clothes.

Passive: The clothes can be washed by Nishant.

Active: Nishant should wash the clothes.

Passive: The clothes should be washed by Nishant.

- **Special Constructions in Passive Voice**

Let us now look at some special sentence types and how they are changed to passive voice. These include statements with implied agents, questions, commands, and passive constructions where the subject is not clearly mentioned.

1. Sentence with Impersonal Construction

Example:

Active: It is time to close the performance.

Passive: It is time for the performance to be closed.

Note: *The phrase "It is time to..." stays unchanged. The verb "close" is made passive using "to be + past participle."*

2. Passive Constructions Using "It" as Subject

Example:

Active:	The Indian team is expected to win the trophy.
Passive:	It was expected by the Indian team that it would win the trophy.

Note: Use "it" in the passive voice when the thing being talked about (to win the trophy) is a full action or idea, not a single noun.

3. Sentence with General Public as the Agent

Example:

Active:	*Everyone* expected India to win the trophy.
Passive:	It was expected by *everyone* that India would win the trophy.

Note: The agent here is "everyone".

4. Interrogative sentence (with "who")

Examples:

Active:	Who called you a coward?
Passive:	By whom were you called a coward?
Active:	Who taught you swimming?
Passive:	By whom were you taught swimming?

5. Passive Sentences with Implied or Unknown Subjects (Rewriting in Active)

Examples:

Passive:	Our secret has been exposed.
Active:	Someone has exposed our secret.

Note: When the doer is unknown or not clearly mentioned in the passive sentence, an assumed subject like "someone' can be used when converting to active voice.

Passive:	Our basketball team has been defeated.
Active:	*The rivals* have defeated our basketball team.

Note: Choose an appropriate agent based on the context for the active voice. Here, "the rivals" becomes an appropriate agent to mean the opposing team.

Passive:	Our troops were defeated.
Active:	The enemy defeated our troops.

Note: Similar to the previous example, choose an appropriate agent based on the context. In this case, since "troops" implies a military setting, "the enemy" is a suitable agent.

6. Imperative Sentence (Commands, Orders, Requests, Advice, Instructions)

Example:

Active:	Give the order.
Passive:	*Let* the order be given.
Active:	Open the door.
Passive:	*Let* the door be opened.
Active:	Do the homework.
Passive:	*Let* the homework be done.

Note: Imperative sentences begin with the base verb in the active voice. The passive structure becomes:

Let + object + be + past participle (V3) + (by + subject, if needed)

Tips to Remember

1. Always use the third form of the verb (V3) in passive voice.
   - The clothes were washed by Nishant. (Not *washes* or *washing*)
2. By + agent" (the doer of the action) is added only when the agent is important, known, or necessary.
   - The song was composed by A R Rahman. (Known agent)
   - The window was broken. (Agent unknown or unimportant. So "by someone" is not needed.)
3. The tense of the sentence remains the same in passive voice; only the verb structure changes.
   - Active: Nishant washes the clothes. (Simple present)
   - Passive: The clothes are washed by Nishant. (Still simple present — only verb structure has changed)
4. Only transitive verbs (those that take an object) can be changed to passive.
   - He slept early. (No object – no passive form)
   - He closed the window. (Sentence has an object - "window"; so, it can be changed to passive form à The window was closed (by him).
5. Remember the pronoun changes when converting from active to passive:

Active Pronoun	Passive Form	Example - Active Voice	Conversion to Passive Voice
I	me	I wrote the poem.	The poem was written by me.
He / She	him / her	She painted the wall.	The wall was painted by her.
We	us	We ate the fruits.	The fruits were eaten by us.
They	them	They served lunch.	Lunch was served by them.
You	you	You drove the car.	The car was driven by you.

6. Passive voice is generally not used with certain continuous tenses, as the constructions become awkward and grammatically incorrect. Observe the passive forms in the following continuous sentences.

Present Perfect Continuous

Example:
Active: Trisha has been cleaning her room. ✓
Passive: The room has been being cleaned by Trisha. ×

Past Perfect Continuous

Example:
Active: The engineers had been building the dam. ✓
Passive: The dam had been being building by the engineers. ×

Future Continuous.

Example:
Active: The Prime Minister will be delivering a speech. ✓
Passive: A speech will be being delivered by the Prime Minister. ×

- To avoid such awkward passive forms, it is best to rewrite the sentence in a simpler tense, such as present perfect or past perfect, instead.

SUBJECT-VERB AGREEMENT

What is the Subject-Verb agreement?

Subject-verb agreement means that the subject and verb in a sentence must match in number (singular or plural). In other words, a singular subject (he, Prannoy, the sun) takes a singular verb (is, reads, rises), whereas a plural subject (animals, birds, students) takes a plural verb (run, fly, study).

Examples:

Singular subject with Singular verb

She runs fast.

Plural subject with Plural verb

They run fast.

There are several exceptions, which are discussed in the rules below.

1. **Two or more singular nouns or pronouns joined by 'and' take a plural verb.**
   (a) *Neelima and I* are childhood friends.
   (b) *Jealousy and hate* are negative emotions.
   (c) Are *Vihaan and Aryan* in the library?
2. **Two singular nouns joined by 'and' that refer to one idea take a singular verb.**
   (a) *Bread and butter* is my breakfast on Sundays.
   (b) *Peace and quiet* is all I want.
   (c) *Rice and dal* is my favourite meal.
   (d) *Honour and glory* on the battlefield was his reward.
   (e) *Slow and steady* wins the race.
   (f) *Law and order* is essential for a peaceful society.

Exception: When the nouns are treated as separate items, use a plural verb.

Example:

Bread and butter are made from wheat and milk, respectively.

(Here, bread and butter are treated as different items.)

3. **Two singular nouns referring to the same person or thing take a singular verb.**
   (a) The famous *novelist and poet* has died.
   (b) The *singer and music composer* is expected any time now.

Note: If the article 'the' is repeated, the two nouns refer to two different subjects.

The singer and *the music composer* are expected any time now.

4. **Subjects joined by 'or', 'nor', 'either...or', or 'neither...nor' take a verb that agrees with the subject closest to it.**
   (a) Either the cat or the dog makes that noise.
   (b) Neither Ram nor Shyam has failed the exam.
   (c) Either Sonika or Gopal is going to Kanpur tomorrow.
   (d) Either the teacher or the students are in the classroom.
   (e) Either the students or the teacher is in the classroom.
   (f) Neither the captain nor the players were happy with the referee's decision.
   (g) Neither the captain nor the player was happy with the referee's decision.
5. **When subjects joined by 'or' or 'nor' are of different persons (first, second, or third), the verb agrees with the subject nearest to it.**
   (a) *Either* Seetha *or* I am the topper in the exam.
   (b) *Neither* Jasper *nor* you are to step out in this rain.
   (c) *Either* I *or* she is presenting the report.
6. **When two nouns are joined by phrases like 'with,' 'along with', 'as well as', 'in addition to', 'together with', etc., the verb agrees with the main subject (the noun before the phrase).**
   (a) The unstable building, with its furniture, was pulled down.
   (b) The gardener, with all the volunteers, has planted the saplings.
   (c) Wheat as well as sugarcane is grown in Uttar Pradesh.
   (d) The actor, along with her team, was welcomed.
   (e) The principal, in addition to the teachers, is attending the meeting.

Note: A phrase starting with 'with' is not part of the main subject. It is an additional detail. Hence, the verb must agree with the main subject, not the noun (subject) in the added phrase.

The gardener, with all the volunteers, has planted the saplings. – (Not 'have planted' because the main subject is 'the gardener'.)

7. **Words like 'either', 'neither', 'each', 'everyone', and 'many a' take singular verbs.**
   (a) Many a mountaineer has died on the way to Mt Everest.
   (b) Either of the cakes looks delicious.
   (c) Everyone was invited to the party.
   (d) Each of these experiments is important for the examination.
   (e) Neither of the two men was strong.

8. **Collective nouns usually take singular verbs when considered as a single unit.**
   (a) The Lok Sabha has elected its new Speaker.
   (b) The association has submitted the accounts.
   (c) The jury is divided in its opinion.

Exception: If the members act individually, use a plural verb:
The jury were divided in their opinions.

9. **'Police' is always plural when referring to members of the force.**
   (a) The police have arrived at the crime scene.

Exception: When referring to the police force as a single organised unit, it takes a singular verb.

The police force has evidence against the culprit.
Note: Police → plural (individual officers),
Police force → singular (institution or organised unit)

10. **Plural proper nouns denoting single entities take singular verbs.**
    (a) The United States of America is a powerful nation.
    (b) The Olympic Games is held every four years.
    (c) The headquarters of the bank is in Mumbai.
    (d) The Arabian Nights is a classic in literature.

11. **Plural nouns denoting a specific amount, measurement, time, distance or money take singular verbs when considered as a whole.**
    (a) Fifteen kilometres is a long distance.
    (b) Five thousand rupees is too much for a second-hand appliance.

12. **If two singular nouns are joined by 'and' but are also preceded by 'each' or 'every', the verb used is singular. This is because 'each' and 'every' refer to individual items, not a group.**
    (a) *Each* boy *and* girl was given a certificate.
    (b) *Every* nook *and* corner of the airport was occupied.

13. **Words like 'majority' can take singular or plural verbs depending on usage.**
    (a) The majority opinion is in favour of early elections. (refers to opinion)
    (b) he majority of voters are unhappy. (refers to people)

14. **Some nouns are always plural in form and take plural verbs.**
    These include tools, clothing, and instruments like scissors, trousers, glasses, jeans, binoculars, pliers, socks, etc.
    (a) My socks are on the bed.
    (b) Your trousers are dirty.
    (c) These scissors are sharp.
    (d) The jeans are too expensive.

15. **Avoid 'proximity error'- the verb should agree with the actual subject, not the nearby noun.**
    (a) The colour of the flowers was pink. (subject is colour, not flowers)

16. **'No one' and 'none' used in responses must agree with what is being referred to.**
    (a) Is there a doctor on the flight? No, there is no one.
    (b) Are there any doctors on the flight? No, there are none.

17. **Phrases like 'a number of', 'a great number of', 'a large number of', and 'a variety of' take plural nouns and plural verbs.**

(a) A number of shops are open.
(b) A variety of animals live in this forest.

However, when these phrases begin with 'the', they take singular verbs.

(a) The number of COVID cases is decreasing.
(b) The variety of programmes on TV is impressive.

18. When the same singular noun is repeated before and after certain prepositions, the whole phrase is treated as singular and takes a singular verb.

(a) Movie after movie was screened at the event.
(b) Rule by rule is being checked.
(c) Battle over battle shaped the course of history.
(d) Tree beside tree stands tall in the garden.
(e) Hill beyond hill is covered in mist

Note: This applies when the noun repetition forms a pattern that suggests sequence or continuity.
E.g. Step by step, day after day.
Common prepositions that follow this pattern include: *after, behind, beneath, beside, between, beyond, by, over, under, upon, with.*

19. In hypothetical, imaginary or unreal situations, often introduced with words or phrases like 'if', 'as if', 'I wish', 'as though', 'suppose' – 'were' is used instead of 'was', even with singular subjects like *I, he*, or *she*.

(a) If I were a bird, I would fly over the mountains.
(b) I wish she were here to see this.
(c) He spoke as if he were a scientist.
(d) She danced as though she were on stage.
(e) Suppose I were taller, I could play basketball better.

20. 'Both', 'both of', and 'a few' take plural verbs.

(a) Both horses are in good health.
(b) Both of my cousins live abroad.
(c) A few students have turned up for the session.

21. 'A lot of' takes a singular or plural verb based on whether the noun is countable or uncountable.

(i) With countable nouns - plural nouns + plural verb
  (a) A lot of books have been donated to the library.
  (b) A lot of people work in this company.
(ii) With uncountable nouns - uncountable noun + singular verb
  (a) A lot of trash is lying on the street.
  (b) A lot of water is wasted when the tap is left open.

22. Words like 'most', 'some', 'lots of', 'enough', and 'plenty' follow the same rule as 'a lot of'- plural verbs with countable nouns and singular verbs with uncountable nouns.

(a) Most residents are free this Sunday. (countable – plural)
(b) Some vegetables have gone bad. (countable – plural)
(c) Plenty of food is in the refrigerator. (uncountable – singular)
(d) Some water has soaked into the carpet. (uncountable – singular)
(e) Most of the property belongs to him (uncountable – singular)

23. In sentences that begin with 'here' or 'there', the verb agrees with the subject that follows.

(a) There is a pen in my bag.
(b) There are pens in my bag.
(c) Here comes the bride.
(d) Here come the dancers.

24. Gerunds (verbs + ing) used as subjects take singular verbs.

(a) Cycling is a good exercise.
(b) Reading helps you improve your vocabulary.
(c) Playing cricket in the rain is fun.

25. Words like 'amount' and 'quantity', when referring to uncountable nouns, take a singular verb.

(a) This amount of money is enough for the trip.
(b) The amount of work yesterday was overwhelming.
(c) A small quantity of juice was spilt on the floor.
(d) This quantity of data stored on the computer is massive.

26. Use a singular verb when 'amount' or 'quantity' is singular, even if it refers to countable things.

The amount / The quantity is a singular verb
(a) The quantity of plastic bottles in the oceans has increased.
(b) The amount of emails in my inbox is overwhelming.

27. Use a plural verb when the subject is 'amounts' or 'quantities' (plural)

(a) Large amounts of money were spent on COVID research.
(b) Small quantities of snacks are being packed for the trip.

DIRECT TO INDIRECT SPEECH

What is Direct Speech?

The exact reproduction of a speaker's words, enclosed within quotation marks, is called Direct Speech.

Example: Gopi said, "I am going to play badminton."

What is Indirect Speech?

Also known as Reported Speech, indirect speech conveys the meaning of what someone said without quoting their exact words, and without the use of quotation marks.

Example: Gopi said that he was going to play badminton.

IMPORTANT RULES TO REMEMBER

Rule 1:

When the reporting verb of direct speech is in the past tense (e.g. said), then the present tense in the reported sentence changes to the past tense in indirect speech.

Direct: Hari *said*, "I am hungry."
Indirect: Hari said that he was hungry.

Exceptions:

(a) *If the reporting verb is in the present tense, the tense of the reported speech does not change.*

Direct: He *says*, "I am a mechanical engineer."

Indirect: He *says* that he is a mechanical engineer.

(b) *If the reporting verb is in the future tense, the tense does not change.*

Direct: He *will say*, "I am hardworking."

Indirect: He *will say* that he is hardworking.

(c) *If the sentence expresses a universal truth, the tense does not change, even if the reporting verb is in the past.*

Direct: He *said*, "The sun rises in the east."

Indirect: He *said* that the sun rises in the east.

Rule 2: Changes from Present Tense to Past Tense

(a) *Simple present changes to simple past*

Direct: Anushka said, "I am not creative."

Indirect: Anushka said that she was not creative.

(b) *Present Perfect changes to Past Perfect*

Direct: Aditya told me, "I have been to Ladakh."

Indirect: Aditya told me that he had been to Ladakh.

(c) *Present Continuous changes to Past Continuous*

Direct: "I am taking the online class," my teacher announced.

Indirect: My teacher announced that he was taking the online class.

(d) *Present Perfect Continuous changes to Past Perfect*

Direct: She said, "I have been studying all night."

Indirect: She said that she had been studying all night.

Rule 3: Changes from Past Tense to Past Perfect Tense

(a) *Simple Past changes to Past Perfect*

Direct: The principal said, "Samrat studied hard for the exam."

Indirect: The principal said that Samrat had studied hard for the exam.

(b) *Past Continuous changes to Past Perfect Continuous*

Direct: "We were practising for the concert," the team leader said.

Indirect: The team leader said that they had been practising for the concert.

Note: Pronouns like "we" change to "they" to reflect the shift in perspective. Similarly,

- "I" becomes he or she,
- "My" becomes his or her,
- "You" becomes I, we, he, she, or they depending on context.

Rule 4: Changes from Future Tense to Conditional Tense

(a) *Future Simple changes to Conditional (would + verb)*

Direct: Rohan said, "I will visit my grandparents tomorrow."

Indirect: Rohan said that he would visit his grandparents the next day.

(b) *Future Continuous changes to Conditional Continuous (would be + verb-ing)*

Direct: The coach said, "I will be training the team next week."

Indirect: The coach said that he would be training the team the following week.

Note: Time words like *tomorrow* and *next week* change to *the next day* and *the following week*, respectively.

Rule 5: Changes in Interrogative Sentences

(a) *When the direct speech sentence begins with a helping /auxiliary verb, use 'if' or 'whether' to join the clauses.*

Direct: Param said, "Will you come for a drive?"

Indirect: Param asked if I would come for a drive. or

Param asked if we would come for a drive.

(b) *When the direct speech begins with a question word (when, what, where), no conjunction is used.*

Direct: "Where do you work?" asked my neighbour.

Indirect: My neighbour asked where I worked.

(c) *When the reporting verb is 'said', it usually changes to 'asked' or 'enquired'.*

Direct: Ria said to her friend, "What are you reading?"

Indirect: Ria asked her friend what she was reading.

Rule 6: Changes in Modals

(a) *'Can becomes Could*

(b) *May becomes Might*

(c) *Must becomes Had to / Would have to*

Direct: Dhoni said, "Chennai Super Kings can win."

Indirect: Dhoni said that Chennai Super Kings could win.

Direct: Taneesha said, "I may go to the cinema."

Indirect: Taneesha said that she might go to the cinema.

Direct: Purbita said, "I must visit the physiotherapist."

Indirect: Purbita said that she had to visit the physiotherapist.

(d) *Modals that do not change*

Would, Could, Should, Might, Ought to – remain the same

Direct: Yashaswi said, "I should visit the exhibition."

Indirect: Yashaswi said that she should visit the exhibition.

Direct: Srinivas said, "I could do with some dessert."

Indirect: Srinivas said that he could do with some dessert.

("Could do" here expresses a desire or preference.)

Rule 7: What happens to the Pronoun in Reported Speech?

(a) *First person changes according to the subject of the reporting verb.*

Direct: He said, "I am employed as a detective."

Indirect: He said that he was employed as a detective.

(b) *Second person changes according to the object of the reporting verb.*

Direct: Neelanjana said to them, "You have done a great job."

Indirect: Neelanjana told them that they had done a great job.

(c) *Third person remains the same.*

Direct: Namrata said, "He sculpts beautifully."

Indirect: Namrata said that he sculpted beautifully.

Rule 8: Exclamation, Request, Wish, Commands

In indirect speech, 'said' or 'said to' are often replaced with verbs that match the tone or intention of the original words: advised, requested, suggested, ordered, commanded, forbade, or *exclaimed.*

Direct: The officer said to the soldiers, "Stand at attention."

Indirect: The officer ordered the soldiers to stand at attention.

Direct: Sarla said to her daughter, "Please finish your lunch."

Indirect: Sarla requested her daughter to finish her lunch.

Direct: The doctor said, "Do not eat sweets."

Indirect: The doctor forbade me from eating sweets.

Direct: He said, "What a cute dog it is!"

Indirect: He exclaimed in wonder that it was a very cute dog.

Direct: She said, "Alas! I lost my purse."

Indirect: She exclaimed sadly that she had lost her purse.

Rule 9: Changes in Time Descriptions

When changing direct speech into indirect speech, time words often need to be changed to reflect the shift in perspective.

Direct Speech	Indirect Speech
Today →	That day
Tomorrow →	The next day
Yesterday →	The day before
Now →	Then
This →	That
Next week →	The following week

Example:
Direct: Garima said, "Saurabh's medical reports came yesterday."
Indirect: Garima said that Saurabh's medical reports had come the day before.

Practice Questions

1. Salman said, "I am going to the market."
2. The teacher said, "You must submit your assignments on time."
3. "I will call you later," Manish said to Geetanjali.
4. "We have finished our work," they told me.
5. Sayali said, "I am studying for my exams."

Answer Key

1. Salman said that he was going to the market.

   Explanation: The present continuous tense "am going" changes to "was going" in indirect speech.
2. The teacher said that we had to submit our assignments on time.

   Explanation: "You" changes to "we" based on the context, and the modal verb "must" changes to "had to."
3. Manish told Geetanjali that he would call her later.

   Explanation: The future tense "will" changes to "would" in indirect speech.
4. They told me that they had finished their work.

   Explanation: The present perfect tense "have finished" changes to "had finished" in indirect speech.
5. Sayali said that she was studying for her exams.

   Explanation: The present continuous tense "am studying" changes to "was studying" in indirect speech.

Chapter 6: Degrees of Comparison

What is a Degree of Comparison?

Degrees of Comparison describe the **intensity or extent** of an adjective or adverb. They are used to compare people, things, or actions.

There are three degrees of comparison

Positive

Expresses a quality in the simplest form (No comparison).

E.g. This book is interesting.

Comparative

Compares two persons or things.

E.g. This book is more interesting than that one.

Superlative

Shows the highest degree among three or more. E.g. This is the most interesting book of all.

Rules for Forming Degrees of Comparison

1. The Regular Way

(a) With one-syllable adjective, add **-er** / **-est**.

- short → shorter → shortest
- fast → faster → fastest

(b) If the adjective ends in **-e**, add **-r** / **-st**.

- large → larger → largest
- wise → wiser → wisest

(c) If the adjective ends in **consonant** + **y**, change **y** to **i** + **-er** / **-est**.

- happy → happier → happiest
- busy → busier → busiest

(d) If the word follows a **consonant–vowel–consonant** pattern, double the last consonant.

- big → bigger → biggest
- hot → hotter → hottest

(e) For most two-syllables (not ending in **-y**) and for three or more syllables, use **more** / **most**.

- careful → more careful → most careful
- expensive → more expensive → most expensive

2. Irregular Comparisons

Positive	Comparative	Superlative
good	better	best
bad / ill	worse	worst
little	less	least
much/many	more	most
far	farther/ further	farthest/ furthest
old	older/ elder	oldest/ eldest

Note:

☞ Use *farther/farthest* for physical distance and *further/furthest* for figurative distance (time, degree, extent, discussion, etc.)

> ***Examples***:
> - Delhi is farther from Chennai than from Hyderabad. (physical distance)
> - We need to discuss this matter further. (figurative: extent of discussion)

☞ Use *elder/eldest* for family relationships and *older/oldest* for general use.

> ***Examples***:
> - My elder sister is a doctor. (family)
> - He is older than me. (general)

3. Use of *than* with Comparative Degree

Always use "than" when comparing two things.

Wrong: She is taller her brother.

Right: She is taller than her brother.

4. Double Comparatives and Double Superlatives

Do not use **more** / **most** with adjectives already in comparative / superlative form.

Wrong: This book is more better than that.

Correct: This book is better than that.

5. Adjectives Without Degrees

Some adjectives are absolute. They describe an ultimate state and are not used for comparison.

> ***Examples***: *unique, perfect, supreme, round, square, eternal, impossible.*

Wrong: more perfect, most unique.

Correct: perfect, unique.

6. Comparatives of Equality and Inequality

(a) **Equality:** as + adjective + as
- She is as sensible as her mother.

(b) **Inequality:** not as/so + adjective + as
- He is not as adventurous as his brother.

7. Two Qualities in the Same Person/Thing

Use **more + adjective** when one noun has two qualities.

- He is more creative than wise. (His creativity is greater than his wisdom.)

8. Use of 'the' with Superlatives

Always use 'the' before a superlative adjective.

- She is the tallest girl in the class.

9. Comparatives for Parallel Increase

Structure: the + comparative ... the + comparative

- The more you study, the more you learn.
- The higher we go, the cooler it becomes.

10. Superlatives in Groups

- Superlative → for three or more
- Comparative → for two.

- Between *the two* sisters, she is the taller one. (not tallest)
- Among the *four*, she is the tallest.

11. Special Phrasal Comparisons

- Preferable **to** (not than)
  - This plan is preferable to that one.
- Senior/junior **to** (not than)
  - He is senior to me.
- Inferior/superior **to**
  - This cloth is superior to that.
- Elder/younger to (for family)
  - She is elder to her sister by three years.

12. Compound Comparatives are used to show proportion.

Used to show proportion or parallel increase.

- He became more and more impatient.
- The sooner, the better.

13. Comparative without 'than'.

Sometimes a comparative structure implies a superlative meaning.

- *Nothing* could be better. (It means it is the best possible)

Practice Exercises

1. This road is long. (Use *longer*)
   Answer: This road is longer than that one.
2. This road is longer than the other roads in the city (Use *longest*)
   Answer: This road is the longest in the city.
3. This book is interesting. (Use *more*)
   Answer: This book is more interesting than that one.
4. She is the tallest girl in the class. (Begin with *No other*)
   Answer: No other girl in the class is as tall as she is.
5. He is wiser than his two brothers. (Change to superlative degree)
   Answer: He is the wisest of the three brothers.
6. Mount Everest is the highest peak in the world. (Change to comparative degree)
   Answer: Mount Everest is higher than any other peak in the world.
7. This house is bigger than that one. (Change to *not as...as*)
   Answer: That house is not as big as this one.
8. No other city in India is as big as Mumbai. (Change to superlative degree)
   Answer: Mumbai is the biggest city in India.
9. This car is the most expensive in the market. (Use *more*)
   Answer: This car is more expensive than any other car in the market.
10. No other flower is as beautiful as the rose. (Change to comparative degree)
    Answer: The rose is more beautiful than any other flower.

ICSE TEST PAPER 1

Tenses:

1. Fill in each of the numbered blanks with the correct form of the verb given in brackets.

One morning, I received a letter, ...(0) (write) in pale ink, on glassy, blue-lined note paper, and ...(1) (bear) the postmark of a little Nebraska village. This letter looked ...(2) (wear) out, as though it ...(3) (carry) for some days in a coat-pocket that was none too clean, and was from my Uncle Howard. It ...(4) (inform) me that his wife ...(5) (leave) a small legacy by a bachelor relative who had recently ...(6) (die) and that it had become necessary for her to ...(7) (come) to Boston to attend to the settling of the estate. He ...(8) (request) me to meet her at the station.

Answer: (0) written

Prepositions:

2. Fill in the blanks with the appropriate prepositions.

(a) A human heart beats 72 times per minute .... average.

(b) The wrestlers grappled .... each other in the arena.

(c) Mukul did not confess .... the crime.

(d) Mukul was let .... when no evidence was found against him.

(e) Priya was convicted .... the crime.

(f) Did you fall asleep .... the movie?

(g) Did you fall asleep .... the movie hall?

(h) My school is .... the end of the road.

Join the Sentences:

3. Choose the correct option to make one complete sentence without using *and, but or so.*

1. My grandfather is very old. He is very active.

(a) Although my grandfather is very old, he is very active.

(b) My grandfather is very old provided he is very active.

(c) Either my grandfather is very old or very active.

(d) Even though my grandfather is very active, he is very old.

2. He lived in the city for many years. He could not find his way about.

(a) Despite living in the city for many years, he could not find his way about.

(b) Although he lived in the city for many years, he could find his way about.

(c) Although he could not find his way about, he lived in the city for many years.

(d) He lived in the city for many years, therefore he could not find his way about.

3. Captain is my pet dog. He is scared of the dark.

(a) Captain, my pet dog, is scared of the dark.

(b) Being my pet dog, Captain is scared of the dark.

(c) In spite of being my pet dog, Captain is scared of the dark.

(d) Captain is my pet dog yet he is scared of the dog.

4. They heard the news. They informed us.

(a) No sooner did they heard the news than they informed us.

(b) Hardly had they heard the news when they inform us.

(c) Scarcely they heard the news before they informed us.

(d) As soon as they heard the news, they informed us.

Transformation of Sentences:

4. Choose the correct option and rewrite the sentence according to the instruction given after each.

1. He replied curtly. (Begin with *His*)

(a) His reply was curtly.

(b) His reply was curt.

(c) His reply is curt.

(d) His replied was curt.

2. If you train a dog early, it will not cause a nuisance. (Begin with *Unless*)

(a) Unless you train a dog early, it will not cause a nuisance.

(b) Unless a dog will not cause a nuisance, do not train it early.

(c) Unless you do not train a dog early, it will causes a nuisance.

(d) Unless you train a dog early, it will cause a nuisance.

3. Meenakshi said to me, "Let us go out for dinner."

(a) Meenakshi suggested to me that we could go out for dinner.

(b) Meenakshi suggested to me to go out for dinner.

(c) Meenakshi suggested to me that we should go out for dinner.

(d) Meenakshi suggested to me that we may go out for dinner.

4. He will say, "I am fine." (Change to indirect speech)

(a) He will say that I am fine.
(b) He will say that he was fine.
(c) He will say that I was fine.
(d) He will say that he is fine

5. Everybody will admit that they struggled hard throughout their life. (Begin with *Nobody*)
(a) Nobody will deny that they struggled hard throughout their life.
(b) Nobody will admit that they had not struggled hard throughout their life.
(c) Nobody will admit that they struggled hard throughout their life.
(d) Nobody will deny that they did not struggle hard throughout their life.

6. He kept on persevering and kept scaling great heights. (Begin with *The more*)
(a) The more heights he scaled, the greater he persevered.
(b) The more he persevered, the greater heights he scaled.
(c) The more and more he persevered, the greater heights he scaled.
(d) The more he persevered, the great heights he scaled.

7. When you are older, you will realise what is best for you. (Use *until*)
(a) You will not realise what is best for you until you are older.
(b) You will not be older until you realise what is best for you.
(c) You will realise what is best for you until you are older.
(d) You will not realise what is best for you not until you are older.

8. Galileo said, "The earth revolves around the sun." (Change to reported speech)
(a) Galileo said that the earth revolved around the sun.
(b) Galileo said that the earth will revolve around the sun.
(c) Galileo said that the earth has revolved around the sun.
(d) Galileo said that the earth revolves around the sun.

ANSWER KEY

1. Tenses
1. bearing
2. worn
3. had been carried
4. informed
5. had been left
6. died
7. come
8. requested

2. Prepositions
(a) on
(b) with
(c) to
(d) off
(e) of
(f) during
(g) in
(h) at

3. Join the Sentences
1. (a)
2. (a)
3. (a)
4. (d)

4. Transformation of Sentences
1. (b)
2. (d)
3. (c)
4. (d) (If the reporting verb is in the future (will say), the tense in reported speech does not change.
5. (a)
6. (b)
7. (a)
8. (d) (Because this is a scientific fact / universal truth, so the tense does not change in reported speech.)

ICSE TEST PAPER 2

Tenses:

1. Fill in each of the numbered blanks with the correct form of the verb given in brackets.

The Baroness ...(0) (shrug) her plump shoulders. "There are always legends ...(1) (hang) about these old places. They are not difficult to invent and they ...(2) (cost) nothing. In this case, there is a story that when anyone ...(3) (die) in the castle all the dogs in the village ...(4) (howl) the night long."

"The story is not as you have ...(5) (tell) it," said Amalie. Everyone ...(6) (turn) and looked at her in astonishment. She was wont to sit silent, never ...(7) (speak) unless someone ...(8) (speak) to her.

Answer: (0) shrugged

Prepositions:

2. Fill in the blanks with the appropriate prepositions.

(a) The landlord distributed fertilisers ..... the farmers.
(b) Divide the notebooks .... Ram and Shyam.
(c) It was difficult to part ...... her family when she went to college.
(d) The shirt is priced .... ₹2500.
(e) Rohan inherited his fondness ..... cricket from his father, Sunil Gavaskar.
(f) He kept staring .... the food without eating.
(g) He has written a book ..... American politics.
(h) My friend was named ..... actor Salman Khan.

Join the Sentences:

3. Choose the correct option to make one complete sentence without using *and, but or so.*

1. The reporter was the first to reach the spot. He was the first to interview the police commissioner.
   (a) While the reporter was the first to reach the spot, he was the first to interview the police commissioner.
   (b) The reporter was not only the first to reach the spot but also the first to interview the police commissioner.
   (c) The reporter was the first to reach the spot yet the first to interview the police commissioner.
   (d) Though the reporter was the first to reach the spot, he was the first to interview the police commissioner.
2. Smoking is injurious to health. Rajat smokes.
   (a) Smoking is injurious to health because Rajat smokes.
   (b) Although smoking is injurious to health, Rajat smokes.
   (c) Despite of the fact that smoking is injurious to health, Rajat smokes.
   (d) In spite the fact that smoking is injurious to health, Rajat smokes.
3. I bought a new violin. Immediately, I took music lessons.
   (a) I bought a new violin yet immediately took music lessons.
   (b) No sooner did I buy a new violin when I took music lessons.
   (c) Hardly did I buy a new violin than I took music lessons.
   (d) As soon as I bought a new violin, I took music lessons.
4. He was a weak man. He could not stand the fight.
   (a) Being a weak man, he cannot stand the fight.
   (b) Being a weak man, he could not stand the fight.
   (c) He was a weak man, though unable to stand the fight.
   (d) He was a weak man since he could not stand the fight.

Transformation of Sentences:

4. Choose the correct option and rewrite the sentence according to the instruction given after each.

1. He will pay only under compulsion. (Use *compelled*)
   (a) He will pay unless he is compelled.
   (b) He will not pay only if compelled.
   (c) He will not pay unless he is compelled.
   (d) He will pay unless he is not compelled.
2. He is too tired to dance. (Use *so*)
   (a) He is so tired that he cannot dance.
   (b) He is so tired to dance.
   (c) He is so tired that he will not dance.
   (d) He is so tired that he can dance.
3. The students are writing an examination now. (Begin with *An*)
   (a) An examination is being written by the students now.
   (b) An examination now was being written by the students.
   (c) An examination is written by the students now.
   (d) An examination is to be written by the students now.
4. The teacher scolded him for coming late. (Begin with *He*)
   (a) He is scolded by the teacher for coming late.
   (b) He is being scolded by the teacher for coming late.

(c) He was being scolded by the teacher for coming late.
(d) He was scolded by the teacher for coming late.

5. He has disgraced his family. (Begin with *He is*)
(a) He is a disgrace to his family.
(b) He has disgrace to his family.
(c) He is a disgrace for his family.
(d) He is a disgrace among his family.

6. He will fail the exam. (Add a question tag)
(a) He will fail the exam, won't he?
(b) He will fail the exam, will he?
(c) He will fail the exam, isn't it?
(d) He will fail the exam, is it?

7. It costs 2000 rupees. (Use *cost*)
(a) It cost 2000 rupees.
(b) Its cost was 2000 rupees.
(c) 2000 rupees is it's cost.
(d) Its cost is 2000 rupees.

8. He is not a painter. He is not a sculptor. (Use *neither*)
(a) He is neither a painter nor a sculptor.
(b) He is neither a painter nor he is a sculptor.
(c) He is neither a painter or a sculptor.
(d) He is neither painter nor is sculptor.

ANSWER KEY

1. Tenses
1. hanging
2. cost
3. dies
4. howl
5. told
6. turned
7. speaking
8. spoke

2. Prepositions
(a) among
(b) between
(c) from (shows separation or moving away)
(d) at
(e) for
(f) at
(g) on (*on* here indicates the subject being discussed or referred to)
(h) after

3. Join the Sentences
1. (b)
2. (b)

Why: (The two ideas contrast each other — smoking is bad, yet Rajat smokes. To show contrast, we use "although", "though", or "in spite of" correctly.)

3. (d)
4. (b)

4. Transformation of Sentences
1. (c)
2. (a)
3. (a)
4. (d)
5. (a)
6. (a)

Why: (the helping verb here is WILL. So the tag must use the negative form WON'T.)

7. (d) (c option is wrong because it should be its)
8. (a)

ICSE TEST PAPER 3

Tenses:

1. Fill in each of the numbered blanks with the correct form of the verb given in brackets.

In India, particularly in villages, even a few decades back, women without children ...(0) (look) down upon. Such women were not invited for naming ceremonies, and ...(1) (taunt) as barren women. Nobody ...(2) (understand) the hurt and trauma they ...(3) (undergo). When I ...(4) (be) a child, I ...(5) (have) a teacher called Gowramma. She was kind and warm. She ...(6) (use) to teach us Sanskrit and ...(7) (will) tell lots of stories in the class. But students ...(8) (be) not interested in her stories.

Answer: (0) were looked

Prepositions:

2. Fill in the blanks with the appropriate prepositions.

(a) Egged ... by his wife, Macbeth committed a crime.
(b) He showed great courage in the face ..... danger.
(c) Right now, he will be .... work.
(d) He stood .... every word he said.
(e) The company will enter ... an agreement with you.
(f) The PM embarked ... a process of financial reforms.
(g) He sat ... the movie even though it was boring.
(h) He knows nothing ..... the theft.

Join the Sentences:

3. Choose the correct option to make one complete sentence without using *and, but or so.*

1. They bought a new car. They can travel long distances.
   (a) Since they have bought a new car, they can travel long distances.
   (b) As soon as they bought a new car, they travelled long distances.
   (c) Provided they bought a new car, they can travel long distances.
   (d) Besides buying a new car, they can travel long distances.
2. He was very nervous. He could not perform well in the exam.
   (a) He was too nervous to perform well in the exam.
   (b) He was too nervous to not perform well in the exam.
   (c) Though he was very nervous, he could not perform well in the exam.
   (d) Besides being nervous, he could not perform well in the exam.
3. The task was not pleasant. It was not easy either.
   (a) The task was neither pleasant or easy.
   (b) The task was neither pleasant nor easy.
   (c) The task was either not pleasant or not easy.
   (d) Though the task was not pleasant, it was not easy either.
4. I love to eat ice cream. I love to eat cake.
   (a) Since I love to eat ice cream, I love to eat cake as well.
   (b) I love to eat ice cream yet I love to eat cake.
   (c) I love to eat ice cream with cake.
   (d) I love to eat ice cream as well as cake.

Transformation of Sentences:

4. Choose the correct option and rewrite the sentence according to the instruction given after each.

1. "I am preparing dinner," he said. (Change to reported speech)
   (a) He said that he was preparing dinner.
   (b) He said that he is preparing dinner.
   (c) He said that I am preparing dinner.
   (d) He said that I was preparing dinner.
2. As soon as the function concluded, the children ran out of the auditorium. (Begin with *Hardly*)
   (a) Hardly had the function concluded than the children ran out of the auditorium.
   (b) Hardly had the function concluded when the children ran out of the auditorium.
   (c) Hardly did the function concluded when the children ran out of the auditorium.
   (d) Hardly does the function conclude than the children run out of the auditorium.
3. Mukesh is too ill to come to school. (Begin with *Mukesh is so*)
   (a) Mukesh is so ill that he cannot come to school
   (b) Mukesh is so ill yet he came to school.
   (c) Mukesh is so ill that he will not come to school.
   (d) Mukesh is so ill that he can come to school.
4. Roopa said to her, "Ask whoever you want." (Change to reported speech)
   (a) Roopa told her to ask whoever she wanted to.
   (b) Roopa told her to ask whoever she want to.
   (c) Roopa told her to ask whoever you want to.
   (d) Roopa told her to ask whoever you wanted to.
5. With age, his eyesight did not improve. (Begin with *His eyesight*)
   (a) His eyesight became worse with age.

(b) His eyesight did not show improvement with age.

(c) His eyesight became worst with age.

(d) His eyesight showed a lack of improvement with age.

6. You are as good as I. (Begin with *I am not*)

(a) I am not very good than you.

(b) I am not good as you.

(c) I am not worse as you.

(d) I am not better than you.

7. He worked hard but he did not clear the exam. (Begin with *Notwithstanding*)

(a) Notwithstanding his hard work, he did not clear the exam.

(b) Notwithstanding his working hard, he did not clear the exam.

(c) Notwithstanding his hard work, he cleared the exam.

(d) Notwithstanding clearing the exam, he worked hard.

8. His efforts were successful. (Begin with *He achieved*)

(a) He achieved successful efforts.

(b) He achieved efforts that were successful.

(c) He achieved success in his efforts.

(d) He achieved his success in the efforts.

ANSWER KEY

1. Tenses

1. were taunted
2. understood
3. underwent
4. was
5. had
6. used
7. would
8. were

2. Prepositions

(a) on (shows encouragement/influence)

(b) of

(c) at

(d) by (shows commitment)

(e) into

(f) on

(g) through

(h) about (shows subject of knowledge)

3. Join the Sentences

1. (a)
2. (a)
3. (b)
4. (d)

4. Transformation of Sentences

1. (a)
2. (b)
3. (a)
4. (a)
5. (b)
6. (d)
7. (a)
8. (c)

ICSE TEST PAPER 4

Tenses:

1. Fill in each of the numbered blanks with the correct form of the verb given in brackets.

It was in the days when France's power was already ...(0) (break) upon the seas and when more of her three-deckers lay ...(1) (rot) in the Medway than were to be ...(2) (find) in Brest harbour. But her frigates still ...(3) (scour) the ocean, closely ...(4) (follow) by those of her rival. These vessels ...(5) (shatter) each other. It had blown hard in the night but the wind ...(6) (drop) with the dawning, and now the ...(7) (rise) sun ...(8) (tint) the fringe of the storm-wrack.

Answer: (0) broken

Prepositions:

2. Fill in the blanks with the appropriate prepositions.

(a) The channel was too narrow for the ship to sail ......
(b) You could compensate for the losses ..... the gains.
(c) You can meet him ..... your own risk.
(d) The captain entered .... a pact with the players.
(e) We invested our money ... the textile industry.
(f) A wooden barrier was placed .... the road.
(g) Unjust criticism was levelled .... the manager.
(h) Our school is famous .... its achievements in music.

Join the Sentences:

3. Choose the correct option to make one complete sentence without using *and, but or so.*

1. Anil is not intelligent. He is not hardworking.
   (a) Though Anil is not intelligent, he is not hardworking.
   (b) Anil is neither intelligent nor hardworking.
   (c) Anil is not intelligent but he is not hardworking.
   (d) Anil is not intelligent provided he is not hardworking.
2. I was very busy. I could not talk to her.
   (a) I was too busy to talk to her.
   (b) I was too busy to not talk to her.
   (c) I was very busy, I could not talk to her too.
   (d) Besides being very busy, I could not talk to her.
3. I will get ready. Do not go till then.
   (a) I will get ready till you go.
   (b) Neither I will get ready nor you go till then.
   (c) Do not go because I will get ready.
   (d) Do not go till I get ready.
4. I was very busy. I could talk to her.
   (a) Despite very busy, I could talk to her.
   (b) Because I was very busy, I could talk to her.
   (c) I was too busy to talk to her.
   (d) Though I was very busy, I could talk to her.

Transformation of Sentences:

4. Choose the correct option and rewrite the sentence according to the instruction given after each.

1. If I had known about the meeting earlier, I would have prepared better. (Begin with *Had*)
   (a) Had I known about the meeting earlier, I would have prepared better.
   (b) Had I know about the meeting earlier, I would have prepared better.
   (c) Had I known about the meeting, I would have prepared better earlier.
   (d) Had I known about the meeting, I would had prepared better.
2. I need not stay long. (Add a question tag)
   (a) I need not stay long, do I?
   (b) I need not stay long, need I?
   (c) I need not stay long, don't I?
   (d) I need not stay long, isn't it?
3. Instead of studying science, I would pursue a career in journalism. (Begin with *I would rather*)
   (a) I would rather study science than pursue a career in journalism.
   (b) I would rather pursue a career in journalism instead of studying science.
   (c) I would rather a career in journalism than study science.
   (d) I would rather pursue a career in journalism than study science.
4. Writing a book was the best thing I have ever done in my life. (Begin with *No other*)
   (a) No other book I have ever written was the best thing I have done in my life.
   (b) No other best thing I have ever done in my life was writing a book.
   (c) No other thing I have ever done in my life was as good as writing a book.
   (d) No other thing I have ever done was as good as writing a book in my life.
5. I prepared lunch and washed the clothes. (Use *Not only*)
   (a) Not only did I prepare lunch but I also washed the clothes.

(b) Not only did I prepared lunch but also washed the clothes.
(c) Not only I prepared lunch and also washed the clothes.
(d) Not only had I prepared lunch but also washed the clothes.

6. You alone were to blame for this. (Begin with *None*)
(a) None but you only were to blame for this.
(b) None but you alone were to blame for this.
(c) None but you were to blame for this.
(d) None of you were to blame for this.

7. No sooner had Shah Rukh Khan entered the auditorium than his fans mobbed him. (Begin with *Hardly*)
(a) Hardly had Shah Rukh Khan entered the auditorium when his fans mobbed him.
(b) Hardly did Shah Rukh Khan enter the auditorium when his fans mob him.
(c) Hardly had Shah Rukh Khan entered the auditorium than his fans mobbed him.
(d) Hardly had Shah Rukh Khan enter the auditorium when his fans mobbed him.

8. "Sir, may I go to the library?" asked Munish. (Change to reported speech)
(a) Munish asked Sir if he may go to the library.
(b) Munish asked Sir if he might go to the library.
(c) Munish asked Sir if he can go to the library.
(d) Munish asked Sir if I might go to the library.

ANSWER KEY

1. Tenses
1. rotting
2. found
3. scoured
4. followed
5. shattered
6. had dropped
7. rising
8. tinted

2. Prepositions
(a) through (shows movement from one side to the other)
(b) with
(c) at (used to show manner or consequence)
(d) into
(e) in
(f) across (shows something extending from one side to the other – the barrier stretches across the road, blocking it; "on" would be incorrect as it would mean the barrier is merely resting on the surface, not blocking the road.)
(g) against
(h) for

3. Join the Sentences
1. (b)
2. (a)
3. (d)
4. (d)

4. Transformation of Sentences
1. (a)
2. (b)
3. (d)
4. (c)
5. (a)
6. (c)
7. (a)
8. (b)

ICSE TEST PAPER 5

Tenses:

1. Fill in each of the numbered blanks with the correct form of the verb given in brackets.

Aditya ...(0) (walk) into his 18th floor office early that morning. The Indiscape office ... (1) (be) a newer and more open office that made liberal use of glass. Aditya had two lavish cabins, one on each floor. He ...(2) (try) calling Sundeep a few times but his phone ...(3) (switch) off. Natasha, Sundeep's wife, was away in Delhi, ...(4) (visit) her parents. After ...(5) (deposit) his bag in his cabin, by force of habit, he ...(6) (walk) towards the washroom. The light in Sundeep's room was on. ...(7) (assume) that he ...(8) (forget) to switch it off, Aditya ignored it and walked straight into the washroom.

Answer: (0) walked

Prepositions:

2. Fill in the blanks with the appropriate prepositions.

(a) I do not want you to engage ... that rowdy group.

(b) He disposes .... the garbage at night.

(c) He turned his eyes .... from her.

(d) Their insurance claim has been turned ....

(e) He spooned .... a small portion of the ice cream for himself.

(f) He turned ... at my office last week.

(g) He was accused of siphoning ... money from the firm.

(h) I hope you will not indulge ... any unethical activity.

Join the Sentences:

3. Choose the correct option to make one complete sentence without using *and, but or so*.

1. He is a good writer. He is a good musician.
   (a) He is not only a good writer but also a good musician.
   (b) Beside being a good writer, he is a good musician.
   (c) He is a good writer yet he is a good musician.
   (d) He is a good writer though he is a good musician.
2. She is very clumsy. She cannot handle pets carefully.
   (a) Though she is very clumsy, she cannot handle pets carefully.
   (b) Besides being very clumsy, she cannot handle pets carefully.
   (c) She is too clumsy to handle pets carefully.
   (d) Either she is very clumsy or she cannot handle pets carefully.
3. They are colleagues. They are close friends.
   (a) They are colleagues yet close friends.
   (b) They are not only colleagues but also close friends.
   (c) Besides they are colleagues, they are close friends.
   (d) Beside colleagues, they are also close friends.
4. Ravi makes beautiful pots. He earns a lot.
   (a) Ravi makes beautiful pots to earn a lot.
   (b) Ravi earns a lot by making beautiful pots.
   (c) Ravi earns a lot to make beautiful pots.
   (d) Ravi makes beautiful pots because he earns a lot.

Transformation of Sentences:

4. Choose the correct option and rewrite the sentence according to the instruction given after each.

1. He was the only one who knew the killer. (Begin with *None*)
   (a) None despite he knew the killer.
   (b) None but only he knew the killer.
   (c) None knew the killer but he.
   (d) None but he knew the killer.
2. None of your friends play cricket. (Add a question tag)
   (a) None of your friends play cricket, doesn't he?
   (b) None of your friends play cricket, do they?
   (c) None of your friends play cricket, don't they?
   (d) None of your friends play cricket, do none?
3. He succeeded in his efforts to win the case. (Begin with *His efforts*)
   (a) His efforts to win the case were successful.
   (b) His efforts to win the case was successfully met.
   (c) His efforts to win the case were succeeded.
   (d) His efforts to win the case are succeeding.
4. The policeman asked, "Why are you lying on the pavement in this manner?" (Change to reported speech)
   (a) The policeman asked why he was lying on the road in that manner.
   (b) The policeman asked why he was lying on the road in this manner.
   (c) The policeman asked why are you lying on the road in that manner.
   (d) The policeman asked why you are lying on the road in this manner.
5. If it were not for his injury, Ahmed would have been included in the team. (Begin with *But for*)
   (a) But for injury, Ahmed would have been included in the team.
   (b) But for his injury, Ahmed would have been included in the team.

(c) But for not his injury, Ahmed would have been included in the team.
(d) But for his injury, Ahmed would not have been included in the team.

6. Praveen could not go to school because of dengue. (End with *to school*)
(a) Dengue allowed Praveen from not going to school.
(b) Notwithstanding dengue, Praveen could not go to school.
(c) But for dengue, Praveen could not go to school.
(d) Dengue prevented Praveen from going to school.

7. This monsoon has been the wettest in the last twenty years. (Begin with *No other*)
(a) No other monsoon has been as wet as this monsoon in the last twenty years.
(b) No other monsoon has been more wet as this monsoon in the last twenty years.
(c) No other monsoon has been wetter as this monsoon in the last twenty years.
(d) No other monsoon has been as wettest as this monsoon in the last twenty years.

8. The news is so good that it cannot be true. (Use *too*)
(a) The news is too good to be true.
(b) The news is too good to be not true.
(c) The news is too good that it can be true.
(d) The news is too good that it cannot be true.

ANSWER KEY

1. Tenses
1. was
2. had tried
3. was switched
4. visiting
5. depositing
6. walked
7. Assuming
8. had forgotten

2. Prepositions
(a) with
(b) of
(c) away
(d) down (turned down = rejected)
(e) out
(f) up (turn up - used to show appearance)
(g) off
(h) in

3. Join the Sentences
1. (a)
2. (c)
3. (b)
4. (b)

4. Transformation
1. (d)
2. (b)
3. (a)
4. (a)
5. (b)
6. (d)
7. (a)
8. (a)

ICSE TEST PAPER 6

Tenses:

1. Fill in each of the numbered blanks with the correct form of the verb given in brackets.

The gorilla .... (0) (be) something of a paradox in the African scene. One ... (1) (think) one ...(2) (know) him very well. For a hundred years or more, he ...(3) (capture), imprisoned in zoos and has also been killed. His bones ...(4) (mount) in natural history museums everywhere, and he has always ...(5) (exert) a strong fascination upon scientists and romantics alike. Yet the fact ...(6) (be) we know very little about gorillas. Carl Akeley the American naturalist ...(7) (lead) two expeditions in the 1920s and now is ...(8) (bury) among the animals he loved so well.

Answer: (0) is

Prepositions:

2. Fill in the blanks with the appropriate prepositions.

(a) The case is .... trial.
(b) The post is up .... grabs.
(c) It is 6 pm .... my watch.
(d) I shall return .... an hour.
(e) The houses in Japan are made .... wood.
(f) Paper is made .... trees.
(g) This dish is made .... organically grown pulses and herbs.
(h) Her necklace is made .... silver.

Join the Sentences:

3. Choose the correct option to make one complete sentence without using *and, but or so.*

1. Meenakshi fell ill. She could not take the examination.
   (a) Meenakshi fell ill yet she could not take the examination.
   (b) Having fallen ill, Meenakshi could not take the examination.
   (c) Though Meenakshi fell ill, she could not take the examination.
   (d) As soon as Meenakshi fell ill, she could not take the examination.
2. It was raining heavily. The children continued to play football.
   (a) Because it was raining heavily, the children continued to play football.
   (b) If it was raining heavily, the children continued to play football.
   (c) Despite the heavy rain, the children continued to play football.
   (d) Since it was raining heavily, the children continued to play football.
3. He is, no doubt, very clever. He still makes small mistakes.
   (a) Although he is not clever, he still makes small mistakes.
   (b) If he is clever, he still makes small mistakes.
   (c) He is clever so he still makes small mistakes.
   (d) In spite of being very clever, he still makes small mistakes.
4. I know him very well. I don't like him.
   (a) I know him too well to like him.
   (b) I don't like him, so I know him very well.
   (c) Besides knowing him very well, I don't like him.
   (d) I know him very well, yet I like him.

Transformation of Sentences:

4. Choose the correct option and rewrite the sentence according to the instruction given after each.

1. He studied all night and felt confident going into the exam. (Begin with *Having*)
   (a) Having studied all night, he felt confident to go into the exam.
   (b) Having felt confident going into the exam, he studied all night.
   (c) Having studied all night, he felt confident going into the exam.
   (d) Having all night study, he felt confident going into the exam.
2. The news is too good to be true. (Use *so*)
   (a) The news is so good that it cannot be true.
   (b) The news is so good that it can be true.
   (c) The news is so good that it will not be true.
   (d) The news is so good to be true.
3. The teacher said, "Akhtar, why were you absent yesterday?" (Change to reported speech)
   (a) The teacher asked Akhtar why he was absent the previous day.
   (b) The teacher asked Akhtar why are you absent yesterday.
   (c) The teacher asked Akhtar why he had been absent the previous day.
   (d) The teacher asked Akhtar why were you absent yesterday.

4. Her heart is so full that she cannot express her feelings. (Use *too*)
   (a) Her heart is too full that she cannot express her feelings.
   (b) Her heart is too full to express her feelings.
   (c) Her heart is too full to not express her feelings.
   (d) Her heart is too full and cannot express her feelings.
5. Jumping over the fence to get to the yard is dangerous. (Begin with *It is*)
   (a) It is jumping over the fence to get to the yard dangerous.
   (b) It is dangerous to jump over the fence to get to the yard.
   (c) It is dangerous to jumping over the fence to get to the yard.
   (d) It is dangerous to get to the yard if you jump over the fence.
6. He made several efforts yet he did not succeed. (Begin with *Notwithstanding*)
   (a) Notwithstanding several efforts, he did succeed.
   (b) Notwithstanding several efforts, yet he did not succeed.
   (c) Notwithstanding he made several efforts, he did not succeed.
   (d) Notwithstanding several efforts, he did not succeed.
7. If you are polite, you will be accepted by the group. (Begin with *Unless*)
   (a) Unless you are not polite, you will be accepted by the group.
   (b) Unless you are polite, you will not be accepted by the group.
   (c) Unless you are not polite, you will not be accepted by the group.
   (d) Unless you are polite, you will be accepted by the group.
8. If you take the medicine, you will feel better. (Begin with *Provided*)
   (a) Provided you take the medicine, you will not feel better.
   (b) Provided if you take the medicine, you will not feel better.
   (c) Provided you take the medicine, you will feel better.
   (d) Provided you do not take the medicine, you will feel better.

ANSWER KEY

1. Tenses
0. is
1. thinks
2. knows
3. has been captured
4. have been mounted
5. exerted
6. is
7. led
8. buried

2. Prepositions
(a) under (shows something ongoing, e.g., a trial in progress)
(b) for (shows availability or demand)
(c) by (means *according to*, shows reference point for time; "on" would be incorrect because it is used for specific days/dates, not reference points)
(d) in
(e) of (made "of" - used when the material or qualities remain unchanged)
(f) from (made "from" - used when the material is transformed)
(g) with (made "with" - used for ingredients in food)
(h) of

3. Join the Sentences
1. (b)
2. (c)
3. (d)
4. (a)

4. Transformation of Sentences
1. (c)
2. (a)
3. (c)
4. (b)
5. (b)
6. (d)
7. (b)
8. (c)

ICSE TEST PAPER 7

Tenses:

1. Fill in each of the numbered blanks with the correct form of the verb given in brackets.

Rain ...(0) (fall). A damp cutting wind was racing about the garden, ...(1) (howl) and ...(2) (give) the trees no rest. The banker ...(3) (strain) his eyes. ...(4) (go) to the spot where the lodge stood, he twice ...(5) (call) the watchman. No answer ...(6) (come). Evidently the watchman ...(7) (seek) shelter from the weather and was now asleep. He ...(8) (feel) in the darkness for the steps and the door.

Answer: (0) was falling.

Prepositions:

2. Fill in the blanks with the appropriate prepositions.

(a) I enjoyed sitting in the shade .... the tree.
(b) He lives in the city .... joy, Kolkata.
(c) He has a sensible head .... his shoulders.
(d) I enjoyed sitting .... the tree.
(e) Go and sit .... the last bench.
(f) The authorities did not allow him to sit ... the committee.
(g) The manager was angry that he had sat ... the work for so long.
(h) The patient was gasping .... breath.

Join the Sentences:

3. Choose the correct option to make one complete sentence without using *and, but or so.*

1. The team arrived at the stadium. The rain started.
   (a) Though the team arrived at the stadium, the rain started.
   (b) Hardly had the team arrived at the stadium when the rain started.
   (c) No sooner did the team arrived at the stadium than the rain started.
   (d) As soon as the team arrive at the stadium, the rain started.
2. He is not a singer. He is not a dancer.
   (a) He is neither a singer nor a dancer.
   (b) He is neither a singer nor he a dancer.
   (c) He is neither a singer or a dancer.
   (d) He is neither a singer nor dancer.
3. The sun had set. We had not finished our game.
   (a) Though the sun had set, we had not finished our game.
   (b) While the sun had set, we had not finished our game.
   (c) The sun had set hence we had not finished our game.
   (d) If the sun had set, we had not finished our game.
4. Submit your project. Only then can you appear for the test.
   (a) Unless you submit your project, you cannot appear for the test.
   (b) Unless you submit your project, you can appear for the test.
   (c) Until you submit your project, you can appear for the test.
   (d) Until you appear for the test, you cannot submit your project.

Transformation of Sentences:

4. Choose the correct option and rewrite the sentence according to the instruction given after each.

1. He was late to the meeting and missed the most important discussion. (Begin with *Being*)
   (a) Being missing at the most important discussion, he was late to the meeting.
   (b) Being late to the meeting, missed the most important discussion.
   (c) Being was late to the meeting and missed the most important discussion.
   (d) Being late to the meeting, he missed the most important discussion.
2. No other detective is as sharp as Karamchand in Patna. (Use *sharpest*)
   (a) Karamchand is the sharpest detective in Patna.
   (b) Karamchand is sharpest detective in Patna.
   (c) All other detectives are not as sharpest as Karamchand in Patna.
   (d) No other detective is sharpest than Karamchand in Patna.
3. He is a talented musician and excels at sports. (Use *Not only*)
   (a) Not only is he a talented musician but also excels at sports.
   (b) Not only does he excel at sports but he is a talented musician.
   (c) Not only he is a talented musician but also excels at sports.
   (d) Not only is he a talented musician but also excel at sports.

4. It is so cold that I cannot step out. (Use *too*)
   (a) It is too cold not to step out.
   (b) It is too cold to step out.
   (c) It is too cold that I cannot step out.
   (d) It is too cold that I can step out.
5. The movie was a delight. (Add a question tag)
   (a) The movie was a delight, was it?
   (b) The movie was a delight, is it?
   (c) The movie was a delight, isn't it?
   (d) The movie was a delight, wasn't it?
6. Mohan tried his level best to clean the kitchen but failed. (Begin with *Even*)
   (a) Even though Mohan failed, he tried his level best to clean the kitchen.
   (b) Even though Mohan tried his level best to clean the kitchen, he failed.
   (c) Even though Mohan tried his level best to clean the kitchen, Mohan failed.
   (d) Even though Mohan tried his level best to clean the kitchen, he had failed.
7. As soon as she entered the room, her dog ran to her. (Begin with *She had hardly*)
   (a) She had hardly entered the room than her dog ran to her.
   (b) She had hardly entered the room yet her dog ran to her.
   (c) She had hardly entered the room when her dog ran to her.
   (d) She had hardly entered the room then her dog ran to her.
8. Discarded plastic and tar were mixed to build the road. (Begin with *They*)
   (a) They discarded plastic and tar to mix and build the road.
   (b) They built the road with mixed and discarded plastic and tar.
   (c) They mixed to build the road by discarding plastic and tar.
   (d) They built the road by mixing discarded plastic and tar.

ANSWER KEY

1. Tenses

1. howling
2. giving
3. strained
4. Going
5. called
6. came
7. had sought
8. felt

Prepositions

(a) of
(b) of
(c) on
(d) under
(e) on
(f) on (sit on committee = be part of the committee)
(g) on (sit on work = delaying or holding off work)
(h) for

Join the Sentences

1. (b)
2. (a)
3. (a)
4. (a) (*Appearing for the test* is **conditional** on *project submission*. This option restates the same condition using "unless," which means "if not.")

Transformation

1. (d)
2. (a)
3. (a)
4. (b)
5. (d)
6. (b)
7. (c)
8. (d)

ICSE TEST PAPER 8

Tenses:

1. Fill in each of the numbered blanks with the correct form of the verb given in brackets.

It ...(0) (be) the summer of 1947. A local moneylender ...(1) (murder) and suspicion ...(2) (fall) upon Juggut Singh, the village gangster who ...(3) (be) in love with a Muslim girl. When a train ...(4) (arrive), ...(5) (carry) the bodies of dead Sikhs, the village ...(6) (transform) into a battlefield, and the police were not able to stem the ...(7) (rise) tide of violence. It is left to Singh ...(8) (redeem) himself and reclaim peace for his village.

(*Excerpt from Khushwant Singh's 'Train to Pakistan'*)

Answer: (0) was

Prepositions:

2. Fill in the blanks with the appropriate prepositions.

(a) The workers have to queue .... for their wages.

(b) He placed his hand .... my shoulder.

(c) She put her arms .... her mother.

(d) My gardener waters the plants .... Sundays.

(e) I dislike the way he lords .... his colleagues.

(f) The pace of work at the construction site has picked ....

(g) I managed to paint the door .... a day.

(h) Both of us arrived .... the same time.

Join the Sentences:

3. Choose the correct option to make one complete sentence without using *and, but or so.*

1. Play well. You will win the match.
   (a) Besides playing well, you will win the match.
   (b) Play well if you will win the match.
   (c) Unless you play well, you will not win the match.
   (d) Unless you play well, you will win the match.
2. I warned Suresh not to drive rashly. He still did so.
   (a) In spite of my warning, Suresh drove rashly.
   (b) I warned Suresh not to drive rashly though he still did so.
   (c) Despite I warned Suresh not to drive rashly, he still did so.
   (d) As soon as I warned Suresh not to drive rashly, he still did so.
3. The fire was put out. This took only an instant.
   (a) This took only an instant to put out the fire.
   (b) The fire was put out besides this took only an instant.
   (c) Though the fire was put out, this took only an instant.
   (d) The fire was put out in an instant.
4. Miss Kavita is unwell. She will take the class today.
   (a) Though Miss Kavita will take the class today, she is unwell.
   (b) Though Miss Kavita is unwell, she will take the class today.
   (c) Despite of Miss Kavita's unwellness, she will take the class today.
   (d) Miss Kavita will take the class today yet she is unwell.

Transformation of Sentences:

4. Choose the correct option and rewrite the sentence according to the instruction given after each.

1. Kochi has the best coastline among cities in India. (Use *better*)
   (a) No other city in India has a better coastline than Kochi.
   (b) No cities in India have better coastline than Kochi.
   (c) No other city in India has good coastline than Kochi.
   (d) No other city in India has the best coastline like Kochi.
2. Sriya ran to the station but she missed the train. (Begin with *Although*)
   (a) Although Sriya ran to the station, Sriya missed the train.
   (b) Although Sriya ran to the station, she missed the train.
   (c) Although Sriya ran to the station but she missed the train.
   (d) Although Sriya missed the train, she ran to the station.
3. She never failed to reach in time.
   (a) Did she ever failed to reach in time?
   (b) Did she never fail to reach in time? (Begin with *Did she*)
   (c) Did she fail to reach in time?
   (d) Did she ever fail to reach in time?
4. As he is intelligent, he can aim to top the exam. (Begin with *Being*)
   (a) Being he is intelligent, he can aim to top the exam.
   (b) Being intelligent, he can aim to top the exam.

(c) Being intelligent, he is aiming to top the exam.
(d) Being full of intelligence, he can aim to top the exam.

5. He admitted his guilt. (Begin with *He admitted*)
(a) He admitted that guilt of his.
(b) He admitted that he was guilt.
(c) He admitted that he was guilty.
(d) He admitted that he was of guilty.

6. I entered the house and saw a cat drinking milk. (Begin with *Entering*)
(a) Entering the house, I saw a cat drinking milk.
(b) Entering the house, I have seen a cat drinking milk.
(c) Entering the house, I saw a cat drink milk.
(d) Entering the house, I see a cat drinking milk.

7. The manager approves the proposal. (Change to passive voice)
(a) The approval of the proposal is done by the manager.
(b) The proposal was approved by the manager.
(c) The proposal is approved by the manager.
(d) The manager gets the proposal approved.

8. We decided to cook at home instead of going out for dinner. (Begin with *Rather*)
(a) Rather go out for dinner, we decided to cook at home.
(b) Rather than going out for dinner, we decided to cook at home.
(c) Rather than cooking at home, we decided to go out for dinner.
(d) Rather than cook at home, we decided to go out for dinner.

ANSWER KEY

1. Tenses

1. was murdered
2. fell
3. was
4. arrived
5. carrying
6. was transformed
7. rising
8. to redeem

2. Prepositions

(a) up
(b) on
(c) around
(d) on
(e) over
(f) up
(g) in
(h) at

3. Join the Sentences

1. (c)
2. (a)
3. (d)
4. (b)

4. Transformation

1. (a)
2. (b)
3. (d)
4. (b)
5. (c)
6. (a)
7. (c)
8. (b)

ICSE TEST PAPER 9

Tenses:

1. **Fill in each of the numbered blanks with the correct form of the verb given in brackets.**

Jim was never late. Della ...(0) (double) the chain in her hand and ...(1) (sit) on the corner of the table near the door that he always ...(2) (enter). Then she ...(3) (hear) his step on the stair away down on the first flight, and she turned white for just a moment. She had a habit of ...(4) (say) a little silent prayer about the simplest every-day things, and now she ...(5) (whisper): "Please God, ...(6) (make) him think I am still pretty."

The door opened and Jim ...(7) (step) in. Poor fellow, he was only twenty – and to be ...(8) (burden) with a family!

Answer: (0) doubled

Prepositions:

2. **Fill in the blanks with the appropriate prepositions.**
   (a) The artist has an eye .... detail.
   (b) The team has a leg ... on the competition because of injuries in the rival side.
   (c) Thanks for listening. I wanted to get this ... my chest.
   (d) A positive person always keeps his chin ...
   (e) Even as an infant, she had an ear .... music.
   (f) The refugees were packed shoulder ... shoulder on the relief aircraft.
   (g) He cannot put his finger ... the problem.
   (h) Once your exams are over, you can let your hair ....

Join the Sentences:

3. **Choose the correct option to make one complete sentence without using *and, but or so.***
   1. The fans were on. It felt hot and humid.
      (a) In spite of the fans being on, it was feeling hot and humid.
      (b) It felt hot and humid, but the fans were on.
      (c) It felt hot and humid despite the fans being on.
      (d) Due to it feeling hot and humid, the fans were being put on.
   2. He scored a century. He got out immediately.
      (a) While he scored a century, he got out immediately.
      (b) He scored a century while he got out immediately.
      (c) As soon as he scored a century, he got out immediately.
      (d) As soon as he scored a century, he got out.
   3. He began his speech. The fire alarm went off.
      (a) No sooner did he begin his speech than the fire alarm went off.
      (b) As soon as he began his speech when the fire alarm went off.
      (c) He began his speech yet the fire alarm went off.
      (d) No sooner did he begin his speech when the fire alarm went off.
   4. The rain stopped. The cricketers could start playing.
      (a) The cricketers could start playing once the rain stopped.
      (b) The rain being stopped, the cricketers could start playing.
      (c) The rain stopped as the cricketers could start playing.
      (d) The rain having stopped, the cricketers could start playing.

Transformation of Sentences:

4. **Choose the correct option and rewrite the sentence according to the instruction given after each.**
   1. As soon as the old sailor killed the bird, he brought bad luck to the crew. (Begin with *No sooner*)
      (a) No sooner was the bird killed than it brought bad luck to the crew.
      (b) No sooner had the old sailor kill the bird than he brought bad luck to the crew.
      (c) No sooner did the old sailor kill the bird than he brought bad luck to the crew.
      (d) No sooner did the old sailor killed the bird, than he brought bad luck to the crew.
   2. Unless something goes wrong with the new car, I hope to reach Mumbai by evening. (Begin with *If*)
      (a) If anything goes right with the new car, I will not reach Mumbai by evening.
      (b) If something goes right with the new car, I hope to reach Mumbai by evening.
      (c) If nothing goes wrong with the new car, I hope to reach Mumbai by evening.
      (d) If everything goes wrong with the new car, I will not reach Mumbai by evening.
   3. No other institution is as good as Harvard. (Use *better*)
      (a) Harvard is better than any other institution.
      (b) Any other institution is better than Harvard.

(c) Harvard is better than no other institution.
(d) Harvard is better as no other institution.

4. "Will you help me carry the box?" my neighbour said to me. (Change to indirect speech)
(a) My neighbour told me for helping her carry the box.
(b) My neighbour said to me to carry the box.
(c) My neighbour asked me that I would help her carry the box.
(d) My neighbour asked me if I would help her carry the box.

5. As soon as he heard the news, he rushed home (Begin with *No sooner*)
(a) No sooner he heard the news than he rushed home.
(b) No sooner did he hear the news when he rushed home.
(c) No sooner did he heard the news than he rushed home.
(d) No sooner did he hear the news than he rushed home.

6. Please switch off the lights. (Change to passive voice)
(a) You are requested to please switch off the lights.
(b) You are requested to switch off the lights.
(c) Please the lights may be switched off.
(d) Let the lights to be switched off.

7. "What a forgetful person you are!" he angrily remarked. (Change to reported speech)
(a) He angrily remarked what a forgetful person I was.
(b) He angrily remarked you are a very forgetful person.
(c) He angrily remarked that I was a very forgetful person.
(d) He angrily remarked that I am a very forgetful person.

8. The principal asked the students, "Have you completed this assignment?" (Change into reported speech)
(a) The principal asked the students if they had completed that assignment.
(b) The principal asked the students if they have completed this assignment.
(c) The principal asked the students whether they have completed that assignment.
(d) The principal asked the students whether they had completed their assignment.

ANSWER KEY

1. Tenses
1. sat
2. entered
3. heard
4. saying
5. whispered
6. make
7. stepped
8. burdened

2. Prepositions
(a) for
(b) up (means to have an advantage)
(c) off (get something off your chest = talk about something that has been worrying, upsetting, or burdening you, so you feel relieved)
(d) up
(e) for
(f) to (shoulder to shoulder = very crowded)
(g) on (put finger on = to identify or pinpoint)
(h) down (let your hair down = relax and enjoy yourself without worrying about rules or formality)

3. Join the Sentences
1. (c)
2. (d)
3. (a)
4. (d)

4. Transformation
1. (c)
2. (c)
3. (a)
4. (d)
5. (d)
6. (b)
7. (c)
8. (a)

ICSE TEST PAPER 10

Tenses:

1. Fill in each of the numbered blanks with the correct form of the verb given in brackets.

The ribbon-vendor and his two friends ..(0) (stand) at the market gate and ...(1) (enjoy) the sight immensely as the blind man ...(2) (struggle) to find his way about. He stood ...(3) (root) to the spot, ...(4) (wave) his stick. He ...(5) (feel) as if he were hanging in mid-air. He was wailing. He ...(6) (try) to cross the road, came near being run over by a dozen vehicles, and ...(7) (tumbled) and ...(8) (gasp).

Answer: (0) stood

Prepositions:

2. Fill in the blanks with the appropriate prepositions..

(a) He spent the night, curled .... on the sofa.

(b) Your request is .... consideration.

(c) I hate being laughed ....

(d) I often find him absorbed .... thought.

(e) This is a luxury .... my income.

(f) He parted .... his friends at the end of the trip.

(g) You should not deviate ...... your objective.

(h) .... the long run, hard work will pay off.

Join the Sentences:

3. Choose the correct option to make one complete sentence without using *and, but or so.*

1. He bought a camera. He clicked his selfie immediately.
   (a) As soon as he bought a camera, he clicked his selfie immediately.
   (b) He bought a camera yet he clicked his selfie immediately.
   (c) No sooner did he bought a camera than he clicked his selfie.
   (d) As soon as he bought a camera, he clicked his selfie.
2. Suman planted the sapling. Rakesh watered it.
   (a) Suman and Rakesh planted the sapling as well as watered it.
   (b) As soon as Suman plant the sapling, Rakesh watered it.
   (c) No sooner did Suman planted the sapling than Rakesh watered it.
   (d) While Suman planted the sapling, Rakesh watered it.
3. The teacher did not know the answer to the question. The students did not know the answer to the question.
   (a) Neither the teacher nor the students know the answer to the question.
   (b) Neither the teacher nor the students knows the answer to the question.
   (c) Neither the teacher nor the students knew the answer to the question.
   (d) Neither the teacher nor the students did not know the answer to the question.
4. I woke up at 5:30 am. I went for a walk.
   (a) Having woken up at 5:30 a.m., I went for a walk.
   (b) After waking up, I went for a walk at 5:30 a.m.
   (c) Being woken up at 5:30 a.m., I went for a walk.
   (d) At 530 a.m., I woke up to went for a walk.

Transformation of Sentences:

4. Choose the correct option and rewrite the sentence according to the instruction given after each.

1. She is the youngest in the family and often gets the most attention. (Begin with *Being*)
   (a) Being the youngest in the family, gets the most attention for her.
   (b) Being youngest in the family, oftens gets her the most attention.
   (c) Being the youngest in the family, she gets most attention often.
   (d) Being the youngest in the family, she often gets the most attention.
2. He finished his exercise and put away the books. (Begin with *Having*)
   (a) Having finished his exercise, he put away his books.
   (b) Having put away the books, he finished his exercise.
   (c) Having finished his exercise, he puts away his books.
   (d) Having put away the books, he has finished his exercise.
3. The shelf is so high that I cannot reach it. (Use *too*)
   (a) This shelf is too high that I cannot reach it.
   (b) This shelf is too high for me to reach.
   (c) This shelf is too high to reach me.
   (d) This shelf is too much high to reach.
4. He said, "Let me have some food." (Change to reported speech)

(a) He told that he wanted to have some food.
(b) He said that let me have some food.
(c) He wished that he might have some food.
(d) He said that let him have some food.

5. There is no time to waste (Change to passive voice)
(a) No time to be wasted by there.
(b) There is no time to be wasted.
(c) No time is to be wasted.
(d) No time to be wasted there.

6. The doctor said to the patient, "I hope you remembered to take the medicines." (Change to indirect speech)
(a) The doctor said to the patient that he hoped that he had remembered to take the medicines.
(b) The doctor said the patient that he hoped that he had remembered to take the medicines.
(c) The doctor said to the patient that he hoped that he remembered to take the medicines.
(d) The doctor said to the patient that he had hoped that he remembered to take the medicines.

7. Respect the elderly. (Change the voice)
(a) The respect for the elderly.
(b) The elderly are respected.
(c) The elderly have been respected.
(d) The elderly should be respected.

8. The teacher explains the lesson clearly. (Change the voice)
(a) The lesson has been explained by the teacher clearly.
(b) The lesson is explained clearly by the teacher.
(c) The lesson explains the teacher clearly.
(d) The lesson was explained clearly by the teacher.

ANSWER KEY

1. Tenses
1. enjoyed
2. struggled
3. rooted
4. waving
5. felt
6. tried
7. tumbled
8. gasped

2. Prepositions
(a) up
(b) under
(c) at
(d) in
(e) beyond
(f) from
(g) from
(h) In

3. Join the Sentences
1. (d)
2. (d)
3. (c)
4. (a)

4. Transformation of Sentences
1. (d)
2. (a)
3. (b)
4. (c)
5. (b)
6. (a)
7. (d)
8. (b)

ICSE TEST PAPER 11

Tenses:

1. Fill in each of the numbered blanks with the correct form of the verb given in brackets.

The next day, I ...(0) (arrive) at Park Lane punctual to the moment, but was ...(1) (tell) by the butler that Lady Alroy has just ...(2) (go) out. I ...(3) (go) down to the club quite unhappy and very ...(4) (puzzle) and after long consideration, ...(5) (write) her a letter, ...(6) (ask) if I might ...(7) (allow) to ...(8) (try) my chance some other afternoon.

Answer: (0) arrived

Prepositions:

2. Fill in the blanks with the appropriate prepositions.

(a) He was stopped by the police for driving .... 100km/hour.

(b) He was found driving .... a seatbelt.

(c) The loud noise drove .... the birds.

(d) He was stopped by the police for driving .... the wrong lane.

(e) On the way to school, we had to drive .... a railway bridge.

(f) I just drove .... the hospital on my way to the office.

(g) You should keep .... the left of the road.

(h) He was stopped by the police for driving ...... the speed limit.

Join the Sentences:

3. Choose the correct option to make one complete sentence without using *and, but or so.*

1. There was heavy snowfall this winter. The plants survived.
   (a) Besides heavy snowfall this winter, the plants survived.
   (b) As soon as there was heavy snowfall this winter, the plants survived.
   (c) Even though heavy snowfall this winter, the plants survived.
   (d) Despite heavy snowfall this winter, the plants survived.

2. The movie was entertaining. It was thought-provoking.
   (a) While the movie was entertaining, it was thought-provoking.
   (b) The movie was entertaining yet it was thought-provoking.
   (c) As soon as the movie was entertaining, it was thought-provoking.
   (d) The movie was not only entertaining but also thought-provoking.

3. You can have dessert. You need to finish the vegetables first.
   (a) You can have dessert, otherwise, you need to finish the vegetables first.
   (b) While you can have dessert, you need to finish the vegetables first.
   (c) You can have dessert provided you finish the vegetables first.
   (d) Unless you finish the vegetables first, you can have dessert.

4. I speak the truth. I am not afraid of it.
   (a) I am not afraid to speak the truth.
   (b) I speak the truth however, I am not afraid of it.
   (c) I am not afraid of the truth to speak it.
   (d) I speak the truth, yet I am not afraid of it.

Transformation of Sentences:

4. Choose the correct option and rewrite the sentence according to the instruction given after each.

1. We not only need a batsman but also a fast bowler. (Begin with *In addition*)
   (a) In addition to a batsman, we need a fast bowler.
   (b) In addition, we need a batsman and a fast bowler.
   (c) In addition, we not only need a batsman and a fast bowler.
   (d) Not only we need a batsman in addition to a fast bowler.

2. The police started firing and the mob dispersed immediately. (Begin with *No sooner*)
   (a) No sooner did the police start firing than the mob dispersed.
   (b) No sooner did the police started firing than the mob dispersed.
   (c) No sooner did the police start firing than the mob dispersed immediately.
   (d) No sooner did the police started firing, than the mob dispersed.

3. Neelima cannot decide, you have to tell her all the facts. (Use *Unless*)
   (a) Unless you tell Neelima all the facts, she cannot decide.
   (b) Unless you do not tell Neelima all the facts, she cannot decide.

(c) Unless you tell her all the facts, Neelima can decide.
(d) Neelima cannot decide unless you do not tell her all the facts.

4. As soon as my pet hears a knock at the door, he starts barking. (Begin with *No sooner*)
(a) No sooner than my pet hear a knock at the door, he starts barking.
(b) No sooner does my pet hear a knock at the door than he starts barking.
(c) No sooner did my pet hear a knock at the door than he started barking.
(d) No sooner does my pet hears a knock at the door than he starts barking.

5. All his friends laughed at him. (Change the voice)
(a) He was laughed by all his friends.
(b) He is laughed at by all his friends.
(c) He will be laughed at by all his friends.
(d) He was laughed at by all his friends.

6. He is so timid that he cannot be a soldier. (Use *too*)
(a) He is too timid to be a soldier.
(b) He is so timid that he too cannot be a soldier.
(c) He is too timid for a soldier.
(d) He is too timid that he can be a soldier.

7. This study space looks neat and tidy. (Add a question tag)
(a) This study space looks neat and tidy, isn't it?
(b) This study space looks neat and tidy, is it?
(c) This study space looks neat and tidy, doesn't it?
(d) This study space looks neat and tidy, does it?

8. He said to me, "I expect you to attend the function." (Change into indirect speech)
(a) He told me that he had expected me to attend the function.
(b) He told me that he expected me to have attended the function.
(c) He told me that he expected me to attend the function.
(d) He told me that he expected me attending the function.

ANSWER KEY

1. Tenses
1. told
2. gone
3. went
4. puzzled
5. wrote
6. asking
7. be allowed
8. try

2. Prepositions
(a) at
(b) without
(c) away
(d) in
(e) under
(f) past (*by* also possible in casual speech (I drove *by* the hospital), but *past* is more precise.
(g) to
(h) over (*above* also correct, though less common than *over; beyond* is incorrect – *beyond* is fine for distance or scope (e.g., *beyond* the hills, *beyond* repair, but not for traffic limits)

3. Join the sentences
1. (d)
2. (d)
3. (c)
4. (a)

4. Transformation of Sentences
1. (a)
2. (a)
3. (a)
4. (b)
5. (d)
6. (a)
7. (c)
8. (c)

ICSE TEST PAPER 12

Tenses:

1. Fill in each of the numbered blanks with the correct form of the verb given in brackets.

The epidemic of ...(0) (shoot) of New York City police officers was a remarkable affair. It ...(1) (become) one of the horror mysteries of the time. In two short weeks, over a hundred police officers ...(2) (shoot) in the legs by their own revolvers. Inspector Jones did not ...(3) (solve) the mystery but it was his idea that finally ...(4) (outwit) Gluck. On his recommendation, the police officers ...(5) (cease) ...(6) (carry) revolvers and no more accidental shootings ... (7) (occur). Everyone ... (8) (heave) a sigh of relief.

Answer: (0) shooting

Prepositions:

2. Fill in the blanks with the appropriate prepositions.

(a) The poet's mother was attacked ... a dog.
(b) I think he will take ... as Acting Principal.
(c) Please write ... what I say otherwise you will forget.
(d) A probe against him is now ... progress.
(e) I told him that these are tears .... joy.
(f) The book has been withdrawn ... circulation.
(g) She shouted angrily ... the disobedient boy.
(h) The dog was hiding ... the bed.

Join the Sentences:

3. Choose the correct option to make one complete sentence without using *and, but or so.*

1. You may get lost. Follow the guide.
   (a) Follow the guide if you don't want to get lost forever.
   (b) You may get lost unless you follow the guide.
   (c) You may follow the guide and get lost.
   (d) You should not get lost; do follow the guide.
2. She finished her meal. She immediately received a phone call.
   (a) No sooner did she finish her meal than she received a phone call.
   (b) No sooner did she finished her meal than she received a phone call.
   (c) No sooner did she finish her meal than she immediately received a phone call.
   (d) No sooner she did finish her meal than she received a phone call.
3. He may ignore me. I will greet him.
   (a) He may ignore me or I will greet him.
   (b) He may ignore me for I will greet him.
   (c) He may ignore me yet I will greet him.
   (d) He may ignore me when I will greet him.
4. It had snowed heavily. The roads to Shimla were blocked.
   (a) As it had snowed heavily, the roads to Shimla were blocked.
   (b) As it snowed heavily, the roads to Shimla were blocked.
   (c) It was snowing heavily however, the roads to Shimla were blocked.
   (d) Though it snowed heavily, the roads to Shimla were blocked.

Transformation of Sentences:

4. Choose the correct option and rewrite the sentence according to the instruction given after each.

1. Priyank said to me, "Please do not leave your place till I tell you what is to be done." (Change into reported speech)
   (a) Priyank requested me not to leave my place till he told me what was to be done.
   (b) Priyank ordered me not to leave the place till he told me what was to be done.
   (c) Priyank told me not to leave the place till he told you what is to be done.
   (d) Priyank told me not to leave the place till I told you what was to be done.
2. He was scolded because he neglected his work. (Begin with *Had he*)
   (a) Had he not neglected his work, he would have been scolded.
   (b) Had he not neglected his work, he could have been scolded.
   (c) Had he not neglected his work, he would not have been scolded.
   (d) Had he neglected his work, he would have been scolded.
3. Radha said to Madhavi, "I like your saree." (Change into indirect speech)
   (a) Radha told Madhavi that she likes your saree.
   (b) Radha told Madhavi that she liked your saree.
   (c) Radha told Madhavi that she liked her saree.
   (d) Radha told Madhavi that she likes her saree.
4. Everybody put up their hands. (Begin with *There was*)
   (a) There was nobody who should up their hands.
   (b) There was nobody who did not put up their hands.

(c) There was nobody whom did not put up their hands.
(d) There was nobody who put up their hands.

5. As soon as the whistle blew, the game stopped. (Begin with *No sooner)*
(a) No sooner did the whistle blow, the game stopped.
(b) No sooner did the whistle blew than the game stopped.
(c) No sooner did the whistle blow than the game stopped.
(d) No sooner than the whistle blew, the game stopped.

6. Instead of following the crowd, he chose to take his own path. (Begin with *Rather*)
(a) Rather than taking his own path, he chose following the crowd.
(b) Rather than taking his own path, he chose to follow the crowd.
(c) Rather following the crowd, he chose to take his own path.
(d) Rather than following the crowd, he chose to take his own path.

7. In spite of the waterlogging the traffic was heavy. (Begin with *Despite*)
(a) Despite of the waterlogging, the traffic was heavy.
(b) Despite of waterlogging, there was heavy traffic.
(c) Despite the traffic being heavy, there was waterlogging.
(d) Despite the waterlogging, the traffic was heavy.

8. The priest said to me, "May God bless you." (Change into reported speech)
(a) The priest prayed that God might bless you.
(b) The priest prayed for me that God might bless me.
(c) The priest prayed that God may bless me.
(d) The priest prayed that God might bless me.

ANSWER KEY

1. Tenses
1. became
2. were shot
3. solve
4. outwitted
5. ceased
6. carrying
7. occurred
8. heaved

2. Preposition
(a) by
(b) over (means to assume the post of)
(c) down
(d) in (means it is going on)
(e) of
(f) from
(g) at
(h) under

3. Join the sentences
1. (b)
2. (a)
3. (c)
4. (a)

4. Transformation
1. (a)
2. (c)
3. (c)
4. (b)
5. (c)
6. (d)
7. (d)
8. (d)

ICSE TEST PAPER 13

Tenses:

1. Fill in each of the numbered blanks with the correct form of the verb given in brackets.

The dog ... (0) (sleep) nearby. He ...(1) (stir) by the smell of food. He ...(2) (get) up, came out of his shelter and ...(3) (stand) before the blind man, ...(4) (wag) his tail and ...(5) (gaze) expectantly at the bowl, as he was eating his sparse meal. The blind man ...(6) (sweep) his arms about and asked : "Who is there?" At which the dog ...(7) (go) up and ...(8) (lick) his hand.

Answer: (0) was sleeping

Prepositions:

2. Fill in the blanks with the appropriate prepositions.

(a) I am sure she did this .... purpose.
(b) We are heading .... the eastern direction.
(c) The performance of the class did not come .... to the expectations of the teacher.
(d) She was crying .... her misfortune.
(e) I am flirting ..... the idea of taking a year off regular work.
(f) Prithvi is longing .... meet his coach.
(g) I was taken .... by his sweet words.
(h) The government has brought .... many changes.

Join the Sentences:

3. Choose the correct option to make one complete sentence without using *and, but or so.*

1. There was a power cut. We took the stairs.
   (a) Unless there was a power cut, we took the stairs.
   (b) There was a power cut yet we took the stairs.
   (c) Though there was a power cut, we took the stairs.
   (d) As there was a power cut, we took the stairs.
2. He anchored the event. He sang a song.
   (a) Besides anchoring the event, he sang a song.
   (b) He anchored the event yet he sang a song.
   (c) Though he anchored the event, he sang a song.
   (d) Apart anchoring the event, he sang a song.
3. Jatin did not come to office. He did not inform anyone.
   (a) Neither Jatin did come to office nor he did inform anyone.
   (b) Jatin did not come to office since he did not inform anyone.
   (c) Neither did Jatin come to office nor did he inform anyone.
   (d) Jatin did not come to office besides he did not inform anyone.
4. The dog is a very faithful animal. The dog is the most loving pet.
   (a) Having been a very faithful animal, the dog is the most loving pet.
   (b) Besides being a very faithful animal, the dog is the most loving pet.
   (c) Since the dog is a very faithful animal, it is the most loving pet.
   (d) Not only faithful but dog is the most loving pet.

Transformation of Sentences:

4. Choose the correct option and rewrite the sentence according to the instruction given after each.

1. He decided to sleep instead of studying economics. (Begin with *Rather*)
   (a) Rather to sleep, he did not study economics.
   (b) Rather than decide to sleep, he studied economics.
   (c) Rather than studying economics, he decided to sleep.
   (d) Rather than sleeping, he decided study economics.
2. If she had studied well, she would have cleared the exam. (Begin with *Had*)
   (a) Had she studied well, she would have cleared the exam.
   (b) Had she had studied well, she would have cleared the exam.
   (c) Had she studied well, she would had cleared the exam.
   (d) Had she studied well, she would have cleared exam.
3. She will come at 5 pm. (Add a question tag)
   (a) She will come at 5 pm, isn't it?
   (b) She will come at 5 pm, would she?
   (c) She will come at 5 pm, will she?
   (d) She will come at 5 pm, won't she?
4. The log is too heavy to be lifted. (Use *so*)
   (a) The log is so very heavy to lift it.
   (b) The log is so heavy to be lifted.
   (c) The log is so heavy that I can lift it.
   (d) The log is so heavy that it cannot be lifted.
5. He did not know that this decision would change his life. (Begin with: *Little did* ...)
   (a) Little did he know, despite this decision would change his life.
   (b) Little did he know and this decision would change his life.

(c) Little did he know that this decision would change his life.

(d) Little did he know this decision changed his life already.

6. He said to his friend, "Please wait here till I return." (Convert to indirect speech)

(a) He asked his friend to please wait there till he returned.

(b) He requested his friend to wait there till he returned.

(c) He pleaded with his friend to wait here till he returned.

(d) He ordered his friend to wait there till he returned.

7. "I have an appointment next week," said Chandana. (Change into reported speech)

(a) Chandana said that she will have an appointment next week.

(b) Chandana said that she has an appointment the following week.

(c) Chandana said that she had an appointment next week.

(d) Chandana said that she had an appointment the following week.

8. Tapish said, "What a hot day!" (Change into reported speech)

(a) Tapish exclaimed with grief that it was a hot day.

(b) Tapish said that it was a hot day.

(c) Tapish exclaimed that it was a hot day.

(d) Tapish exclaimed excitedly that it was a hot day.

ANSWER KEY

1. Tenses

1. was stirred
2. got
3. stood
4. wagging
5. gazing
6. swept
7. went
8. licked

2. Prepositions

(a) on

(b) in (*in* the eastern direction or *towards* the east. *Towards* the eastern direction is incorrect because "towards" already means "in the direction of.")

(c) up

(d) over

(e) with

(f) to

(g) in

(h) about

3. Join the sentences

1. (d)
2. (a)
3. (c)
4. (b)

4. Transformation of Sentences

1. (c)
2. (a)
3. (d)
4. (d)
5. (c)
6. (b)
7. (d)
8. (c)

ICSE TEST PAPER 14

Tenses:

1. Fill in each of the numbered blanks with the correct form of the verb given in brackets.

In India, particularly in villages, even a few decades back, women without children ...(0) (look) down upon. Such women were not invited for naming ceremonies, and ...(1) (taunt) as barren women. Nobody ...(2) (understand) the hurt and trauma they ....(3)....(undergo). When I ...(4) (be) a child, I had a teacher called Gowramma. She was kind and warm. She ...(5) (use) to ...(6) (teach) us Sanskrit and ...(7) (will) tell lots of stories in the class. But students were not ...(8) (interest) in her stories.

Answer: (0) were looked

Prepositions:

2. Fill in the blanks with the appropriate prepositions.

(a) Mahatma Gandhi travelled to Dandi .... foot.

(b) "I am .... the bus to Pune," Ravinder said to his friend.

(c) Mona is a positive influence .... Shreyas.

(d) Rakesh is .... the guidance of his manager.

(e) I have told Dinesh and he is ..... the job.

(f) It is a fantastic team you work ....

(g) The bank manager was not ... his desk.

(h) I cannot meet you as I will be ... work in the afternoon.

Join the Sentences:

3. Choose the correct option to make one complete sentence without using *and, but or so.*

1. The daughter cut the vegetables. The son cooked.

(a) While the daughter cut the vegetables, the son cooked.

(b) Though the daughter cut the vegetables, the son cooked.

(c) Although the daughter cut the vegetables, the son cooked.

(d) The daughter cut the vegetables yet the son cooked.

2. The place was very noisy. I couldn't hear anything properly.

(a) Though the place was very noisy, I couldn't hear anything properly.

(b) The place was very noisy yet I couldn't hear anything properly.

(c) The place was too noisy to hear anything properly.

(d) The place was so noisy to hear anything properly.

3. Mala is not in the classroom. Mala is not in the library.

(a) Mala is neither in the classroom nor in the library.

(b) Mala is neither in the classroom or in the library.

(c) Either Mala is not in the classroom or in the library.

(d) Mala is not in the classroom, she is neither in the library.

4. Ravi disliked cockroaches. He disliked the ridicule of his classmates more.

(a) Ravi disliked cockroaches, provided he disliked the ridicule of his classmates more.

(b) Ravi disliked the ridicule of his classmates more than he disliked cockroaches.

(c) Ravi disliked cockroaches more than he disliked the ridicule of his classmates.

(d) Ravi disliked cockroaches, yet he disliked the ridicule of his classmates more.

Transformation of Sentences:

4. Choose the correct option and rewrite the sentence according to the instruction given after each.

1. Asha sang well. (Add a question tag)

(a) Asha sang well, didn't she?

(b) Asha sang well, did she?

(c) Asha sang well, had she?

(d) Asha sang well, hadn't she?

2. A pizza tastes better than a burger. (Change the voice)

(a) A burger tastes good as a pizza.

(b) A burger taste is worst than a pizza.

(c) A burger does not taste as good as a pizza.

(d) A burger tastes better than a pizza.

3. Kamal was unable to do anything until the following year. (Begin with *Not until*)

(a) Not until the following year was Kamal able to do anything.

(b) Not until the following year Kamal was unable to do anything.

(c) Not until the following year Kamal was able to do anything.

(d) Not until the following year was Kamal unable to do anything.

4. This book is beautifully printed and is free from mistakes also. (Begin with *Besides*)
   (a) Besides being beautifully printed, this book is free from mistakes.
   (b) Besides being free from mistakes, this book is beautifully printed.
   (c) Besides beautifully printed, this book is free from mistakes also.
   (d) Besides being beautifully printed, this book is also free from mistakes.
5. He is Mexican by birth, but he speaks Bengali like his mother tongue. (Begin with *In spite*)
   (a) In spite of being Mexican by birth, yet he speaks Bengali like his mother tongue.
   (b) In spite of being Mexican by birth, he speaks Bengali like his mother tongue.
   (c) In spite of being Mexican by birth, but he speaks Bengali like his mother tongue.
   (d) In spite being Mexican by birth, he speaks Bengali like his mother tongue.
6. "I went to the meeting yesterday," said Sunil. (Change into indirect speech)
   (a) Sunil said that he had gone to the meeting the previous day.
   (b) Sunil told that he went to the meeting the day before.
   (c) Sunil said that he had gone to the meeting yesterday.
   (d) Sunil said that he went to the meeting yesterday.
7. "I may never meet you again," he whispered to Prasad. (Change into reported speech)
   (a) He whispered to Prasad that he will never meet him again.
   (b) He whispered to Prasad that he may never meet him again.
   (c) He whispered to Prasad that he might never meet you again.
   (d) He whispered to Prasad that he might never meet him again.
8. The tree is too high for me to climb. (Use *so*)
   (a) The tree is so high for me to climb.
   (b) The tree is so high that I cannot climb it.
   (c) The tree is so high that I can climb it.
   (d) The tree is so high that I can climb.

ANSWER KEY

1. Tenses

1. were taunted
2. understood
3. underwent
4. was
5. used
6. teach
7. would
8. interested

2. Prepositions

(a) on
(b) on ("on" for larger public/shared transport (bus, train, plane, ship) → *on* the bus, *on* the train; "in" for smaller private vehicles (car, taxi, van) → *in* the car, *in* a van)
(c) on
(d) under
(e) on
(f) with
(g) at
(h) at

3. Join the sentences

1. (a)
2. (c)
3. (a)
4. (b)

4. Transformation of Sentences

1. (a)
2. (c)
3. (a)
4. (a)
5. (b)
6. (a)
7. (d)
8. (b)

ICSE TEST PAPER 15

Tenses:

1. Fill in each of the numbered blanks with the correct form of the verb given in brackets.

After a long while, the game ...(0) (stop) and the door ...(1) (bang). I ...(2) (sleep) because I was dead ...(3) (tire). Otherwise I should have ...(4) (prefer) to have kept awake. When the morning ...(5) (come), I went to my own room and ...(6) (prepare) to pack after ...(7) (note) down the facts of the case. And then I ...(8) (hear) the game begin again.

Answer: (0) stopped

Prepositions:

2. Fill in the blanks with the appropriate prepositions.

(a) He refused to part ..... his books.
(b) He is standing .... the window.
(c) He is .... the phone right now.
(d) He stays .... a village near Pune..
(e) He was mistaken .... someone else.
(f) He rushed .... the conference room and greeted everyone.
(g) Sheela went to Lucknow ... air.
(h) He insisted that he needed to get .... the next flight.

Join the Sentences:

3. Choose the correct option to make one complete sentence without using *and, but or so.*

1. He earns very little. He cannot buy a house.
   (a) He earns very little to buy a house.
   (b) Though he earns very little, he can buy a house.
   (c) Though he earns very little, he cannot buy a house.
   (d) He earns too little to buy a house.
2. They had just finished eating. The waiter brought the bill.
   (a) They had just finished eating while the waiter brought the bill.
   (b) Hardly had they finished eating than the waiter brought the bill.
   (c) Hardly they had finished eating when the waiter brought the bill.
   (d) Hardly had they finished eating when the waiter brought the bill.
3. She was not happy with the results. She was not satisfied with the results.
   (a) She was neither happy nor satisfied with the results.
   (b) While she was not happy with the results, she was also not satisfied.
   (c) She was not happy yet not satisfied with the results.
   (d) In spite of not being happy with the results, she was not satisfied.
4. I warned him several times. Yet, he broke the school rules.
   (a) Although I warned him several times, he broke the school rules.
   (b) Although I warned him several times, yet he broke the school rules.
   (c) Although I had warned him several times, still he broke the school rules.
   (d) Although I warned him several times, but he broke the school rules.

Transformation of Sentences:

4. Choose the correct option and rewrite the sentence according to the instruction given after each.

1. A charity event is organised by the Diwali committee. (Change the voice)
   (a) The Diwali committee has been organising a charity event.
   (b) The Diwali committee organises a charity event.
   (c) The Diwali committee organised a charity event.
   (d) The Diwali committee has organised a charity event.
2. As soon as Madhu sat down to study, the lights went off. (Begin with *No sooner*)
   (a) No sooner did Madhu sit down to study then the lights went off.
   (b) No sooner did Madhu sit down to study than the lights went off.
   (c) No sooner did Madhu sat down to study than the lights went off.
   (d) No sooner had Madhu sit down to study than the lights went off.
3. She rang the bell and welcomed everyone. (Begin with *Having*)
   (a) Having rings the bell, she welcomed everyone.
   (b) Having rung the bell, she welcomed everyone.
   (c) Having ringing the bell, she welcomed everyone.
   (d) Having rang the bell, she welcomed everyone.
4. If you don't ask him, he will not help you. (Begin with *Unless*)
   (a) Unless you don't ask him, he will not help you.
   (b) Unless you ask him, he will help you.

(c) Unless you don't ask him, he will help you.
(d) Unless you ask him, he will not help you.

5. He hasn't been running in this weather. (Add a question tag)
(a) He hasn't been running in this weather, isn't he?
(b) He hasn't been running in this weather, is he?
(c) He hasn't been running in this weather, has he?
(d) He hasn't been running in this weather, hasn't he?

6. We completed the project early and had extra time to relax. (Begin with *Having*)
(a) Having completed the project, we had extra time to relax.
(b) Having the project early, we completed with extra time to relax.
(c) Having completed the project early, we had extra time to relax.
(d) Having extra time to relax, we completed the project early.

7. Rather than spending money on new clothes, she chose to save for a vacation. (Use *instead*)
(a) She chose to save for a vacation instead of spending money on new clothes.
(b) She chose to spend money on new clothes instead of saving for a vacation.
(c) She chose to spending money on new clothes instead of saving for a vacation.
(d) Instead of saving for a vacation, she chose to spend money on new clothes.

8. Had he arrived on time, he wouldn't have missed the presentation. (Begin with *If*)
(a) If he hadn't missed the presentation, he would have arrived on time.
(b) If he had arrived on time, he wouldn't have missed the presentation.
(c) If he had arrived on time, he wouldn't had missed the presentation.
(d) If he arrived on time, he wouldn't have missed the presentation.

ANSWER KEY

1. Tenses
1. banged
2. slept
3. tired
4. preferred
5. came
6. prepared
7. noting
8. heard

2. Prepositions
(a) with (part with = giving something up)
(b) at, beside, near, by
(c) on (on the phone = talking on the phone)
(d) at (Use *in* for large places (cities, towns, countries). Use *at* for small places (villages, small stops, points on a map). E.g. She lives *in* Delhi (big city). He stays *at* a village near Pune (small place).
(e) for
(f) into ("To" is used when we mean to say he ran up to the door/entrance of the room, but not necessarily inside. "Into" means he actually entered the room. The action of greeting everyone shows he was already inside. So, the correct choice is: *into*.)
(g) by
(h) on (Use "on" for vehicles (flights, trains, buses) in general conversation. "*Onto*" – He insisted that he needed to get <u>onto</u> the next flight. – though grammatically correct, "onto" emphasises movement onto a surface or more formal contexts, e.g., The cat jumped *onto* the roof.)

3. Join the Sentences
1. (d)
2. (d)
3. (a)
4. (a) (Yet will not be used with Though or Although)

4. Transformation
1. (b)
2. (b)
3. (b)
4. (d)
5. (c)
6. (c)
7. (a)
8. (b)

ICSE TEST PAPER 16

Tenses:

1. Fill in each of the numbered blanks with the correct form of the verb given in brackets.

On paper, it ...(0) (go) to be an open and shut case. But still, Sartaj ...(1) (study) Chetanbhai Patel's chequebook as the jeep ...(2) (wind) its way through the traffic. Sartaj ...(3) (bend) the book and the pages ...(4) (flurry) by. Earlier, when Kshitij ...(5) (open) the door to the apartment, he ...(6) (hold) a dumbbell and ... (7) (dress) in a white banian and shorts which ...(8) (hang) off his thin waist.

Answer: (0) was going

Prepositions:

2. Fill in the blanks with the appropriate prepositions.

(a) The incessant rains should stop .... the weekend.

(b) The doctor sees patients .... 2 pm and 4 pm.

(c) How long have you been .... a diet?

(d) I will get .... the bottom of this scandal.

(e) The question came .... in the Tripura Assembly last week.

(f) I want a clerk familiar .... typewriting.

(g) The Second World War broke .... in 1939.

(h) But .... my uncle's support, I couldn't have succeeded.

Join the Sentences:

3. Choose the correct option to make one complete sentence without using *and, but or so.*

1. He is sensible. He is kind.
   (a) Though he is sensible, he is kind.
   (b) He is sensible yet he is kind.
   (c) He is not only sensible but also kind.
   (d) Since he is sensible, he is kind.
2. We are not allowed to play in the sun. We are not allowed to play in the rain.
   (a) We are not allowed to play in the sun nor the rain.
   (b) We are neither allowed to play in the sun nor in the rain.
   (c) We are not allowed to play in sun and rain.
   (d) We are not allowed to play in the sun and the rain.
3. The minister neglected his duties. It was foolish.
   (a) It was foolish of the minister to neglect his duties.
   (b) It was foolish by the minister to neglect his duties.
   (c) The minister neglected his duties though it was foolish.
   (d) The minister neglected his duties hence it was foolish.
4. The bell rang. The students rushed out.
   (a) Hardly had the bell ring when the students rushed out.
   (b) As soon as the bell rang, the students rushed out.
   (c) No sooner did the bell rang than the students rushed out.
   (d) The students rushed out since the bell rang.

Transformation of Sentences:

4. Choose the correct option and rewrite the sentence according to the instruction given after each.

1. "I could do the cooking," Divya said. (Change into indirect speech)
   (a) Divya said that she will cook.
   (b) Divya said that she might do the cooking.
   (c) Divya said that she can do the cooking.
   (d) Divya said that she could do the cooking.
2. Anil is inviting each of his classmates. (Begin with *Each*)
   (a) Each of his classmates is invited by Anil.
   (b) Each of Anil's classmates is been invited by Anil.
   (c) Each of his classmates has been invited by Anil.
   (d) Each of his classmates is being invited by Anil.
3. "I am sorry I gave you the wrong number," said Prasad to Srinivas. (Change into reported speech)
   (a) Prasad apologised saying he gave Srinivas the wrong number.
   (b) Prasad apologised saying he was sorry for having given Srinivas the wrong number.
   (c) Prasad apologised to Srinivas for having given him the wrong number.
   (d) Prasad apologised and felt sorry for giving the wrong number.
4. We started rowing in this lake in 2019. (Begin with *We have*)
   (a) We have been rowing in the lake from 2019.
   (b) We have rowed in this lake since 2019.
   (c) We have been rowing in this lake since 2019.
   (d) We have rowed in this lake from 2019.
5. Aeroplanes fly faster than birds. (Begin with *Birds*)
   (a) Birds are slower flying than aeroplanes.
   (b) Birds fly as fast as aeroplanes.

(c) Birds do not fly faster as aeroplanes.
(d) Birds do not fly as fast as aeroplanes.

6. She always praises her neighbours. (Change the voice)
(a) Her neighbours are always praised by her.
(b) Her neighbours are always being praised by her.
(c) Her praise always is for her neighbours.
(d) Her neighbours praise her.

7. If you convince the members, they will take action. (Begin with *Unless*)
(a) Unless you take action, they will convince the members.
(b) Unless you do not convince the members, they will not take action.
(c) Unless you convince the members, they will not take action.
(d) Unless you convince the members, they will not take action.

8. He was away from Delhi, yet he sent across a gift. (Use *although*)
(a) He send across a gift although he was away from Delhi.
(b) He was away from Delhi although he sent across a gift.
(c) Although he was away from Delhi, he sends across a gift.
(d) Although he was away from Delhi, he sent across a gift.

ANSWER KEY

1. Tenses
1. studied
2. wound
3. bent
4. flurried
5. had opened
6. was holding
7. was dressed
8. hung

2. Prepositions
(a) by (by = not later than a certain time)
(b) between
(c) on
(d) to
(e) up
(f) with
(g) out
(h) for

3. Join the sentences
1. (c)
2. (b)
3. (a)
4. (b)

4. Transformation of Sentences
1. (d)
2. (d)
3. (c)
4. (c)
5. (d)
6. (a)
7. (c)
8. (d)

ICSE TEST PAPER 17

Tenses:

1. Fill in each of the numbered blanks with the correct form of the verb given in brackets.

Feld, the shoemaker, ...(0) (annoy) that his helper, Sobel, was so insensitive to his reverie that he ...(1) (will) not for a minute ...(2) (cease) his fanatic ...(3) (pound) at the other bench. He ...(4) (give) a look but Sobel's bald head ...(5) (bend) over the last as he ...(6) (work), and he did not ...(7) (notice). The shoemaker simply .... (8) (shrug).

Answer: (0) was annoyed

Prepositions:

2. Fill in the blanks with the appropriate prepositions.

(a) Can we agree .... the main points?
(b) This makes ..... a good ending to the movie.
(c) I have come ..... the conclusion that this candidate is not fit for the job.
(d) I am confident .... success in the genetics project.
(e) I am confident ..... your abilities to handle all these tasks.
(f) The plane touched .... at Mumbai airport at 10 am.
(g) Have you arrived ..... a decision?
(h) I am confident ..... the film.

Join the Sentences:

3. Choose the correct option to make one complete sentence without using *and, but or so.*

1. I finished my homework. I switched on the TV.
(a) I finished my homework yet I switched on the TV.
(b) No sooner did I finished my homework than I switched on the TV.
(c) As soon as I finished my homework, I switched on the TV.
(d) No sooner did I finish my homework than I switch on the TV.

2. The baby ate his breakfast. He went to sleep.
(a) Having eaten his breakfast, the baby went to sleep.
(b) By eating his breakfast, the baby went to sleep.
(c) Having eaten his breakfast, he went to sleep.
(d) Eating his breakfast, the baby went off to sleep.

3. The car was expensive. My uncle bought it.
(a) Though the car was expensive, my uncle bought it.
(b) In spite of the expensive car, my uncle bought it.
(c) Either the car was expensive or my uncle bought it.
(d) The car was expensive, therefore my uncle bought it.

4. It rained heavily. There was no waterlogging.
(a) It rained heavily because there was no waterlogging.
(b) Since there was no waterlogging, it rained heavily.
(c) Though it rained heavily, there was no waterlogging.
(d) It rained heavily, thus there was no waterlogging.

Transformation of Sentences:

4. Choose the correct option and rewrite the sentence according to the instruction given after each.

1. Lissy played all day and was exhausted. (Begin with *Having*)
(a) Having played all day, Lissy was exhausted.
(b) Having played on the day, Lissy was exhausted.
(c) Having played during the day, Lissy was exhausted.
(d) Having played all day, Lissy has been exhausted.

2. The children played football in the park. (Change the voice)
(a) Football was played by the children in the park.
(b) Playing of football in the park was done by the children.
(c) Football is played by the children in the park.
(d) In the park, the children have played football.

3. I am as tall as you. (Begin with *You are*)
(a) You are not taller than me.
(b) You are taller as me.
(c) You are tall as me.
(d) You are taller than me.

4. These rooms need painting again. (Begin with *These rooms*)
(a) These rooms will require painting.
(b) These rooms need for painting again.
(c) These rooms will have to be painted again.
(d) These rooms will be needing painting again.

5. Who can question the principal's integrity? (Change the voice)
(a) By whom the principal's integrity can be questioned?
(b) By whom could the principal's integrity be questioned?

(c) By whom can the principal's integrity be questioned?
(d) By whom can question the principal's integrity?

6. He is the rudest man I have ever met. (Change the degree)
(a) I have never met a ruder man than him.
(b) I have ever met a ruder man than him.
(c) I have never met a rudest man than him.
(d) I have never met a rude man as him.

7. You love ice cream. (Add a question tag)
(a) You love ice cream, do you?
(b) You love ice cream, don't you?
(c) Do you love ice cream, don't you?
(d) You love ice cream, isn't it?

8. He is too proud to beg. (use *so*)
(a) He is so proud that he will beg.
(b) He is so proud that he cannot beg.
(c) He is so proud that he will not beg.
(d) He is so proud to beg.

ANSWER KEY

1. Tenses

1. would
2. cease
3. pounding
4. gave
5. was bent
6. worked
7. notice
8. shrugged

2. Prepositions

(a) on
(b) for
(c) to
(d) of (confident *of* = when referring to facts, outcomes, results, not abilities)
(e) in (confident *in* = to express trust or belief in someone's skills, qualities, or abilities)
(f) down
(g) at
(h) about (confident *about* = used for general opinion or attitude)

3. Join the sentences

1. (c)
2. (a)
3. (a)
4. (c)

4. Transformation of Sentences

1. (a)
2. (a)
3. (a)
4. (c)
5. (c)
6. (a)
7. (b)
8. (b) ("*cannot beg*" = emphasises incapability; his pride makes it impossible for him. "*will not beg*" = emphasises choice/refusal; his pride leads him to refuse, but doesn't strictly make it impossible.

So, in a strict grammatical sense, option (b) is closer to "too proud to beg," because "too ... to" usually implies inability rather than mere refusal.)

ICSE TEST PAPER 18

Tenses:

1. Fill in each of the numbered blanks with the correct form of the verb given in brackets.

A sense of loneliness ...(0) (creep) over me. I ...(1) (arise), ...(2) (move) on tiptoe about the room, doing stealthily what I had to do, as I were environed by sleeping enemies whose slumbers it would be fatal ...(3) (break). I covered up in bed, lay ...(4) (listen) to the rain and wind and the faint ... (5) (creak) of distant shutters, till they ...(6) (lull) me to sleep. I ....(7) (sleep) profoundly but how long I do not ...(8) (know)

Answer: (0) crept

Prepositions:

2. Fill in the blanks with the appropriate prepositions.

(a) There is no exception .... this rule.
(b) Why are you averse ... hard work?
(c) Though he had promised to come, he never turned ....
(d) I am counting .... you today.
(e) The phone call was made to him .... mistake.
(f) The brothers have fallen .... over division of property.
(g) He was at a loss .... words.
(h) I am looking forward .... your visit.

Join the Sentences:

3. Choose the correct option to make one complete sentence without using *and, but or so.*

1. He escaped from prison. He looked for a place to hide.
   (a) He escaped from prison, yet he looked for a place to hide.
   (b) After escaping from prison, he looked for a place to hide.
   (c) Looking for a place to hide, he escaped from prison.
   (d) Though he escaped from prison, he looked for a place to hide.
2. The field was wet. The match was called off.
   (a) The field being wet, the match was called off.
   (b) Though the field was wet, the match was called off.
   (c) The field was wet, yet the match was called off.
   (d) The match was called off, provided the field was wet.
3. I lost all my money. I asked my friend for help.
   (a) I lost all my money, yet I asked my friend for help.
   (b) Though I lost all my money, I asked my friend for help.
   (c) Having lost all my money, I asked my friend for help.
   (d) Besides losing all my money, I asked my friend for help.
4. The lift was out of order. We walked up the stairs.
   (a) The lift was out of order, yet we walked up the stairs.
   (b) We walked up the stairs as the lift was out of order.
   (c) The lift was out of order while we walked up the stairs.
   (d) Walking up the stairs, the lift was out of order.

Transformation of Sentences:

4. Choose the correct option and rewrite the sentence according to the instruction given after each.

1. The dog is more faithful than all other creatures. (Use *most faithful*)
   (a) The dog is most faithful than any other creature.
   (b) No other creature is most faithful than the dog.
   (c) The dog is the most faithful than any other creature on earth.
   (d) The dog is the most faithful creature.
2. He is as brave as any soldier in the army. (Change the degree)
   (a) He is more brave than any soldier in the army.
   (b) No soldier in the army is brave as him.
   (c) He is braver than any soldier in the army.
   (d) No soldier in the army is braver than him.
3. He insisted that he was innocent. (Use *innocence*)
   (a) Insistence on innocence was done by him.
   (b) Innocence was insisted upon by him.
   (c) He insisted on his innocence.
   (d) He insisted on innocence.
4. But for the timely treatment, the cancer would have cost his life. (Begin with *Had*)
   (a) Had it not been for the timely treatment, the cancer would have cost his life.
   (b) Had it not been for the cancer, the timely treatment would have cost his life.
   (c) Had the cancer not treated on time, it would have cost his life.

(d) Had the treatment of cancer not been given timely, the cancer would have cost his life.

5. It rained so heavily that they could not go for the picnic. (Use *too*)
   (a) It rained too heavily that they could not go for the picnic.
   (b) It rained too heavily for them to go for the picnic.
   (c) It rained too heavily for their picnic.
   (d) It rained too heavily for them not to go for the picnic.

6. Why would you suspect me of committing fraud? (Change to passive voice)
   (a) Why would I be suspected of committing fraud by you?
   (b) Why would you be suspected of committing fraud by me?
   (c) Why would I suspect you of committing fraud?
   (d) Why am I suspected of committing fraud by you?

7. The price of milk has risen recently. (End with *milk*)
   (a) There has been recent price rise in milk.
   (b) There has been a recent rise in the price of milk.
   (c) There has been a rising price in milk.
   (d) There has been a recent rice in the price of milk.

8. Although it was a holiday, the manager was very busy. (Begin with *Despite*)
   (a) Despite a holiday, the manager was very busy.
   (b) Despite being busy, it was a holiday.
   (c) Despite it being a holiday, the manager was very busy.
   (d) Despite the manager's business, it was a holiday.

ANSWER KEY

1. Tenses
1. arose
2. moving
3. to break
4. listening
5. creaking
6. lulled
7. slept
8. know

2. Prepositions
(a) to
(b) to (averse to = having a reluctance to)
(c) up (turn up = arrive)
(d) on (count on = to rely on or depend on someone)
(e) by
(f) out (fall out = have a difference of opinion or quarrel)
(g) for (loss for words = unable to think of anything to say, usually due to shock, surprise, admiration, etc.)
(h) to

3. Join the Sentences
1. (b)
2. (a)
3. (c)
4. (b)

4. Transformation of Sentences
1. (d)
2. (d)
3. (c)
4. (a)
5. (b)
6. (a)
7. (b)
8. (c)

ICSE TEST PAPER 19

Tenses:

1. Fill in each of the numbered blanks with the correct form of the verb given in brackets.

Our cart ...(0) (rumble) over the boulders of the street and we were soon at the village square. Javni was running behind the cart, with tears ...(1) (roll) down her cheeks. For one full week, I ...(2) (see) her ...(3) (weep) all the time, all the time ...(4) (dread) the day when we ... (5) (leave) her and she ... (6) (see) us no more. She was breathless but she walked fast, ...(7) (keep) pace with the bullocks. My sister was sad. In her heart, she ...(8) (know) she was leaving a friend.

Answer: (0) rumbled

Prepositions:

2. Fill in the blanks with the appropriate prepositions.

(a) I asked them to provide us .... a guide.
(b) She burst ... tears when she heard the news.
(c) It has been raining .... an hour.
(d) I hope he complies .... the wishes of his parents.
(e) South Africa is famous .... its diamonds.
(f) My parents were longing .... meet me.
(g) Truth always prevails .... the long run.
(h) She wanted to be a novelist but she never put pen .... paper.

Join the Sentences:

3. Choose the correct option to make one complete sentence without using *and, but or so.*

1. He is too headstrong. He will not listen to advice.
   (a) He is so headstrong that he will not listen to advice
   (b) Unless he is too headstrong, he will not listen to advice.
   (c) While he is too headstrong, he will not listen to advice.
   (d) As he is too headstrong, he will not listen to advice.
2. The hero appeared on screen. The audience clapped.
   (a) Though the hero appeared on screen, the audience clapped.
   (b) As soon as the hero appeared on screen, the audience clapped.
   (c) Hardly had the hero appear on screen when the audience clapped.
   (d) No sooner did the hero appeared on screen than the audience clapped.
3. The coffee isn't strong. It won't keep us awake.
   (a) The coffee isn't strong yet it won't keep us awake.
   (b) The coffee isn't strong despite it won't keep us awake.
   (c) The coffee isn't strong enough to keep us awake.
   (d) Though the coffee isn't strong, it won't keep us awake.
4. Mohan opened his bag. He found the laptop missing.
   (a) Mohan opened his bag when the laptop was missing.
   (b) When Mohan opened his bag, he found the laptop missing.
   (c) Mohan opened his bag then he found the laptop missing.
   (d) The laptop was missing after Mohan opened his bag.

Transformation of Sentences:

4. Choose the correct option and rewrite the sentence according to the instruction given after each.

1. In spite of the heavy rain, we reached home early. (Begin with *Despite*)
   (a) Despite the heavy rain, we reached home early.
   (b) Despite of the heavy rain, we reached home early.
   (c) Despite it rained, we reached home early.
   (d) Despite we reached home early, it rained.
2. Shweta has gone to the market to buy milk. (Add a question tag)
   (a) Shweta has gone to the market to buy milk, isn't it?
   (b) Shweta has gone to the market to buy milk, didn't she?
   (c) Shweta has gone to the market to buy milk, hadn't she?
   (d) Shweta has gone to the market to buy milk, hasn't she?
3. He spoke too fast to be understood. (Use *so*)
   (a) He spoke so fast to be understood.
   (b) He spoke so fast that he could not be understood.
   (c) He spoke so fast that he cannot be understood.
   (d) He spoke so fast so that he could not be understood.
4. I did not know that she would be such a liar. (Begin with *Little*)

(a) Little did not I know that she would be such a liar.
(b) Little do I know that she would be such a liar.
(c) Little did I know that she would be such a liar
(d) Little did I know that she would not be such a liar.

5. No sooner had the manager arrived than the guard went to the canteen. (Begin with *As soon as*)
(a) As soon as the manager arrived, then the guard went to the canteen.
(b) As soon as the manager arrived when the guard went to the canteen.
(c) As soon as the manager arrive, the guard went to the canteen.
(d) As soon as the manager arrived, the guard went to the canteen.

6. Lissy is delivering today's lecture. (Change the voice)
(a) Today's lecture is being delivered by Lissy.
(b) Today's lecture is delivered by Lissy.
(c) Today's lecture is delivering by Lissy.
(d) Today's lecture will be delivered by Lissy.

7. Only an artist can make such a masterpiece. (Begin with *None*)
(a) None but an artist can make such a masterpiece.
(b) None other than but an artist can make such a masterpiece.
(c) None only an artist can make such a masterpiece.
(d) None an artist cannot make such a masterpiece.

8. As soon as the rain stopped, the match began. (Begin with *Hardly*)
(a) Hardly did the rain stop than the match began.
(b) Hardly did the rain stopped when the match began.
(c) Hardly had the rain stopped when the match began.
(d) Hardly had the rain stopped than the match began.

ANSWER KEY

1. Tenses
1. rolling
2. had seen
3. weeping
4. dreading
5. would leave
6. would see
7. keeping
8. knew

2. Prepositions
(a) with
(b) into
(c) for
(d) with (comply *with* = obey or follow rules, instructions, or requests)
(e) for
(f) to
(g) in
(h) to

3. Join the Sentences
1. (a)
2. (b)
3. (c)
4. (b)

4. Transformation of Sentences
1. (a)
2. (d)
3. (b)
4. (c)
5. (d)
6. (a)
7. (a)
8. (c)

ICSE TEST PAPER 20

Tenses:

1. **Fill in each of the numbered blanks with the correct form of the verb given in brackets.**

   That night, when Aksynonof ...(0) (lie) on his bed and just ...(1) begin) to doze, someone ...(2) (come) quietly and ...(3) (sit) down on his bed. He ...(4) (peer) through the darkness and ...(5) (recognise) Makar.

   "What more do you ...(6) (want) of, me? asked Aksyonof. "Why have you ...(7) (come) here?"

   "It was I who ...(8) (kill) the merchant."

Answer: (0) was lying

Prepositions:

2. **Fill in the blanks with the appropriate prepositions.**
   (a) Be prepared .... a test on Monday.
   (b) He managed to get .... the shock pretty soon.
   (c) An accident is holding .... traffic on MG Road.
   (d) The robbers are still .... large.
   (e) He broke .... hearing the bad news.
   (f) I am surprised that you fell .... that trick.
   (g) I will call .... my uncle when I am in Mumbai next.
   (h) Call me .... when you have time.

Join the Sentences:

3. **Choose the correct option to make one complete sentence without using *and, but or so.***
   1. He muttered something under his breath. I heard him.
      (a) He muttered something under his breath, for I heard him.
      (b) I heard something he muttered under his breath.
      (c) Because he muttered something under his breath, I heard him.
      (d) Though he muttered something under his breath, I heard him.
   2. He cooked lunch today. He cleaned the kitchen.
      (a) He cooked lunch today besides he cleaned the kitchen.
      (b) Since he cooked lunch today, yet he cleaned the kitchen.
      (c) Though he cooked lunch today, he cleaned the kitchen.
      (d) Besides cooking lunch today, he cleaned the kitchen.
   3. The man was running fast. The police caught him.
      (a) Although the man was running fast, the police caught him.
      (b) The police caught the man in spite he was running fast.
      (c) Despite his running fast, the man caught up with the police.
      (d) The man was running fast, although the police caught him.
   4. You helped Sonika. She will always be grateful.
      (a) Sonika will always be grateful for your help.
      (b) You helped Sonika since she will always be grateful.
      (c) Sonika will always be grateful for helping her.
      (d) You helped Sonika for always being grateful.

Transformation of Sentences:

4. **Choose the correct option and rewrite the sentence according to the instruction given after each.**
   1. Do not beat the dog. (Change into passive voice)
      (a) Let the dog be beaten.
      (b) Let the dog not beat you.
      (c) Let the dog not be beaten.
      (d) May you not beat the dog.
   2. We will always remember our leader. (Change to negative)
      (a) We will always never remember our leader.
      (b) We will never memorise our leader.
      (c) We will never forget our leader.
      (d) We will always not remember our leader.
   3. Roma says, "I am studying." (Change into indirect speech)
      (a) Roma said that she is studying.
      (b) Roma says that she is studying.
      (c) Roma says that she was studying.
      (d) Roma said that she was studying.
   4. The moment the chief guest hoisted the flag, we all saluted. (Begin with *Hardly*)
      (a) Hardly had the chief guest hoisted the flag when we all saluted.
      (b) Hardly had the chief guest hoist the flag when we all saluted.
      (c) Hardly had the chief guest hoisted the flag than we all saluted.
      (d) Hardly had the chief guest hoisted the flag immediately we all saluted.
   5. When he met Anita, he promised to give her a gift. (Use *assured*)
      (a) He promised to give an assured gift to Anita.
      (b) Meeting Anita, he gave an assured gift.

(c) He assured of giving a gift when he was meeting Anita.

(d) When he met Anita, he assured her of giving a gift.

6. The inspector said to me, "You are a bad driver." (Change into reported speech)

(a) The inspector told me that I was a bad driver.

(b) The inspector told me that you are a bad driver.

(c) The inspector said to me that I were a bad driver.

(d) The inspector told me that I am a bad driver.

7. We walked only one kilometre and they stopped us. (Begin with *Barely*)

(a) Barely we had walked one kilometre when they stopped us.

(b) Barely had we walked one kilometre when they stopped us.

(c) Barely had we walked one kilometre then they stopped us.

(d) Barely had we walked only one kilometre when they stopped us.

8. We must hurry or we will be late to catch the train. (Begin with *If*)

(a) If we do not hurry, we will be late to catch the train.

(b) If we hurry, we will be late to catch the train.

(c) If we do not hurry, we will not be late to catch the train.

(d) If we are late to catch the train, we must hurry.

ANSWER KEY

1. Tenses Answer key

1. began
2. came
3. sat
4. peered
5. recognised
6. want
7. come
8. killed

2. Prepositions

(a) for

(b) over (means to recover)

(c) up (means to create a traffic jam)

(d) at (means they still have not been caught or apprehended by the police)

(e) down (means he cried)

(f) for (means you got cheated)

(g) on (means to visit)

(h) up (means to make a phone call)

3. Join the Sentences

1. (b)
2. (d)
3. (a)
4. (a)

4. Transformation

1. (c)
2. (c)
3. (b)
4. (a)
5. (d)
6. (a)
7. (b)
8. (a)

ISC TEST PAPER 1

Tenses:

1. Fill in the blanks in the passage given below with the appropriate form of the verb given in the brackets.

The college friends .... (1) (plan) their annual trekking trip for months. They ..... (2) (decide) on a challenging trail in the Himalayas. The team leader, Arjun, ... (3) (make) sure that everyone ...... (4) (get) all the necessary gear. One evening, as they were discussing the route, their friend Maya, who was an experienced mountaineer, ... (5) (tell) them that the weather forecast .... (6) (predict) heavy snowfall for the coming week. She said, "You all must ..... (7) (be) very careful. I suggest you .... (8) (reconsider) your plan." But the others .... (9) (not/listen) to her and .... (10) (go) ahead with the trip.

Phrasal Verbs

2. Fill in the blanks with the correct phrasal verbs.

(a) The speaker had to break .... the complex topic for the audience.

(b) She tried to gloss .... her mistake during the presentation.

(c) The teacher told the noisy students to pipe .... during the lecture.

(d) The tech company rolled .... its new product with much fanfare.

(e) Despite the obstacles, the young entrepreneur pulled .... the deal successfully.

(f) The manager asked us to run .... the report one last time before printing.

(g) The minister called .... the reporters for spreading false news.

(h) She turned .... the job offer because it did not match her expectations.

(i) After months of planning, the scientists finally carried .... the complex experiment.

(j) The politician managed to get .... a difficult question by changing the topic.

Rewrite as Directed

3. Rewrite the following sentences according to the instructions given in the brackets.

(a) She sings better than anyone else in the class. (Begin with *No one*)

(b) People say that she writes beautiful poetry. (Change to passive voice)

(c) If you do not water the plants, they will die. (Begin with *Unless*)

(d) He seldom goes out on weekends. (Add a question tag)

(e) The sight of the mountains was amazing. (Rewrite as an exclamatory sentence)

ANSWER KEY

1. Tenses

1. had been planning
2. had decided
3. had made
4. got
5. told
6. was predicting/predicted (Both acceptable: Past continuous if the forecast is viewed as ongoing; Simple past if treated as a completed factual statement.)
7. be
8. reconsider
9. did not listen
10. went

Note:

- For (1) *had been planning* → a long action continuing before another past event ("for months").
- *were planning* → could work, but it only shows the action as ongoing in the past, not necessarily stretching over a long duration before the warning. That is why *had been planning* is more precise.

2. Phrasal Verbs

(a) down (*break down = simplify*)

(b) over (*gloss over = avoid or hide mistakes*)

(c) down (*pipe down = be quiet*)

(d) out (*roll out = launch or introduce*)

(e) off (*pull off = succeed against odds*)

(f) through (*run through = review/check*)

(g) out (*call out = openly criticise*)

(h) down (*turn down = reject*)

(i) out (*carry out = perform or execute a task*)

(j) around (*get around = avoid dealing with*)

3. Rewrite as Directed

(a) No one else in the class sings as well as she does.

(b) It is said that she writes beautiful poetry.

(c) Unless you water the plants, they will die.

(d) He seldom goes out on weekends, does he?

(e) What an amazing sight the mountains were!

ISC TEST PAPER 2

Tenses:

1. **Fill in the blanks in the passage given below with the appropriate form of the verb given in the brackets.**

   Some years ago, we had a forestry officer in this town who .... (1) (scoff) at things. He was ....(2) (send) by his department for some special work in Mempi Forest and he had his headquarters here. He had spent a couple of years abroad, and after ....(3) (return) home, he was full of contempt for all our practices. He was rational, which ....(4) (mean) that he ... (5) (believe) only in things he could ... (6) (touch) or ...(7) (see). God did not .... (8) (pass) any of these tests, at any rate, the God we .... (9) (believe) in. According to most of us, God .... (10) (reside) in the Anjaneya Temple.

Phrasal Verbs

2. **Replace the incorrect words in CAPITAL LETTERS to make the sentence meaningful and grammatically correct.**
   (a) The doctor is attending FOR the patient.
   (b) In the shot, the heroine was required to blush and look OUT.
   (c) These flowers are OFF no value.
   (d) The bright student fell DOWN in studies due to his illness.
   (e) Please put the chemical AWAY of reach of children.
   (f) Their relationship is WITHOUT repair.
   (g) Upon hearing the news, he broke IN tears.
   (h) The player acted WITH his coach's advice.
   (i) He has nothing but contempt OF politicians.
   (j) I hope he lives OFF to your expectations.

Rewrite as Directed

3. **Rewrite the following sentences according to the instructions given in the brackets.**
   (a) People who are homeless deserve our support. (Begin with *The*)
   (b) Everything is bright and beautiful. (Add a question tag)
   (c) Unless Giriraj clears his pending bills by Monday, he will have to vacate his hotel room. (Rewrite using "*...if he...*")
   (d) Baldev was stronger than any other wrestler. (Begin with *No other*)
   (e) In spite of being talented, he could not win the music competition. (Begin with *Notwithstanding*)

ANSWER KEY

1. **Tenses**
   1. scoffed
   2. sent
   3. returning
   4. meant
   5. believed
   6. touch
   7. see
   8. pass
   9. believed
   10. resides / resided

   Note:
   - "Resides" = simple present, showing a timeless fact.
   - "Resided" = simple past, if referring to belief at that time only. Both are acceptable depending on the interpretation.

2. **Phrasal Verbs**
   (a) to (*attend to = take care of*)
   (b) away (*look away = turn aside*; here "away" is the more natural choice, though "look down" could also work depending on context.)
   (c) of (*of no value = worthless*)
   (d) behind (*fall behind = not keep up with work/studies*)
   (e) out (*out of reach = inaccessible*)
   (f) beyond (*beyond repair = cannot be fixed*)
   (g) into (*broke into tears = began crying suddenly*)
   (h) on (*acted on = followed advice*)
   (i) for (*contempt for = dislike of*)
   (j) up (*live up to = meet expectations*)

3. **Rewrite as Directed**
   (a) The homeless people deserve our support.
   (b) Everything is bright and beautiful, isn't it?
   (c) Giriraj will have to vacate his hotel room if he does not clear his pending bills by Monday.
   (d) No other wrestler was as strong as Baldev.
   (e) Notwithstanding his talent, he could not win the music competition.

ISC TEST PAPER 3

Tenses:

1. **Fill in the blanks in the passage given below with the appropriate form of the verb given in the brackets.**

The next morning, Ruskin Bond, a cheerful author of several ghost stories, ... (1) (drop) in for breakfast. I .... (2) (tell) him about my weird encounter. He .... (3) (pale) and grew terribly excited. We ... (4) (decide) to meet Ranjit. We .... (5) (hop) over the boundary wall of the graveyard and could see Ranjit .... (6) (potter) around outside his hut. He saw us .... (7) (come) and burst into peals of laughter, his face .... (8) (cover) with the ashes of yesterday's fire. Suddenly, a piece of twisted metal ....(9) (catch) my eye. "Look," I said to Ruskin, "That's what he .... (10) (hold) in his hand last night."

Phrasal Verbs

2. **Replace the incorrect words in CAPITAL LETTERS to make the sentence meaningful and grammatically correct.**

(a) The Telangana CM is pulling UP illegal structures constructed on lake beds.

(b) He subscribes FOR the Marxist ideology.

(c) I pleaded AGAINST him to tell me the truth.

(d) The cost of the project is pegged FOR 200 crore rupees.

(e) He is flirting FROM the idea of running for the post of Mayor.

(f) The seawater has eaten DOWN the sandbank.

(g) His income comes UP one lakh rupees a week.

(h) May I confide WITH you?

(i) The smell of freshly baked cookies conjured OUT memories of my childhood holidays.

(j) The government is WITH pressure from the opposition on the issue.

Rewrite as Directed

3. **Rewrite the following sentences according to the instructions given in the brackets.**

(a) He will not pay his dues unless he is compelled. (Begin with *Only if*)

(b) If the examination is cancelled, I will let you know. (Begin with *Should*)

(c) Owing to ill luck, he met with an accident on the eve of his birthday. (Begin with *He was*)

(d) Ria is much more intelligent than her brother. (Begin with *Ria's brother*)

(e) The man said, "God is everywhere." (Rewrite in indirect speech)

ANSWER KEY

1. **Tenses**
   1. dropped
   2. told
   3. paled
   4. decided
   5. hopped
   6. pottering
   7. coming
   8. covered
   9. caught
   10. was holding

2. **Phrasal Verbs**

(a) down (*pull down = demolish*)

(b) to (*subscribe to = follow a belief/ideology*)

(c) with (*plead with = beg/entreat*)

(d) at (*pegged at = fixed/estimated at*)

(e) with (*flirt with an idea = toy with/consider it lightly*)

(f) away (*eat away = gradually erode/diminish*).

(g) to (*income comes to = amounts to*)

(h) in (*confide in = trust someone with a secret*)

(i) up (*conjure up = evoke memories/images*)

(j) under (*under pressure = being pressed by circumstances/people*)

3. **Rewrite as Directed**

(a) Only if he is compelled will he pay his dues.

(b) Should the examination be cancelled, I will let you know.

(c) He was unlucky to have met with an accident on the eve of his birthday.

(d) Ria's brother is not as intelligent as she is.

(e) The man said that God is everywhere.

ISC TEST PAPER 4

Tenses:

1. Fill in the blanks in the passage given below with the appropriate form of the verb given in the brackets.

When I .... (1) (go) into a bank, I get rattled. The sight of the money .... (2) (rattle) me. The moment I .... (3) (cross) the threshold of a bank and attempt .... (4) (transact) business there, I .... (5) (become) an irresponsible idiot.

I shambled in and .... (6) (look) timidly round at the clerks. I had an idea that a person about .... (7) (open) an account must .... (8) (consult) the manager.

"Can I see the manager?" I said, and ... (9) (add) solemnly, "alone".

"Certainly" said the accountant, and .... (10) (fetch) him.

Phrasal Verbs

2. Fill in the blanks

(a) Do you have an interest .... music?

(b) Do you have an aptitude .... music?

(c) The baby has grown .... of the habit of thumb sucking.

(d) The experiments on butterflies were carried .... at this lab in Mysuru.

(e) Once he took the painkiller, he was relieved .... the pain.

(f) She has to atone .... her misdeeds.

(g) The family has set out .... a pilgrimage.

(h) Hard work is the key .... success.

(i) Her services were dispensed .... by the company.

(j) The police are .... the case.

Rewrite as Directed

3. Rewrite the following sentences according to the instructions given in the brackets.

(a) As soon as Bharat entered the classroom, his teacher asked him for an explanation. (Begin with *Hardly*)

(b) I study both architecture and statistics. (Begin with *Not only*)

(c) The doctor has not been to the hospital for over a month. (Begin with *It has*)

(d) She was too tired for one more exam. (Begin with *She was so*)

(e) He was so weak that he could not climb the stairs. (Use *...enough...*)

ANSWER KEY

1. Tenses

1. go
2. rattles
3. cross
4. to transact
5. become
6. looked
7. to open
8. consult
9. added
10. fetched

2. Phrasal Verbs

(a) in (*interest in = liking or concern about*)

(b) for (*aptitude for* = natural ability/talent)

(c) out (*grow out of = stop a habit as one matures*)

(d) out (*carry out = perform, conduct*)

(e) of (*relieved of = freed from, rid of*)

(f) for (*atone for = make amends*)

(g) on (*set out on = begin a journey*)

(h) to (*key to = essential element leading to*)

(i) with (*dispense with = do away with, no longer need*)

(j) on (*on the case = actively investigating or handling a matter*)

3. Rewrite as Directed

(a) Hardly had Bharat entered the classroom when his teacher asked him for an explanation.

(b) Not only do I study architecture, but I also study statistics.

(c) It has been over a month since the doctor went to the hospital.

(d) She was so tired that she could not take one more exam.

(e) He was not strong enough to climb the stairs.

ISC TEST PAPER 5

Tenses:

1. **Fill in the blanks in the passage given below with the appropriate form of the verb given in the brackets.**

   Athletics in India has become synonymous with PT Usha. .....(1) (bear) in a poor family, this Kerala girl .....(2) (show) her rare talent in the sub-junior championships. She .....(3) (declare) the individual champion. The man who ....(4) (shape) the raw material into a glittering diamond was her coach, Madhavan Nambiar. His guidance and coaching .....(5) (transform) her into a great athlete. PT Usha showed her athletic prowess at the Asian Games, New Delhi in 1982, where she ....(6) (win) two silver medals. However, the Asian Games in Seoul in 1986 ....(7) (give) her rare international recognition and fame. She ....(8) (bag) four gold medals and her glorious records ....(9) (remain) unbroken by any Indian Athlete so far. Recently, Usha .....(10) (appoint) the President of the Indian Olympic Association.

Phrasal Verbs

2. **Replace the incorrect words in CAPITAL LETTERS to make the sentence meaningful and grammatically correct.**

   (a) This lawyer deals exclusively ON divorce cases.

   (b) I hope you sort UP the misunderstanding.

   (c) His objections to the project were brushed OFF by the Chairman.

   (d) The hospital room smelled WITH antiseptics and medicines.

   (e) After the failure of the mission, the biologists went back WITH the drawing board.

   (f) The actor entered WITH an agreement with the producer.

   (g) The dam official is snowed WITH by reports from over 100 engineers.

   (h) The robbers had walked OVER a trap.

   (i) I will give OFF engineering and focus on cricket instead.

   (j) Raman was mocked ON by everyone.

Rewrite as Directed

3. **Rewrite the following sentences according to the instructions given in the brackets.**

   (a) Both of my brothers are not interested in joining the family business. (Begin with *Neither*)

   (b) If there was no air, we would have died. (Begin with *But for*)

   (c) It looks as if Laxman has gone to the wrong doctor. (Begin with *Laxman seems*)

   (d) He says to me, "I am nervous." (Rewrite in indirect speech)

   (e) My uncle returned home one month ago. (Begin with *It has been*)

ANSWER KEY

1. **Tenses**
   1. born (past participle of *bear)*
   2. showed
   3. was declared
   4. shaped
   5. transformed
   6. won
   7. gave
   8. bagged
   9. remain
   10. was appointed

2. **Phrasal Verbs**

   (a) in / with (*deal in / deal with = to handle or specialise in something*)

   (b) out (*sort out = resolve*)

   (c) aside / away (*brush aside / brush away = dismiss or ignore*)

   (d) of (*smelled of = had the odour of*)

   (e) to (*go back to the drawing board = start over and rethink a plan*)

   (f) into (*enter into = to make or form an agreement*)

   (g) under (*snowed under = overwhelmed with too much work*)

   (h) into (*walked into = got caught in something unexpectedly, often a trap*)

   (i) up (*give up = quit, stop doing something*)

   (j) at (*mocked at = ridiculed or made fun of*)

3. **Rewrite as Directed**

   (a) Neither of my brothers is interested in joining the family business.

   (b) But for air, we would have died.

   (c) Laxman seems to have gone to the wrong doctor.

   (d) He tells me that he is nervous.

   (e) It has been one month since my uncle returned home.

ISC TEST PAPER 6

Tenses:

1. **Fill in the blanks in the passage given below with the appropriate form of the verb given in the brackets.**

   It is hard to ....(1) (say) how Kadambini .... (2) (reach) Ranihat. At first she .... (3) (show) herself to no one, but .... (4) (spend) the whole day in a .... (5) (ruin) temple, ... (6) (starve). When people .... (7) (huddle) into their houses for fear of the impending storm, then Kadambini ... (8) (come) forth. Her heart .... (9) (tremble) as she reached her father-in-law's house and .... (10) (draw) a veil over her face, entered.

Phrasal Verbs

2. **Replace the incorrect words in CAPITAL LETTERS to make the sentence meaningful and grammatically correct.**
   (a) The Prime Minister dashed OUT a letter to the President.
   (b) Her father did not approve OFF Mona's pictures on Instagram.
   (c) Students are expected to be acquainted IN coding if they are pursuing computer engineering.
   (d) Since you are unwell, shall I send IN the doctor?
   (e) Your hostel bill for the month has come FOR Rs 9500.
   (f) The journalist has dug OFF some hidden facts about the pharma company.
   (g) Relatives are not allowed to barge TO the ICU when the patient is being attended to.
   (h) The senior students were told not to pick UP their juniors.
   (i) My computer is acting UPON again.
   (j) It never dawned AT me that my manager was lying.

Rewrite as Directed

3. **Rewrite the following sentences according to the instructions given in the brackets.**
   (a) The Metro rail service has been interrupted by a workers' strike. (Begin with *A workers' strike*)
   (b) The farmers work hard. (Add a question tag)
   (c) As soon as I reach my office, I will inform your parents. (Begin with *No sooner*)
   (d) It looks as if Tuhina has gone to the wrong shop. (Begin with *Tuhina seems)*
   (e) As soon as Geeta saw the snake, she shrieked. (Begin with *On*)

ANSWER KEY

1. **Tenses**
   1. say
   2. reached
   3. showed
   4. spent
   5. ruined
   6. starving
   7. huddled
   8. came
   9. trembled
   10. drawing
2. **Phrasal Verbs**
   (a) off (*dashed off = wrote quickly*)
   (b) of (*approve of = accept / agree with*)
   (c) with (*acquainted with = familiar with*)
   (d) for (*send for = summon / call*)
   (e) to (*come to = amount to*)
   (f) up (*dug up = uncovered / revealed*)
   (g) into (*barge into = enter rudely / forcefully*)
   (h) on (*pick on = bully / harass*)
   (i) up (*acting up = malfunctioning / misbehaving*)
   (j) on (*dawned on = realised / became clear to*)
3. **Rewrite as Directed**
   (a) A workers' strike has interrupted the Metro rail service.
   (b) The farmers work hard, don't they?
   (c) No sooner do I reach my office than I will inform your parents.
   (d) Tuhina seems to have gone to the wrong shop.
   (e) On seeing the snake, Geeta shrieked.

ISC TEST PAPER 7

Tenses:

1. Fill in the blanks in the passage given below with the appropriate form of the verb given in the brackets.

It was a terribly hot afternoon in July, some fifty years ago, in Upper Sind. In the Deccan, cooling showers .... (1) (turn) the hard earth, ...(2) (bake) by the summer winds, into a perfect paradise. The hills rose emerald to the sky, although their summits were often ....(3) (veil) by the monsoon mists and delightful breezes .... (4) (sweep) over the glad earth. In the middle of this region is Sehwan, formerly an important town, but now greatly ....(5) (sink) in importance. One thing it still .... (6) (claim) with justice is that it is one of the hottest places on earth. The train ....(7) (steam) slowly into Sehwan station. The railway on the left bank of the Indus has not been then ... (8) (build), so the railtrack .... (9) (pass) through Sehwan on its way to Karachi. The last carriage of the traffic superintendent was roomier and .... (10) (befit) the quarters of the senior railway official.

Phrasal Verbs

2. Replace the incorrect words in CAPITAL LETTERS to make the sentence meaningful and grammatically correct.

(a) Finish the project BEYOND two days.

(b) Sales of bread have gone FAR this winter.

(c) The police inspector made UPTO the thief and caught him.

(d) Prime Minister Modi has decided to auction FOR the gifts he received to raise funds for Project Namami Ganga.

(e) You are a fool to turn ASIDE such a good job offer.

(f) This was one complication he had not bargained ON.

(g) Will you put UP a word for me?

(h) Why do you keep harping AT the same depressing topic?

(i) After he was found guilty, he was debarred FOR legal practice for two years.

(j) The bicycle can be folded and tucked OFF in a suitcase.

Rewrite as Directed

3. Rewrite the following sentences according to the instructions given in the brackets.

(a) If I don't leave now, I will miss the flight. (Begin with *Unless*)

(b) Only his friends stood by him. (Begin with *None*)

(c) If the weather is humid tomorrow, the pitch will assist the fast bowlers. (Begin with *If the weather is not*)

(d) Anand must not lose his focus, or he will lose the chess match. (Begin with *In the event*)

(e) There is no hope here. (Add a question tag)

ANSWER KEY

1. Tenses

1. had turned
2. baked
3. veiled
4. swept
5. sunk
6. claims
7. steamed
8. built
9. passed
10. befitted

2. Phrasal Verbs

(a) in / within (*finish in/within = complete inside a time limit*)

(b) up / down (*gone up/down = increased/decreased*)

(c) after (*made after = pursued/chased*)

(d) off (*auction off = sell by auction*)

(e) down (*turn down = reject*)

(f) for (*bargained for = expected*)

(g) in (*put in = recommend/mention*)

(h) on (*harping on = talking repeatedly about*)

(i) from (*debarred from = legally prevented*)

(j) away (*tucked away = stored neatly/out of sight*)

3. **Rewrite as Directed**

(a) Unless I leave now, I will miss the flight.

(b) None but his friends stood by him.

(c) If the weather is not humid tomorrow, the pitch will not assist the fast bowlers.

(d) In the event of losing his focus, Anand will lose the chess match.

(e) There is no hope here, is there?

ISC TEST PAPER 8

Tenses:

1. **Fill in the blanks in the passage given below with the appropriate form of the verb given in the brackets.**

The Macphails, condemned .... (1) (spend) a fortnight of idleness at Pago Pago, ... (2) (go) down to the quay and ... (3) (get) out of their boxes a number of books. The doctor ... (4) (call) on the chief surgeon of the naval hospital and ... (5) (go) round the beds with him. They .... (6) (leave) cards for the governor. They ... (7) (pass) Miss Thompson on the road. The doctor ... (8) (take) off his hat, and she .... (9) (give) him a "Good Morning, Doc" greeting in a cheerful voice. She .... (10) (dress) in a white frock and shiny white boots.

Phrasal Verbs

2. **Replace the incorrect words in CAPITAL LETTERS to make the sentence meaningful and grammatically correct.**

(a) The tiger seised the lamb and made THROUGH with it into the thicket.

(b) He hurried to make up TO the time he had lost.

(c) Holidays are drawing UP.

(d) There are many rumours floating FROM her.

(e) As the night drew UP, the three friends quickened their pace.

(f) Did you bring it FOR the Principal's notice?

(g) Someone has made an attempt FOR his life.

(h) They made no attempt IN escape from there.

(i) Chetan Bhagat will bring IN his novel next summer.

(j) The matter was brought IN at the meeting of the Council.

Rewrite as Directed

3. **Rewrite the following sentences according to the instructions given in the brackets.**

(a) Raj is as tall as Vikram. (Begin with *Vikram is not*)

(b) An insect bit his pet dog in the park. (Use *bitten*)

(c) If you come to my house, I can show you beautiful rose plants. (Begin with *Unless*)

(d) The termites did not survive the pest control. (Add a question tag)

(e) He was pleased with the results. (Change into Exclamatory)

ANSWER KEY

1. **Tenses**
   1. to spend
   2. went
   3. got
   4. called
   5. went
   6. left
   7. passed
   8. took
   9. gave
   10. was dressed

2. **Phrasal Verbs**

(a) off (*make off = leave/escape hurriedly*)

(b) for (*make up for = compensate for*)

(c) near (*raw near = approach*)

(d) about (*float about = circulate/spread*)

(e) in (*draw in = become darker/earlier nightfall*)

(f) to (*bring to = bring to someone's notice*)

(g) on (*make an attempt on = try to harm/kill*)

(h) to (*make an attempt to = try/endeavour*)

(i) out (*bring out = publish/release*)

(j) up (*bring up = raise/mention a matter*)

3. **Rewrite as Directed**

(a) Vikram is not taller than Raj.

(b) His pet dog was bitten by an insect in the park. (*Bit* is the past tense of *bite*. *Bitten* is the past participle of *bite*. It is used along with auxiliary verbs like *was, has, have*.)

(c) Unless you come to my house, I cannot show you beautiful rose plants.

(d) The termites did not survive the pest control, did they?

(e) How pleased he was with the results!

ISC TEST PAPER 9

Tenses:

1. **Fill in the blanks in the passage given below with the appropriate form of the verb given in the brackets.**

   Ivan Dmitritch, who .... (1) (live) with his family on an income of twelve hundred a year and was very .... (2) (satisfy) with his lot, ... (3) (sit) down on the sofa after supper and .... (4) (begin) reading the newspaper.

   "I .... (5) (forget) to look at the newspaper today," his wife said to him as she .... (6) (clear) the table.

   .... (7) (look) at his wife, Dmitritch .... (8) (give) a broad smile, like when a baby .... (9) (show) a bright object. His wife .... (10) (smile) too.

Phrasal Verbs

2. **Replace the incorrect words in CAPITAL LETTERS to make the sentence meaningful and grammatically correct.**
   (a) The Army was forging ON along the road.
   (b) He takes OUT more work than is good for him.
   (c) The stand-up comedian waited till the laughter died UP.
   (d) After some discussion, he came DOWN to my views.
   (e) The students requested the teacher to elaborate FORTH the topic.
   (f) The city has embarked WITH an ambitious programme of reform.
   (g) The enemy country spied OVER the defence ministry official for over two years.
   (h) The postman sifts AROUND 1000 letters every day.
   (i) All the guests turned OUT on time.
   (j) The truth dawned AT him.

Rewrite as Directed

3. **Rewrite the following sentences according to the instructions given in the brackets.**
   (a) As soon as I spot him, I will return the money. (Begin with *No sooner*)
   (b) It is most probable that Navin will come to India this summer. (Use *probability*)
   (c) There are eleven players in a hockey team. (Begin with *A hockey team comprises*)
   (d) All of us can convince him. (Add a question tag)
   (e) Who can question the Mayor's honesty? (Begin with *By whom*)

ANSWER KEY

1. **Tenses**
   1. lived
   2. satisfied
   3. sat
   4. began
   5. forgot
   6. cleared
   7. Looking
   8. gave
   9. is shown
   10. smiled

2. **Phrasal Verbs**
   (a) ahead (*forge ahead = move forward steadily / strongly*)
   (b) on (*take on = accept responsibility / work*)
   (c) down (*die down = become less strong*)
   (d) around or round (*come around = change opinion / agree eventually*)
   (e) on / upon (*elaborate on = explain in detail*)
   (f) on / upon (*embark on = begin a project / journey*)
   (g) on (*spy on = watch secretly*)
   (h) through (*sift through = examine carefully*)
   (i) up (*turn up = arrive / appear*)
   (j) upon (*dawn upon = become clear to someone / realise suddenly*)

3. **Rewrite as Directed**
   (a) No sooner do I spot him than I will return the money.
   (b) In all probability, Navin will come to India this summer.
   (c) A hockey team comprises eleven players.
   (d) All of us can convince him, can't we?
   (e) By whom can the Mayor's honesty be questioned?

ISC TEST PAPER 10

Tenses:

1. **Fill in the blanks in the passage given below with the appropriate form of the verb given in the brackets.**

One day, Emperor Akbar and his minister Birbal .....(1) (take) a stroll in the garden. Akbar said, "Birbal, I want to honour all the lazy people in my kingdom. However, I am afraid it ....(2) (go) to be a difficult task." Birbal said, "Let's ....(3) (find) out the lazy ones, your majesty." Soon a messenger went round .....(4) (announce) that all the lazy people in the kingdom should gather near the palace gate the next day. The king wanted to honour them. A very big special pandal ....(5) (erect). Very soon there .... (6) (assemble) a huge crowd at the palace gate. Birbal said to himself, "All these people cannot be really lazy." He asked all of them .... (7) (sit) in the pandal. A few minutes later, the pandal was set on fire. All the people ..... (8) (start) running for their lives. Soon the pandal was almost empty. Birbal went near the pandal and ....(9) (find) two men sitting in a corner, unconcerned about the fire. Birbal said to Akbar, "Your Majesty, these are the ones who are really lazy. You should honour them." Akbar .... (10) (honour) them with good food and clothing and money.

Phrasal Verbs

2. **Replace the incorrect words in capital letters to make the sentence meaningful and grammatically correct.**

(a) Money had been siphoned OUT from the firm for illegal purposes.

(b) Look at how the women are checking her UP.

(c) It is so hot as the temperatures have shot DOWN abnormally this summer.

(d) The event began FROM the national anthem.

(e) I had been told not to allude UP the topic in the presence of the Principal.

(f) The new singer was singled UP for attention at the event.

(g) The director was known to depart TO the written script when he was on location.

(h) The restaurant has brought UP a new manager to improve its sales.

(i) The Centre is being requested to write DOWN debts from backward states.

(j) The sun was beating OUT on the fields.

Rewrite as Directed

3. **Rewrite the following sentences according to the instructions given in the brackets.**

(a) If I had known what to expect earlier, I would have fared better. (Begin with *Had I*)

(b) As soon as you top the class, your classmates will stop humiliating you. (Begin with *No sooner*)

(c) This minister is corrupt, and we can prove it. (Begin with *We can prove*)

(d) Even though Rohini tried to open the door several times, she did not succeed. (Begin with *In spite*)

(e) Pranab worked at the supermarket and studied Statistics at the University. (Begin with *Not only*)

ANSWER KEY

1. **Tenses**
   1. were taking
   2. is going
   3. find
   4. announcing
   5. was erected
   6. assembled
   7. to sit
   8. started
   9. found
   10. honoured

2. **Phrasal Verbs**

(a) off (*siphon off = remove illegally*)

(b) out (*check up on = investigate, keep an eye on*)

(c) up (*shoot up = increase suddenly*)

(d) with (*shoot up = increase suddenly*)

(e) to (*allude to = refer indirectly*)

(f) out (*single out = choose someone specifically*)

(g) from (*depart from = deviate from*)

(h) in (*bring in = appoint, introduce*)

(i) off (*write off = treat as a loss or failure*)

(j) down (*beat down = strike strongly, shine harshly*)

3. **Rewrite as Directed**

(a) Had I known what to expect earlier, I would have fared better.

(b) No sooner do you top the class than your classmates will stop humiliating you.

(c) We can prove that this minister is corrupt.

(d) In spite of trying to open the door several times, Rohini did not succeed.

(e) Not only did Pranab work at the supermarket, but he also studied statistics at the University.

ISC TEST PAPER 11

Tenses:

1. **Fill in the blanks in the passage given below with the appropriate form of the verb given in the brackets.**

   One morning, as he was on his way to Holland Park, where the Mertons .... (1) (live), he .... (2) (drop) in to see a great friend of his, Alan Trevor. Trevor was a painter. But he .... (3) (be) also an artist, and artists are rather rare. When he .... (4) (take) up the brush, he was a real master and his pictures were eagerly .... (5) (seek) after. When Hughie .... (6) (come) in, he .... (7) (find) Trevor .... (8) (put) the finishing touches to a wonderful life-size picture of a beggar-man. The beggar himself was standing on a raised platform with a piteous expression. Over his shoulders was .... (9) (fling) a coarse brown cloak; his thick boots were .... (10) (patch).

Phrasal Verbs

2. **Replace the incorrect words in CAPITAL LETTERS to make the sentence meaningful and grammatically correct.**
   (a) He gambled heavily IN the horses.
   (b) These paintings date ABACK to the 14th century.
   (c) Can you please expand WITH your thought?
   (d) He dug UP his pocket to take out money.
   (e) Please don't say that these books are WITH no value.
   (f) The new President is endowed IN great leadership qualities.
   (g) Please see FOR it that this work is done immediately.
   (h) Working overtime every day will tell TO his health.
   (i) It is better to stick ON what you know.
   (j) Her father clearly disapproved ABOUT Mansi's choice of friends.

Rewrite as Directed

3. **Rewrite the following sentences according to the instructions given in the brackets.**
   (a) The porter found the suitcase too heavy to lift with one hand. (Rewrite using *So...that*)
   (b) "Mrunmayee visited a car museum last Saturday," said Tanieeshka. (Change into indirect speech)
   (c) If you do not drink milk, your teeth will not become strong. (Begin with *Only if*)
   (d) The scissors just grazed Mangala's hand, and her hand started bleeding. (Begin with *Barely*)
   (e) Very few restaurants in the city are as large as the Residency. (Rewrite using *largest*)

ANSWER KEY

1. **Tenses**
   1. lived
   2. dropped
   3. was
   4. took
   5. sought
   6. came
   7. found
   8. putting
   9. flung
   10. patched

2. **Phrasal Verbs**
   (a) on (gamble on = bet on)
   (b) back (date back to = originate from a time)
   (c) on (expand on = elaborate)
   (d) into (dig into (one's) pocket = reach in for money)
   (e) of (of no value = worthless)
   (f) with (endowed with = possessing)
   (g) to (see to (it) = ensure)
   (h) on (tell on = adversely affect)
   (i) to (stick to = adhere to)
   (j) of (disapprove of = not approve)

3. **Rewrite as Directed**
   (a) The porter found the suitcase so heavy that he could not lift it with one hand.
   (b) Tanieeshka said that Mrunmayee had visited a car museum the previous Saturday.
   (c) Only if you drink milk will your teeth become strong.
   (d) Barely had the scissors grazed Mangala's hand when her hand started bleeding. (**Note:** 'Barely did' is incorrect because after negative-adverbials (Barely/Hardly/Scarcely), standard usage is inversion with past perfect.
   (e) The Residency is one of the largest restaurants in the city.

ISC TEST PAPER 12

Tenses:

1. Fill in the blanks in the passage given below with the appropriate form of the verb given in the brackets.

Indian cities must ... (1) (aspire) to be world-class and .... (2) (compete) internationally to attract talent and investments. Most Indian cities do not .... (3) (make) the cut. Before the Aga Khan Trust for Culture .... (4) (take) over the work .... (5) (restore) a necropolis that rulers of the Qutb Shahi dynasty created .... (6) (serve) as their last .... (7) (rest) place, Hyderabad .... (8) (know) only of a handful of tombs and monuments which .... (9) (visit) by local people. Now close to 100 monuments .... (10) (identify).

Phrasal Verbs

2. Replace the incorrect words in CAPITAL LETTERS to make the sentence meaningful and grammatically correct.

(a) Despite the challenges, her determination shone OUT in every project she tackled.
(b) The daughter sided FOR her father.
(c) We are well FROM the deadline.
(d) He had to fork UP a fine of ₹500 for speeding.
(e) I took the bag and emptied it OFF on the bed.
(f) On the fourth day of the Test match, India dictated terms ON Australia.
(g) The police decided not to file a case and let him IN with a warning.
(h) We allowed him to calm UP before starting the discussion again.
(i) He had shaved UP his beard.
(j) She saw him OVER at the railway station.

Rewrite as Directed

3. Rewrite the following sentences according to the instructions given in the brackets.

(a) The captain informed us that the tournament had been postponed the previous year. (Rewrite in direct speech)
(b) If Sarvesh had not given me food and water, I would have collapsed. (Begin with *But*)
(c) My room is too small to accommodate all my friends. (Begin with *My room is not*)
(d) Both the suggestions made by him were not accepted. (Use *Neither*)
(e) He ventured into the jungle despite a warning from his friends. (Begin with *Notwithstanding*)

ANSWER KEY

1. Tenses

1. aspire
2. compete
3. make
4. took
5. to restore
6. to serve
7. resting
8. knew
9. were visited
10. have been identified

2. Phrasal Verbs

(a) through (shone through = become visible / clearly noticeable)
(b) with (side with = support especially in a disagreement or argument)
(c) past (well past = beyond a point in time / deadline)
(d) out (fork out = pay reluctantly | *shell out* means the same)
(e) out (empty out = remove the contents)
(f) to (dictate to = control / dominate the situation)
(g) off (let off = excuse without serious punishment)
(h) down (calm down = become less angry / agitated)
(i) off (shave off = remove facial hair)
(j) off (see off = say goodbye to someone leaving)

3. Rewrite as Directed

(a) The captain informed, "The tournament was postponed last year."
(b) But for Sarvesh giving me food and water, I would have collapsed.
(c) My room is not large enough to accommodate all my friends.
(d) Neither of the suggestions made by him was accepted.
(e) Notwithstanding a warning from his friends, he ventured into the jungle.

ISC TEST PAPER 13

Tenses:

1. Fill in the blanks in the passage given below with the appropriate form of the verb given in the brackets.

A shoemaker .... (1) (name) Simon, lived with his wife and children in a peasant's hut, and ... (2) (earn) his living by his work. What he earned, he ... (3) (spend) on food. Before winter, Simon ... (4) (save) up a little money: a three-rouble note lay .... (5) (hid) in his wife's box and five roubles .... (6) (owe) to him by customers in the village.

So, one morning, he .... (7) (prepare) to go to the village to buy sheepskins. "On the way, I .... (8) (collect) the five roubles that are due to me. That will be enough ... (9) (buy) the sheepskins," he .... (10) (think).

Phrasal Verbs

2. Replace the incorrect words in CAPITAL LETTERS to make the sentence meaningful and grammatically correct.

(a) You need to check TO the hotel by 1 pm.

(b) I have invited the neighbours IN on Saturday.

(c) I could see a dim glow of light emanating IN the room.

(d) The mechanic is tinkering IN the engine of the car.

(e) The forest staff managed to hunt OUT the man-eater leopard.

(f) I do not know why he is always itching WITH a fight.

(g) It seems the country is heading FOR an economic recession.

(h) He wanted to join the Army, but his mother was set FOR the idea.

(i) I blurted AWAY that my nephew had secured a job.

(j) His collar was biting ON his neck.

Rewrite as Directed

3. Rewrite the following sentences according to the instructions given in the brackets.

(a) No sooner did I see the movie than I became rather inspired. (Begin with *As soon as*)

(b) Gautam Roy hosted a dinner last weekend. (Rewrite in passive voice)

(c) Ravinder could not take the exam as his throat infection was very bad. (Use *So*)

(d) Rajeev asked the station master if he could buy the ticket on board the train. (Rewrite in direct speech)

(e) I could not but feel sorry for his plight. (Begin with *I could not help*)

ANSWER KEY

1. Tenses

1. named
2. earned
3. spent
4. saved
5. hidden
6. were owed
7. prepared
8. will collect
9. to buy
10. thought

2. Phrasal Verbs

(a) into (check into = register at a hotel)

(b) over (invite over = ask someone to visit one's home)

(c) from (emanate from = originate from)

(d) with (tinker with = attempt to repair in a casual way)

(e) down (hunt down = track and capture/kill)

(f) for (itching for = eager/to desire strongly)

(g) into (head into = move towards / begin to experience)

(h) against (set against = firmly opposed to)

(i) out (blurt out = say suddenly without thinking)

(j) into (bite into = press into firmly)

3. Rewrite as Directed

(a) As soon as I saw the movie, I became rather inspired.

(b) A dinner was hosted by Gautam Roy last weekend.

(c) Ravinder's throat infection was so bad that he could not take the exam.

(d) Rajeev asked the station master, "Can I buy the ticket on board the train?"

(e) I could not help feeling sorry for his plight.

ISC TEST PAPER 14

Tenses:

1. **Fill in the blanks in the passage given below with the appropriate form of the verb given in the brackets.**

Herman trembled like a leaf as the .... (1) (appoint) hour .... (2) (draw) near. He .... (3) (obey) instructions fully, and .... (4) (reach) the old lady's bedchamber without difficulty. Instead of .... (5) (go) out of the small door behind the screen, however, he .... (6) (conceal) himself in a closet to await the return of the Old Countess.

The hours .... (7) (drag) slowly by. At last, he .... (8) (hear) the sound of wheels. Immediately, lamps .... (9) (light) by the servants. Finally, the old woman .... (10) (totter) into the room, completely exhausted.

Phrasal Verbs

2. **Replace the incorrect words in CAPITAL LETTERS to make the sentence meaningful and grammatically correct.**

(a) The Coldplay concert tickets have been sold OFF.

(b) The hospital is equipped to deal IN any kind of emergency.

(c) The new chief is averse FROM even positive criticism.

(d) The organisers had expected only 500 people but over a thousand showed IN.

(e) The ruling party was voted out FROM office.

(f) I would not put this WITH her as she is a liar.

(g) The doting grandmother is blind FROM Madhav's faults.

(h) Afraid of bungee jumping, he chickened OFF at the last minute.

(i) He decided to dabble WITH politics after he retired from the IAS.

(j) The manager sent OUT his resignation.

Rewrite as Directed

3. **Rewrite the following sentences according to the instructions given in the brackets.**

(a) He said, "I have planned to leave for Washington tonight." (Rewrite in reported speech)

(b) He said, "May you live long!" (Rewrite in reported speech)

(c) Though he has a busy schedule, he always finds time for his parents. (Begin with *Notwithstanding*)

(d) All the boys and girls were given a medal. (Rewrite using *Every boy and every girl*)

(e) The sage said, "God is in every man's heart." (Rewrite in reported speech)

ANSWER KEY

1. **Tenses**

1. appointed
2. drew
3. obeyed
4. reached
5. going
6. concealed
7. dragged
8. heard
9. were lighted/were lit
10. tottered

2. **Phrasal Verbs**

(a) out (sold out = none left for sale)

(b) with (deal with = handle)

(c) to (averse to = opposed to)

(d) up (showed up = arrived)

(e) out of (voted out of office = removed from political power)

(f) past (not put past someone = believe them capable of something bad)

(g) to (blind to = unable to see or unwilling to acknowledge)

(h) out (chickened out = decided not to do due to fear)

(i) in (dabble in = try without serious commitment)

(j) in (sent in = submitted formally)

3. **Rewrite as Directed**

(a) He said that he had planned to leave for Washington that night.

(b) He wished that he might live long.

(c) Notwithstanding his busy schedule, he always finds time for his parents.

(d) Every boy and every girl was given a medal.
(Note: When two nouns are qualified by 'every' or 'each, even when connected by 'and', they take a singular verb.)

(e) The man said that God is in every man's heart.

ISC TEST PAPER 15

Tenses:

1. **Fill in the blanks in the passage given below with the appropriate form of the verb given in the brackets.**

I cannot .... (1) (leave) Meerut without .... (2) (take) the reader to the churchyard of that station. An Indian churchyard .... (3) (present) a very different aspect to a churchyard in England. When first erected, they are generally of plaster which somewhat .... (4) (resemble) Roman cement, but after exposure to only one rainy season, they .... (5) (become) begrimed and black. The birds, ... (6) (fly) from structure to structure, ... (7) (carry) with them the seeds of various plants and herbs, and these if not speedily .... (8) (remove), take root. A stranger .... (9) (wander) in the churchyard of Meerut might not know that I .... (10) (guide) through it by an old pensioner.

Phrasal Verbs

2. **Replace the incorrect words in CAPITAL LETTERS to make the sentence meaningful and grammatically correct.**

(a) I grew up WITH mythological stories.

(b) For illegal practice, the doctor's name can be struck FROM the rolls.

(c) She took out most of her unhappiness AT her husband.

(d) It is better to tear UP old buildings if they cannot be renovated.

(e) You have given me a lot of interesting ideas to chew UP.

(f) I decided to carry UP with the job despite the difficult circumstances.

(g) He was found to be lax WITH his duties.

(h) It is good manners to be sensitive OF other people's feelings.

(i) It was rude OFF him to scream at the elders in public.

(j) The work pressure is beginning to tell IN his health.

Rewrite as Directed

3. **Rewrite the following sentences according to the instructions given in the brackets.**

(a) Jane gave me a present on my last birthday. (rewrite in passive voice)

(b) You feel tired now because you did not sleep well last night. (Begin with *Had you*)

(c) She entered the room. Her son ran to her. (Begin with *Hardly*)

(d) As my father grew older, his handwriting became shakier. (Begin with *The older*)

(e) You are entitled to a discount as long as the offer lasts. (Begin with *So long*)

ANSWER KEY

1. **Tenses**
   1. leave
   2. taking
   3. presents
   4. resembles
   5. become
   6. flying
   7. carry
   8. removed
   9. wandering
   10. was guided

2. **Phrasal Verbs**

(a) on (grow up on = spent childhood being influenced by)

(b) off (struck off =name removed from official register)

(c) on (take it out on = express anger towards)

(d) down (tear down = demolish)

(e) on (chew on = think about carefully)

(f) on (carry on with = continue doing)

(g) in (lax in = careless in duties)

(h) to (sensitive to = aware of others' feelings)

(i) of (rude of someone = improper behaviour)

(j) on (tell on = affect health or condition negatively)

3. **Rewrite as Directed**

(a) I was given a present by Jane on my last birthday.

(b) Had you slept well last night, you would not feel tired now.

(c) Hardly had she entered the room when her son ran to her.

(d) The older my father grew, the shakier his handwriting became.

(e) So long as the offer lasts, you are entitled to a discount.

ISC TEST PAPER 16

Tenses:

1. Fill in the blanks in the passage given below with the appropriate form of the verb given in the brackets.

By .....(1) (walk) out to the first shallow pool that .... (2) (lie) at the foot of the western hill, I could wade across, ... (3) (turn) the flank of the crater, and .... (4) (make) my way inland. Without a moment's hesitation, I .... (5) (march) briskly past the tussocks where Gunga Dass .... (6) (snare) the crows. My first step from the tufts of dried grass .... (7) (show) me how utterly futile was any hope of escape. As I .... (8) (put) my foot down, I .... (9) (feel) an indescribable drawing, ... (10) (suck) motion of the sand below.

Phrasal Verbs

2. Replace the incorrect words in CAPITAL LETTERS to make the sentence meaningful and grammatically correct.

(a) My mood perked WITHIN when I saw my friend.

(b) The accused was shamed FOR an admission by the investigating officer.

(c) It was brave FROM him to take on the robbers single-handedly.

(d) He was slaving UP, running a house and family.

(e) My friend saw me OFF all the hard times.

(f) Ensure you brush OFF on the chapter on Electricity before your Physics exam.

(g) The plants were deprived FROM sunlight and water.

(h) She is rather conscious WITH her looks.

(i) The two companies decided to merge UP each other to expand their market reach.

(j) The smaller startup will merge WITH the larger corporation, adopting its brand and structure.

Rewrite as Directed

3. Rewrite the following sentences according to the instructions given in the brackets.

(a) The artist is not only talented but also well-mannered. (Begin with *Besides*)

(b) Shweta prefers to spend time at home (Rewrite using *would rather*)

(c) If weather permits, the cricket match will be held tomorrow. (Rewrite using *permitting*)

(d) In spite of his injury, Sarandeep Singh played the hockey match. (Begin with *Despite*)

(e) No sooner did it get dark than the children stopped playing. (Begin with *As soon as*)

ANSWER KEY

1. Tenses

1. walking
2. lay
3. turn
4. make
5. marched
6. had snared (this development had already taken place)
7. showed
8. put
9. felt
10. sucking

2. Phrasal verbs

(a) up (PERK UP = become cheerful)

(b) into (shame into = force/compel through embarrassment)

(c) of (brave of someone = showing courage)

(d) away (slave away = work very hard for a long time | *slog* means the same)

(e) through (see some through = support during difficulty)

(f) up (brush up on = revise and improve knowledge)

(g) of (deprived of = lacking something essential)

(h) of (conscious of = aware about / mindful of)

(i) with (merge with = combine together)

(j) into (merge into = absorbed by another entity)

Note:

"Merge with" implies collaboration or joining while both entities remain distinct, as in two companies working together.

"Merge into" implies complete absorption, where one entity is fully incorporated into the other, losing its separate identity.

3. Rewrite as Directed

(a) Besides being talented, the artist is well-mannered.

(b) Shweta would rather spend time at home.

(c) Weather permitting, the cricket match will be held tomorrow.

(d) Despite his injury, Sarandeep Singh played the hockey match. (or)

Despite being injured, Sarandeep Singh played the hockey match.

Note: Both forms are grammatically correct and convey the same meaning. The second form uses the participial phrase "being injured" instead of the noun "his injury".

(e) As soon as it got dark, the children stopped playing.

ISC TEST PAPER 17

Tenses:

1. **Fill in the blanks in the passage given below with the appropriate form of the verb given in the brackets.**

   Manual scavenging work .... (1) (ban) in 2013. Sanitation workers .... (2) (suppose) to be rehabilitated. Yet manual scavenging .... (3) (continue). It is not as if no efforts .... (4) (make). Odisha, for instance, ... (5) (emerge) as the frontrunner in.... (6) (curb) manual scavenging. In 2020, the state government .... (7) (launch) Garima, a scheme for core sanitation workers and their families. It also .... (8) (set) up a State Commission for them. Aspects of Garima .... (9) (include) by the Centre in its own Namaste scheme. It .... (10) (offer) loans and skilling opportunities.

Phrasal Verbs

2. **Replace the incorrect words in CAPITAL LETTERS to make the sentence meaningful and grammatically correct.**

   (a) The new dispensation is determined to root OFF corruption in the tender process.

   (b) All the classmates were envious WITH Avdesh because he had become the School Head Boy.

   (c) She is eligible TO a scholarship.

   (d) After retirement, he decided to settle OFF in his hometown in Uttar Pradesh.

   (e) The train is bound TO Chennai.

   (f) The new government is deaf AGAINST criticism.

   (g) He is eligible FOR vote in the election.

   (h) The waiter waited WITH me at the restaurant.

   (i) We hope that our player will not let us OUT.

   (j) Despite the leader's defeat, his party rallied FOR him.

Rewrite as Directed

3. **Rewrite the following sentences according to the instructions given in the brackets.**

   (a) I will go to sleep as soon as the last guest leaves. (Begin with *No sooner*)

   (b) She has a beautiful house. (Add a question tag)

   (c) It is a pity that I did not take the umbrella. (Begin with *I wish*)

   (d) The train was late, yet Pratiba waited to receive her aunt. (Begin with *Despite*)

   (e) Water your plants regularly, or the flowers will not bloom. (Begin with *Unless*)

ANSWER KEY

1. **Tenses**
   1. was banned
   2. were supposed
   3. continues
   4. have been made
   5. has emerged
   6. curbing
   7. launched
   8. set
   9. have been included / were included
   10. offers / offered

2. **Phrasal verbs**

   (a) out (root out = remove)

   (b) of (envious of = feel jealous)

   (c) for (eligible for = qualified to receive)

   (d) down (settle down = establish oneself)

   (e) for (bound for = heading to)

   (f) to (deaf to = ignore or not respond)

   (g) to (eligible to = having a right to / permitted to do something)

   (h) on (wait on = serve)

   (i) down (let down = disappoint)

   (j) around / behind (rally around / behind = support)

   Note:

   Rallied *around* him → came together in support of him (emphasises unity).

   Rallied *behind* him → actively supported him (emphasises leadership and following).

3. **Rewrite as Directed**

   (a) No sooner does the last guest leave than I will go to sleep.

   (b) She has a beautiful house, doesn't she?

   (c) I wish that I had taken the umbrella.

   (d) Despite the train being late, Pratiba waited to receive her aunt.

   (e) Unless you water your plants regularly, the flowers will not bloom.

ISC TEST PAPER 18

Tenses:

1. **Fill in the blanks in the passage given below with the appropriate form of the verb given in the brackets.**

   The day the cat .... (1) (kill), Maddy .... (2) (watch) her mother wind that old clock with her same little smile, ... (3) (crank) the gold key into its funny hole, as grandma .... (4) (wander) around the dining table in her dressing gown while her nurse .... (5) (read) a pulp fiction on the front step. Meanwhile, her brothers .... (6) (scrap) their forks against the table and .... (7) (drip) the bits of potatoes from their open mouths. The clock had been left by the previous owner. .... (8) (cloak) in pine wood and always .... (9) (count), no one .... (10) (scare) of it.

Phrasal Verbs

2. **Replace the incorrect words in CAPITAL LETTERS to make the sentence meaningful and grammatically correct.**

   (a) The deputy manager has access FOR important files in the bank.

   (b) The army chief apprised the defence minister WITH the situation on the border.

   (c) What is the time ON your watch?

   (d) The company has reposed its trust ON its new manager.

   (e) I want to remind you FOR your role in the movie.

   (f) The students revelled FROM their success.

   (g) The police resorted UPON firing teargas to quell the rioters.

   (h) Everyone says that I TAKE ON my uncle in looks and height.

   (i) The responsibility rests ON the management.

   (j) I want you to get UP with the job of tracking the smugglers.

Rewrite as Directed

3. **Rewrite the following sentences according to the instructions given in the brackets.**

   (a) He will crack the medical entrance exam, and of this, I am certain. (Begin with *I am certain*)

   (b) He saw the dog and ran away immediately. (Begin with *As soon as*)

   (c) The last time Natarajan played in a Test match was in Australia. (Begin with *Natarajan*)

   (d) The association will have to cancel the athletics trials unless it finds a stadium by tomorrow. (Begin with *If*)

   (e) Gurvinder said to me, "Let us skip the gym today." (Rewrite in reported speech)

ANSWER KEY

1. **Tenses**
   1. was killed
   2. watched
   3. cranking
   4. wandered
   5. read
   6. scrapped
   7. dripped
   8. Cloaked
   9. counting
   10. was scared
2. **Phrasal Verbs**

   (a) to (access to = authority or permission to see/use something)

   (b) of (apprise of = inform someone about something)

   (c) by (time by = according to a timepiece)

   (d) in (repose trust in = place confidence or faith in someone)

   (e) of (remind of = bring something to someone's attention)

   (f) in (revel in = take great pleasure or delight in something)

   (g) to (resort to = take an undesirable or unpleasant course of action)

   (h) after (take after = resemble a family member in appearance, character, or behaviour)

   (i) with (rests with = is the responsibility of)

   (j) on (get on with = begin or continue a task)
3. **Rewrite as Directed**

   (a) I am certain that he will crack the medical entrance exam.

   (b) As soon as he saw the dog, he ran away.

   (c) Natarajan last played in a Test match in Australia

   (d) If the association does not find a stadium by tomorrow, it will have to cancel the athletics trials.

   (e) Gurvinder suggested that we (should) skip the gym that day.

ISC TEST PAPER 19

Tenses:

1. **Fill in the blanks in the passage given below with the appropriate form of the verb given in the brackets.**

   Long ago, men .... (1) (spend) most of their time .... (2) (look) for food. They ate anything they could .... (3) (find). Some .... (4) (live) mostly on plants. They .... (5) (eat) the fruit, stems and leaves of some plants and roots of others. Later, men .... (6) (learn) to make weapons with which they could kill larger animals for meat. If they .... (7) (kill) an animal, they would eat the meat and .... (8) (chew) the bones. When they .... (9) (finish) the meal, there was nothing .... (10) (leave).

Phrasal Verbs

2. **Replace the incorrect words in CAPITAL LETTERS to make the sentence meaningful and grammatically correct.**

   (a) Can you dispose AWAY the garbage in the bin?
   (b) It seemed as if he was showing OVER his medals.
   (c) I hope we can slip DOWN before anyone notices.
   (d) Students have handed OUT their assignments for evaluation.
   (e) The election campaign is shaping OUT very well.
   (f) They had covered the holes to shut OFF the water.
   (g) The notice was served TO her three months ago.
   (h) Gaurav set FORTH his gardening task very seriously.
   (i) The new chief minister wants to shake DOWN the working of the irrigation department.
   (j) The commandos smoked the terrorist OFF like a snake.

Rewrite as Directed

3. **Rewrite the following sentences according to the instructions given in the brackets.**

   (a) She did not know that she would be taken into custody. (Begin with *Little*)
   (b) No sooner had he entered the auditorium than the programme began. (Begin with *Hardly*)
   (c) The airline staff will send a message if the flight is delayed. (Begin with *Should*)
   (d) Not only did he buy a new television, but also a laptop. (Begin with *Besides*)
   (e) Shishir said to Salman, "Is this the article you were reading yesterday?" (Rewrite in reported speech)

ANSWER KEY

1. **Tenses**
   1. spent
   2. looking
   3. find
   4. lived
   5. ate
   6. learned
   7. killed
   8. chew
   9. finished
   10. left

2. **Phrasal Verbs**
   (a) of (dispose of = get rid of)
   (b) off (show off = display proudly)
   (c) away/off (slip away/off = leave quietly)
   (d) in (hand in = submit)
   (e) up (shape up = develop or improve)
   (f) out (shut out = prevent)
   (g) on (serve on = deliver a legal document)
   (h) about (set about = start doing something energetically or with a purpose)
   (i) up (shake up = make significant changes)
   (j) out (smoke out = force someone to reveal themselves)

3. **Rewrite as Directed**
   (a) Little did she know that she would be taken into custody.
   (b) Hardly had he entered the auditorium when the programme began.
   (c) Should the flight be delayed, the airline staff will send a message.
   (d) Besides buying a new television, he bought a laptop.
   (e) Shishir asked Salman if that was the article he had been reading the previous day.

ISC TEST PAPER 20

Tenses:

1. **Fill in the blanks in the passage given below with the appropriate form of the verb given in the brackets.**

When Vishwakeshava told his parents that he was .... (1) (consider) processing his own cashew, they .... (2) (support) him wholeheartedly. The family .... (3) (toy) with the idea for a while. His parents had some experience of .... (4) (process). Years ago, they had processed their raw jackfruit and .... (5) (supply) it to a chips factory in Mangalore. Vishwakeshava and his wife .... (6) (get) down to work. They .... (7) (search) for mini cashew processing machines and .... (8) (consult) Manjunath, a farmer in Tumkur, ... (9) (experience) in converting cashews into kernels and .... (10) (market) it.

Phrasal Verbs

2. **Replace the incorrect words in CAPITAL LETTERS to make the sentence meaningful and grammatically correct.**

(a) The children were bundled OF to bed after the long party.

(b) When it comes to legal issues, we should defer FROM a sharp legal brain.

(c) You need to adhere WITH the rules of the college.

(d) The new government needs to shore IN public confidence.

(e) He wears a bracelet to ward OF evil spirits.

(f) I always root WITH the underdog in every match.

(g) Smoking in the hotel room will set UP the fire alarm.

(h) Since he had only ₹500, he had to choose FROM a biography and a novel at the book store.

(i) The tiger seized the lamb and made UP with it into the thicket.

(j) Manohar delighted ON working hard.

Rewrite as Directed

3. **Rewrite the following sentences according to the instructions given in the brackets.**

(a) The shopkeeper said to me, "Would you mind looking after my shop for 15 minutes?" (Change into reported speech)

(b) Bindu is prettier than her sister. (Rewrite using *the prettier*)

(c) As soon as I stepped out, it started raining cats and dogs. (Begin with *No sooner*)

(d) Members with a valid identity card will be allowed to attend the concert. (Rewrite using *without*)

(e) Only a madman would swim in a river infested with crocodiles. (Begin with *None*)

ANSWER KEY

1. **Tenses**
   1. considering
   2. supported
   3. had been toying
   4. processing
   5. supplied
   6. got
   7. searched
   8. consulted
   9. experienced
   10. marketing

2. **Phrasal Verbs**

(a) off (bundle off = send somewhere quickly)

(b) to (defer to = accept someone's opinion / submit to)

(c) to (adhere to = obey or follow)

(d) up (shore up = strengthen, support)

(e) off (ward off = prevent from harming)

(f) for (root for = support / cheer)

(g) off (set off = trigger, e.g., alarm)

(h) between (choose between = select one of two distinct options)

(i) off (make off with = leave hurriedly taking something)

(j) in (delight in = take pleasure from)

3. **Rewrite as Directed**

(a) The shopkeeper asked me if I would mind looking after his shop for 15 minutes.

(b) Bindu is the prettier of the two sisters.

(c) No sooner did I step out than it started raining cats and dogs.

(d) Members without a valid identity card will not be allowed to attend the concert.

(e) None but a madman would swim in a river infested with crocodiles.